ABOVE OR WITHIN?

ABOVE OR WITHIN?

The Supernatural
in Religious Education

20

IAN KNOX

RELIGIOUS EDUCATION PRESS

MISHAWAKA   INDIANA

Acknowledgments

Permission to quote substantially from the following sources is gratefully acknowledged:

From the *Teaching Ministry of the Church* by James D. Smart. Copyright © MCMLIV, by Walter L. Jenkins. Used by permission of The Westminster Press.

From *The Rebirth of Ministry,* by James D. Smart. © Walter L. Jenkins, MCMLX. Used by permission of The Westminster Press.

From *Education for Christian Living,* 2nd ed., by Randolph Crump Miller, © 1963. Used by permission of Prentice-Hall, Inc., Englewood Cliffs, New Jersey.

From *The Gift of Power* by Lewis Joseph Sherrill. Copyright © 1963 by Macmillan Publishing Co., Inc., New York.

Printed in the United States of America

Library of Congress Catalog Card Number: 76–55589

Paper: ISBN: 0–89135–006–3
Hardbound: ISBN 0–89135–010–1

2 3 4 5 6 7 8 9 10

Religious Education Press
Box 364
Mishawaka, Indiana 46544

Religious Education Press, Inc., publishes books and educational materials exclusively in religious education and in areas closely related to religious education. It is committed to enhancing and professionalizing religious education through the publication of significant scholarly and popular books.

FOR MY PARENTS
PERCY AND ELIANE KNOX

Contents

Foreword

Ian Knox is exactly right: "lack of attention to theory has led to a crisis of self-understanding and a fuzziness of identity for the religious education field." His book will not satisfy all those with a point of view on the subject, but it will surely challenge them to produce a better schema, if they can.

He suggests that there are two, and possibly three, basic theoretical approaches: what he calls "transcendist," "immanentist," and "integrationist." The first emphasizes the "aboveness" of God in relation to the world; the second stresses the "withinness" of God; and the third, to the extent that it exists as a separate and distinct position at all, tries to hold the first two biases in some "equilibrium."

The first view corresponds to the orthodox and neo-orthodox movements in Christian theology, Catholic and Protestant alike. The second view corresponds with the liberal movement in early twentieth century American Protestant theology and with some recent trends in Catholic thought. The third view appears as much an ideal as a reality, at most a synthesis in the making. It sees the first two views as not so much contradictory as complementary. This complementarity, Father Knox suggests, offers the most fruitful theological perspective for religious education.

The book does not provide a sustained and vigorous criticism of the transcendist and immanentist views. Yet, both views, taken by themselves and not in tension with the opposite view, are open to such criticism. The transcendist view has been (rightly) taken over the coals again and again in recent times. What needs the fire of tough and sustained criticism today is the immanentist view, particularly as it has emerged in contemporary theological thought. It is this "experiential" approach that seems now to have been so uncritically assimilated by many in religious education programs (although I am well aware that the more traditional view still holds sway in many places). Rather than offering a thoroughgoing criticism of the various theological approaches, the author tries to provide objective descriptions of these approaches as they appear in the works of selected religious educationists. His purpose clearly is to make religious educators reflect on their own personal theological outlook, to encourage them to examine the theological assumptions which lie behind their thinking and teaching, and to engage, where appropriate, in a little self-criticism.

Categorization, of course, is always hazardous. Nuanced and complex positions are not readily adjustable to our particular intellectual designs. Implausible alliances are sometimes artificially forged. But systematization of one sort or another is an intrinsic, and therefore inevitable, component of the human drive for understanding. The author has given us reasons for his choices—and in a commendably tentative fashion at that. His critics will have to do the same if their complaints are to be counted creditable and constructive.

"Religious educators," he writes, "frequently do not act out of a responsible and informed theory, least of all their own theory. It often happens, also, that changes in their actual approach and in their teaching performance are made purely pragmatically and without proper foundation in theory. A further anomaly is that while consciously subscribing to one theory religion teachers choose practices which do not arise from that theory but from a discordant one."

No one concerned about the quality and effectiveness of religious education will lightly regard Father Knox's charge. Indeed, if this book helps us sharpen the issues and elevate the level of argument within the field, he shall have succeeded admirably in his purposes.

RICHARD P. McBRIEN

Director, Institute for the Study
of Religious Education and Service,
Boston College

Preface

What this book is about will be clear enough from a reading of chapter 1 and need not be anticipated here. It is a book for anyone interested in religious education, but it is not one of the "how to do it" variety. In this age of course and curriculum proliferation, harassed religion teachers and religion department heads are already deluged with practical religion packages vying for their attention. This book has been written in the optimistic hope that religion teachers, particularly, appreciate the value and the necessity of reflection and of developing a rationale and a firm theoretical base for their teaching. One cannot successfully proceed with the "how" of religious education until one has firmly established the "why."

Writing a book of this nature one tends to get caught on the horns of a dilemma, that is, whether to write for those with little background in the subject or to write for the "initiated." Attempting to steer a middle course between these two extremes runs the risk of pleasing no one. It is a risk this book will have to live with.

Another dilemma which presented itself was in the choice of terminology. The terms "immanence" and "transcendence" have an accepted theological usage. Following strict grammatical rules the descriptive words which should derive from these terms are "immanentist" and "transcendentist." The word transcendentist suffers from two drawbacks. First, it is awkward (inelegant, if you will), and second, in pronouncing it one tends wrongly to place the accent on the penultimate syllable thus making it sound like something out of a textbook of dentistry. For these reasons the word "transcendist" is used throughout this book even though its grammatical purity is suspect.

For those who want a quick overview of what this book is about, it is suggested that they read the shortest chapters first, namely, chapters 1, 3, and 7. Chapter 2 contains some historical and theological material that may not be of interest to everyone but for a better understanding of what is to follow the final section of chapter is important.

To adequately thank everyone who at various times gave advice, critiqued portions of the manuscript, or offered encouragement would be impossible. Some, in particular, have expressed the wish to remain anonymous. Nevertheless, special mention must be made of Jack McCall and the Boston College Institute for Religious Education and Service whose special charism provided much of the impetus to pursue scholarly work in religious education. Pat Fitzpatrick, C.S.Sp., not only made valuable suggestions and posed some searching questions (not all of which have been answered), but his careful reading of the manuscript picked up several flaws which would otherwise have gone unnoticed. James P. Mackey took an interest in the project from its inception and generously gave permission for the use of ideas (particularly in chapter 7) developed in private correspondence with the author. As well as providing the Protestant "foil" to the author's Roman Catholicism, Rev. Harold Burgess constructively criticized the work and added the much-appreciated dimension of a deep personal friendship. James Michael Lee kindly made available several chapters of *The Content of Religious Instruction* in manuscript form. Thanks must also be offered to the Metropolitan Separate School Board of Toronto for sabbatical leave and financial assistance, and last, but far from least, to the Spiritans of the province of Trans-Canada to whom the author's debt is incalculable.

CHAPTER I

Setting the Scene

A glance at any number of contemporary works on religion and religious topics will reveal that many writers seem intent on examining and cataloging the problems attaching to religious faith. How religious faith can exist and flourish in the context of today's scientific and secularized society seems to be a major concern of a great deal of scholarly and popular writing on religion. Not infrequently one encounters in such writing the somber pronouncement that modern man is rapidly becoming areligious and is losing, or has lost, his capacity, as Harvey Cox puts it, "to live at once in history and in eternity."[1] That concern with the problems of religious faith is a legitimate one need not be questioned. On the other hand, like many other problems connected with religion it is not a particularly new concern. The felt need of reconciling one's God-consciousness, and the religious demands such a consciousness makes, with the realities of one's secular environment is a perennial dilemma and an enduring tension. Particularly is this true for believing Christians whose God-consciousness, though crystalized in the incarnated Christ, is still tinged with that otherworldly dimension of the transcendent beyond. God is simultaneously with us and not with us. Jesus Christ is at once one of us and not one of us. The divine graciously enables, enriches, and sacralizes all of creation while at the same time maintaining a certain quality of aloofness, of mystery, of unreachableness. The God with whom we can confidently have converse in prayer is also he who "dwells in unapproachable light."

Theology has its own terminology for this built-in dilemma of the Christian God-consciousness. It speaks of God's transcendence (from the Latin *transscandere,* to rise above and beyond) which means that God infinitely eclipses all created and contingent reality. The polar opposite of transcendence is immanence (from the Latin *immanere,* to remain in) which refers to God's creative power and presence in everything that is, producing and sustaining all of existence. The problem of reconciling God's transcendence and his immanence in the personal fabric of daily living is, for the serious-minded Christian, a tension-filled experience.

A good example of this tension is to be found in liturgical worship. The very word worship denotes the homage and adoration paid only to God the

1

creator of all being and life; God who is infinitely superior to his creatures who worship him; God whose reality totally surpasses any creaturely experience. The word worship also has the emotive connotations of reverence and veneration, of awe, of wonder, of deference. The God who is worshiped is the transcendent "Other." At the same time, liturgical worship is also a celebration. Particularly is this true of the Christian eucharist with its dimension of the Paschal meal, the Christian *koinonia* gathered around the table of the Lord, the convivial atmosphere of sharing supper and breaking bread as Christ did with his apostles and exhorted them to do in his memory. In this setting the God who is celebrated, and with whom we celebrate, is not so much the transcendent Other as he is the immanent one who is with and in us, our companion and friend.

There are some who would deny that there is any tension here. They would claim that the essential elements of celebration are also the essential elements of worship; that celebration is prayer directed to God intimately present in his mysterious gift of life; that to celebrate is, in fact, to worship the Lord of life. While there may be much validity in this approach, celebration and worship are words which engage different human emotions and evoke different sets of human responses corresponding to different experiences. The particular human need and the facet of human personality which give rise to *eulabeia,* the religious awe of worship, are not the same as those which give rise to the joyful conviviality of celebration. Furthermore, it is a painful fact of experience that joyful celebration too easily becomes mere enthusiasm and that "Man, being predisposed to exaggerated enthusiasms, is tempeted to arrogate to himself the spirit that can only be received as a gift."[2]

The tension inherent in a consideration of how God relates to his creatures can never be fully solved, it can only be assuaged. Whether because of personal temperament, or because of rational conviction, or because of both, some people are more comfortable with transcendence, others with immanence. Some relate better to the God who is "other"; they are more at home with the God who gives meaning to their innate sense of dependence and who is to be adored. Others relate better to the God who is the ground of being, who is immanently and intimately present in all human experience and endeavor. Yet, neither transcendists nor immanentists may be prepared to cling to their preferred emphasis to the exclusion of the other. Neither may be entirely consistent. It is probable that many people may attempt to come to terms with the tension by simultaneously affirming both transcendence and immanence and by striving to hold them in some sort of productive dialectic. Whatever the method, let it be taken as axiomatic that each person develops his or her own *metaperspective* on the transcendence/immanence polarity and uses this metaperspective to bring about some form of personal synthesis which gives meaning to life's experiences.[3]

Metaperspective

A metaperspective is a personal panoramic template or pattern through which people filter their experiences and by which they assign meanings which make sense of the realities that confront them. A metaperspective is an overview, a way of looking at things—specifically, in the context of this book, it is a way of looking at the God/man relationship. It has to do, therefore, with a person's psychological orientation, his or her attitudes and predispositions which to a large extent determine one's approach to and interaction with reality. A metaperspective may be the result of a rationally worked out and consciously adopted posture. It may also be the result of a personality formed and shaped by a particular religious background and early training and, therefore, largely an unconscious attitude. More probably it is a combination of both conscious and unconscious elements. The ingredients which go into the making of a person's metaperspective are immensely complex and variable. Suffice it to say that not only do people tend to screen and sift their experiences so that these experiences fit into an orderly pattern which is personally "manageable," but that this same pattern is also projected in everyone's mode of external self-expression. People, therefore, see what their metaperspective allows them to see and they act in a manner that produces the least possible mental and emotional discordance with their particular overview.

Religious educationists and educators, as well as everyone else, work with, and out of, a metaperspective. This book is largely concerned with examining the metaperspective of prominent religious educationists in so far as such a perspective or stance may be a significant factor in their religious education theory. (Religious educationists are those who, apart from the practical aspect of actual religion teaching are also engaged in the theoretical arena and who have achieved some stature therein. Religious educators, on the other hand, are those who are mainly engaged in the field work of actual teaching or administration). It may be well, at this point, to say a word or two about theory and theorists.

Theory and Theorists

It is a trite saying that ideas rule the world. Whether trite or no this adage is a pithy testimony to the recognition that the greatest influence is wielded by those who think systematically and creatively, by those who construct theories. One has only to ponder, for example, the influence of Thomas Aquinas in theology, Immanuel Kant in philosophy, Sigmund Freud and C. G. Jung in the field of depth psychology, and of Karl Marx in the political realm, to realize the tremendous importance, and indeed the indispensability of the theoretician in any sphere of human endeavor. Constructing a theory means organizing relevant facts, experiential data, concepts, and propositions in a systematic manner so as to indicate relationships among them, which systematic arrangement may be used to explain and predict phenomena. Theory is at the heart of a dialectic; it is born of experience; it is shaped and formed by the intuitive and rational processes; it in turn gives meaning to the very experiences from which it was first drawn, and it forms the mold of intelligibility for future experiences. A theory, therefore, is an instrument of power, for it provides a sense of mastery over facts and situations by allowing one to arrange all the variables into an intelligible and meaningful pattern. A good theory makes for economy of effort in dealing with reality; it also makes for a sense of purpose in what one does. From the systematic arrangement or pattern provided by a theory one is able not only to see a connectedness with other facts and theories, but one is able also to predict the course of future events. It should be evident that a personal metaperspective is intimately connected with one's theories, and, indeed, with one's capacity to theorize. If the metaperspective forms the "hidden agenda" of assumptions and premises on which a person works it seems logical to assume that such an overview will bear a close affinity to the theories a person produces and employs. It should be evident, also, that theory dictates practice and that good theory is eminently practical. In fact, whether consciously or unconsciously, everyone acts out of some theory. Everyone acts out of some theoretical pattern which gives meaning to their acts; people do not act (for the most part, at any rate) in a purely capricious manner. Paradoxical as it may seem, one can only become more practical by becoming more theoretical. The more one can find intelligible and meaningful patterns for one's behavior the more sure-footed and confident one becomes and the better able one is to cope with new experience.

As some writers have indicated, religious education has long exhibited a "bias toward the practical" which to a certain extent has hindered its development and advancement as a unified field of endeavor.[4] The ceaseless cri de coeur of religious educators seems to be: "Tell me what to *do*." Those engaged at the grass roots level of actual teaching seem most frequently to look to the thinkers not for theories, but for prepared packages of practical gimmicks to help them get through the day. One has only to visit the display stands of any religious education convention to have ample evidence of this bias toward the practical. Yet, lack of attention to theory has led to a crisis of self-understanding and a fuzziness of identity for the religious education field. Religious educators frequently do not act out of a responsible and informed theory, least of all their own theory. It often happens, also, that changes in their actual approach and in their teaching performance are made purely pragmatically and without proper foundation in theory. A further anomaly is that while consciously subscribing to one theory religion teachers choose practices which do not arise from that theory but from a another discordant one. Take, for example, the following theoretical position: "That teacher will be able to lead the students to Christ who has already been his companion."[5] Without denying the importance of the teacher's witness, this position appears to be equivalent to saying that holiness makes for competent religion teaching—something which is frequently not borne out by the evidence. Taking such a position to its logical conclusion might mean the neglect of proper teaching practices—something which few religious educators worth their salt would care to subscribe to.

The real point to be made, and made emphatically, is that religious education as a field needs to pay a great deal more attention to theory, which is one reason why this book sets about examining the theories of major religious educationists. If these theorists have had influence in the past, or are influential in the present, or may be so in the future, then it is important to know what elements go into the making of their theories and out of what metaperspective the particular theorists are working. Such an examination of religious education theory will also have the advantage of providing the background for a personal self-examination by every religious educator. Discovery of and conscious attention to one's own basic outlook may, perhaps, provide an explanation of why a particular religious education theory and a particular set of practices are attractive and ring a sympathetic bell, while other theories engender an adverse gut reaction. If one finds oneself concurring with a certain theory then, for example, do one's pedagogical practices fit this particular theory? What do religious educationists have to say on the matter? Does one teach in a certain manner because that is what religious educationists suggest should be done, or because one is more comfortable with a certain way of doing things? What is the rationale for one's own particular approach to the teaching of religion? Everyone engaged in religious education, at whatever level, would profit greatly, first, by a clarification and strengthening of the theory out of which one is working, and second, by an examination of the consistency with which one's actual teaching comes out of a specific theory. An analysis of the religious education theories of major religious educationists will certainly help toward this end.

Theological Themes and Religious Education

In his stimulating volume *Catholicism and Education,* John W. Donohue suggests that "it is because nearly everyone has some . . . convictions about life and education that nearly everyone has a fragmentary education theory."[6] Among the data, concepts, and laws which enter into the making of religious education theory are those which derive from theology. Since nearly everyone has some theological metaperspective, some convictions about theological propositions and constructs, it is more than probable that every religion teacher has some fragmentary religious education theory. For all that, the extent to which theological themes and principles should be allowed to affect religious education theory is a disputed topic. On the one hand, some theorists claim that since theology is concerned with examining and explaining the God/man relationship which is the whole basis of religious education, then it would be ludicrous to suggest that it (theology) could be anything but the heart and core of religious education theory. Contrariwise, other theorists claim that if theology is allowed to be entirely determinative of religious education many absurdities will follow. How, for example, can a nonempirical science such as theology be allowed to determine something as empirical as the teaching act? What theological principles apply to learning theory?

The two poles in this debate, in modern times at any rate, seem to be well represented by Randolph Crump Miller (extremely influential religious educationist and for many years editor of the journal *Religious Education),* and James Michael Lee (originator of the social science approach to religious instruction). For Miller, theology is the "clue" to Christian education, and it is normative for every phase and aspect of religious education theory.[7] Thus, boldly asserts Miller, "Theology, which is the truth-about-God-in-relation-to-man, is *the* determining factor in the development of a philosophy of education, of the techniques to be used, of the goals to be attained, and of the nature of the learners to be taught."[8] This is as clear and as thorough a statement as one could wish on the role of theology in religious education; theology pervades every facet of the entire enterprise. Miller hammers home his point by adding that "Christian education must not be a footnote to secular discoveries."[9]

Such conviction as to the pervasive role of theology in the constructing of religious education theory is not shared by all of Miller's peers. Thus, for example, James Michael Lee would not agree with Miller that theology is the basis and foundation of every aspect of religious education even though he (Lee) admits that theology supplies a significant portion of the substantive content of religious instruction.[10] In fact, Lee specifically situates the essence of religious education outside the boundaries of theological science and locates it within the domain of social science. The fundamental concepts and laws which apply to religious education are those of social science, and specifically those concerned with the teaching-learning process. "At bottom," Lee asserts, "what the social-science approach to religious instruction does is to radicate it in the teaching-learning process."[11] Thus, he argues, "the central task of religious instruction becomes the conscious and deliberative facilitation of behavioral goals," and not merely the inculcation of theological truth.[12] Lee's stance is that religious education is primarily an educational task and not a theological one. Religious education is not a branch of theological science, it is a mode of social science because education is a field which is social scientific in nature and thrust. Theology and social science have different starting points, different methodologies, and different goals. From this stance Lee argues that thinking which is largely derived from theological a priori or authoritative principles should not be allowed to determine educational issues.[13]

Could it be that these divergent opinions as to the role of theology in religious education theory are due to divergent opinions as to the definition and scope of theology itself? Or could it perhaps be due to the selection of a different starting point—biblical revelational truth on the one hand, or empirical, a posteriori experiential evidence on the other? Be that as it may, no matter what viewpoint is advanced, all religious educationists are agreed on the vital importance of theological themes for religious education. Indeed, it would be strange if it were not so. This book sets out to examine a theological theme in its relation to religious education theory; the theme is that of the relationship of the natural and the supernatural. The precise question is: Does adopting a certain metaperspective on the natural/supernatural relationship bear an affinity with a certain religious education theory and the practices which may follow from that theory? Is there any noticeable congruence or correlation between someone's personal theological overview and the theoretical position he or she adopts with respect to religious education?

Assuming for the moment that the natural/supernatural relationship has to do with how God relates to his creation, and even more specifically to man, then it seems evident that this theological theme will be of great importance in religious education theory—of fundamental importance, in fact. An examination of several statements of aims and purposes of religious education indicates that practically all such statements make direct or indirect reference to the God/man relationship. Thus, the God/man relationship may be explicitly referred to as

> to gain a right relationship to God and to all men. (Ferré)[14]

Or it may be stated in terms of relationship with Christ, thus,

> To remake, remold, transform, and reconstruct the experience of the children, youth, and adults with whom we live and work that they will experience their lives as the life of Christ. (Wyckoff)[15]

Or it may be stated in terms of friendship with God

> To lead those to be catechized . . . step by step to a friendship which God Himself wishes to establish with each person and with the whole Christian community. (Hofinger)[16]

Or it may be stated in terms of social religious aims as

Growth of the young toward and into mature and efficient devotion to the democracy of God, and happy self-realization therein. (Coe)[17]

Or it may be stated in terms of response to God's call in love

... that growing children may respond to God's saving love made known in Christ and live in relation to him, commiting their lives to him and finding the gift of the Holy Spirit through the life of the church to empower them in their every relationship. (Cully)[18]

Or it may be stated in purely behavioral terms as

facilitating the modification of the learner's behavior along desired religious lines. (Lee)[19]

In addition to stating the aims of religious education as concerned with the God/man relationship, many writers have drawn attention to the importance of the concept of the supernatural. In his comprehensive survey work *An Invitation to Religious Education,* Harold William Burgess analyzes selected theoretical approaches to religious education in this century. One such approach he calls the Traditional Theological Approach. He notes that the religious education theorists who are representative of this approach strongly stress the dimension of the supernatural as extremely important from the point of view of both religious education theory and practice.[20] There seems to be more than sufficient evidence to state that some aspect of the supernatural is an important factor in *all* theoretical approaches to religious education.

Not only is some aspect of the supernatural an important factor in all theoretical approaches to religious education but some religious educationists have gone out of their way to highlight the natural/supernatural relationship as of basic importance for the religious education task. James Michael Lee, for example, devotes an entire chapter of *The Shape of Religious Instruction* to this theme, and constantly refers to it in his other work.[21] Though he makes clear that chapter 9 of *The Shape* was written to show that a social science approach to religious instruction can in no way be construed as ''secular'' or ''naturalistic,'' his insistence on the compelling importance of the natural/supernatural theme for religious education is abundantly clear. Similarly, Morton Kelsey, a Jungian psychologist who is much concerned with religious education, stoutly insists on the indispensable importance of the supernatural dimension. Especially is he concerned with the experiential aspect of the God/man relationship. His book *Encounter with God* ''puts together a more general framework of understanding—historical, psychological, and philosophical—of man's experience of the supernatural, of God's contact with man.'' He indicates that modern Christianity has failed miserably to communicate this experiential aspect of the supernatural and he incisively indicates how vital and pressing a problem it is for the whole religious education enterprise.[22]

If, as appears evident, religious educationists integrate the natural/ supernatural relationship into their theories then it seems more than likely that they will do so according to the mode of how they themselves perceive and understand this relationship. Thus, a theorist's theological metaperspective or overview will tend to color his or her handling of how God relates to his creatures and the way this relationship is built into religious education theory. All this sounds straightforward enough but things may not be that simple. The problems of delineating cause and effect when it comes to relating a metaperspective to practice, or even to a stated theoretical position, are notorious. No one is ever entirely consistent. There are too many diverse factors, personal or otherwise, which may enter in and tend to addle any neat cause-effect deductions. At most, it must be assumed that, as Randolph Crump Miller points out in a slightly different context, "beliefs which are *habitually* held (and thus taken seriously even when one is not conscious of them) are the normal bases for action."[23]

This book, therefore, makes no attempt to show that adopting a certain theological metaperspective on the natural/supernatural relationship will *necessarily* generate a specific type of religious education theory. It attempts to demonstrate, rather, that such a theological metaperspective is a significant factor (among, perhaps, many other factors) which comes into play in religious education theorizing. Other factors could be, for instance, a theorist's cultural background, epistemological stance, ecclesiastical confession. Thus, a theological metaperspective need not be *totally determinative* of a religious education theory. In other words, it probably would be extremely foolhardy to try to reduce *everything* a religious educationist proposes to a certain theological metaperspective. What is more probable is that there exists an affinity, a certain degree of congruence and correlation, between a metaperspective and a certain type of religious education theory. A theological metaperspective may be looked upon as providing a certain theological "flavor," a tinted horizon against which religious educationists (and indeed everyone) paint their theories. As will be explained later on, a reading of the religious education literature seems to reveal three such "flavors"—the transcendist, the immanentist, and possibly (but rather tentatively) a third, the integrationist.

Religious Educationists

Insofar as everyone normally acts out of some theoretical base and does some thinking on religious education matters, then everyone has the smatterings of a religious education theory, however fragmented and unsystematic. Just the same, the major religious educationists are the ones who have exerted the most influence and whose theories religion teachers follow. Who, then, are major religious educationists?

The answer to this question will depend to a large extent on the criteria that are proposed for making a judgment as to what constitutes a major theorist. Even if such a set of criteria could be drawn up to the satisfaction of all concerned, their application to any particular individual would still entail a subjective judgment on the part of the selector. For the purposes of this book, those religious educationists are considered major theorists who have attempted to develop a reasonably comprehensive approach to religious education theory and practice, who have had a significant impact as judged by their being quoted, discussed, and analyzed by other writers in the field, and who by their writings and by their teaching at important centers have influenced the thinking of individuals concerned with religious education at all levels.

Making most everyone's list of big-name religious educationists would probably be such historical figures as Augustine, author of one of the earliest and most influential treatises on Christian education—*De Catechizandis Rudibus*. Likewise, the framers of the first catechisms which appeared around the period of the Reformation (such as Martin Luther and Peter Canisius) could probably be ranked as major religious educationists. Such catechisms dictated the form and content of Christian education for centuries afterward. Much advantage might be gained from an analysis of the theroies of the early religious educationists. For all that, it seems more profitable, and more helpful to the field in its present state of development, to stick closer to the contemporary period. An examination of the theories of religious educationists who are products more of our modern era will be particularly relevant to religion teachers of the present time. Since it will be impossible to deal with all the major contemporary religious educationists, for the purposes of this book a selection must be made (which, undoubtedly, will not please everyone). The selection is made with the following criteria in mind: (1) that the selected theorists exhibit discernably distinct theological metaperspectives concerning the natural/supernatural relationship, and (2) that the selection be as ecumenical as possible within the confines of the Christian communion. And so, the major religious educationists whose theories are analyzed and described in this book are: Josef Andreas Jungmann, James D. Smart, Johannes Hofinger, George Albert Coe, Gabriel Moran, James Michael Lee, Lewis Joseph Sherrill, Randolph Crump Miller, and Marcel van Caster.

Category System

How does one analyze religious education theory? What are the elements that go into the making of such theory? One basic and necessary procedure in any form of descriptive analysis is the development of some form of category system, some classification scheme, or typological grouping. This is no less true when the data being analyzed are concepts and theoretical positions than when they are the physical and sense-perceptible data of sciences such as physics or biology. Category building is a process which everyone engages in, whether consciously or unconsciously. The world is just a chaotic mass of experiences until those experiences can be successfully slotted into categories which make them intelligible and of some value to each one's personal development. The leaves on a tree are mere biological appurtenances until they can be related to the whole metabolic process of life. The music of Beethoven might sound much like that of Mozart until one learns the criteria which place them in different categories. Calling someone a conservative, or a liberal, may simply be a convenient way of categorizing their political utterances. Category building is an essential process if one is to enhance the richness of experience and to open even further avenues of enrichment.

The importance of developing category systems for use in theory analysis and development in the field of religious education is widely recognized. Unhappily, while most everyone recognizes the need, religious educationists have not yet reached agreement on a common set of categories which cover all the essential points concerned with theory building. Harold William Burgess, for example, details no fewer than seven such category systems proposed by contemporary theorists, and his list is by no means exhaustive.[24] The categories proposed, while having certain features in common, are most often reflective of the individual theorist's personal perspectives and particular preferences. Burgess himself proposes as a category system a group of six zones or areas of educational concern:

> *First,* the aim of religious education, which... will also include such notions as goal, purpose, objective, and the like; *second,* the content of religious education...; *third,* the role of the teacher in the teaching of religion; *fourth,* the student, particularly the manner in which he manifests religious learning outcomes; *fifth,* the function of the environment in religious education; and *sixth,* the means by which religious education may be evaluated.[25]

In particular are these areas crucial to religious education because they relate rather pointedly to the translation of theory into practice. Thus, this grouping of important areas relates to some pressing and very practical questions, viz., toward what is religious education directed? Who teaches, and who is taught? What is taught and what is religious education concerned with? What circumstances affect the teaching-learning process? How is the whole process evaluated; that is, how are stated aims measured against achieved outcomes?

This book makes use of the category system proposed by Burgess. There are several advantages to be gained by so doing. One advantage is that the employment of a category system which has already been developed and analytically used may help to dispel the chronic complaint of the lack of integration in the religious education field. This complaint, one may note, is frequently coupled with the seemingly futile hope that some integration (far more than is presently evident) can ever be achieved.[26] Let it be unequivocally stated that religious educationists have often been guilty of sheer rhetoric. This latter fact is well documented in William Bedford Williamson's gently iconoclastic critique *Language and Concepts in Christian Education*.[27] Reading Williamson's book is a potent reminder that religious educationists have often produced what T. S. Eliot calls "the sleet and hail of verbal imprecisions."[28] Among other things, Williamson calls for a thorough philosophical analysis of these "verbal imprecisions" for purposes of language and concept clarification. A well-understood and accepted language is a sine qua non of fruitful communication, and difficulty in communication seems precisely to be one of the major problems among religious educationists, as evidenced by their failure to develop an agreed-upon set of laws, principles, and categories with which to build religious education theory. One possible way to help clear away some of the chaos (rather than constantly adding to it) is for investigators to use the *same* category system and apply it to the field looked at from different points of view. Such action would promote the solidification of a category system as a useful investigative tool, help to clarify language, provide a basis for comparison and reference in the theoretical arena, and promote the building and further integration of religious education theory. With these advantages in mind, this book investigates different theological metaperspectives on the natural/supernatural relationship which seem characteristic of major religious education theorists by testing the metaperspectives against the critical areas of concern delineated by Burgess. The natural/supernatural relationship is a far more restricted field of inquiry than the broad theoretical positions uncovered in Burgess's work, but there are clearly many points at which they touch base together.

In concluding this chapter let it be reiterated that one of the prime concerns of this book is to help those engaged in religious education at any level to reexamine and make more explicit their own outlook and overview, their own attitudes, assumptions, and presuppositions. Such a reexamination and sharpening will promote the development of a solid theoretical base for one's personal teaching which will be both intelligible and rewarding. The aim is to help teachers of religion to be more fully aware of their own rationale for the way they teach, the selections of material they make, and the experiences they promote. All of these relate to theological metaperspective. This book also endeavors to promote some form of integration in the field of religious education by helping to clarify concepts and solidify a category system for use in building and analyzing religious education theory.

Since the central theme of this investigation is concerned with the natural and the supernatural, the next item on the agenda is an examination of the meaning of these terms in their current and historical uses. Such an examination will provide the background for a useable definition of the terms and for a delineation of different theological metaperspectives which may be adopted by religious education theorists.

NOTES

1. Harvey Cox, *Feast of Fools* (Cambridge, Mass.: Harvard University Press, 1969), p. 43.

2. Klaus Hemmerle, "Enthusiasm," in Karl Rahner, editor, *Sacramentum Mundi: An Encyclopedia of Theology*, Vol. 2 (New York: Herder and Herder, 1970), p. 234.

3. Those interested in pursuing the empirical evidence for what is here taken as axiomatic will find much food for thought in C. David Mortensen's *Communication: The Study of Human Interaction* (New York: McGraw-Hill, 1972). See especially pp. 125–168.

4. See, for example, Harold William Burgess, *An Invitation to Religious Education* (Notre Dame, Indiana: Religious Education Press, 1975), pp. 5–7; see also Charles Melchert, "Hope for the Profession," *Religious Education*, Vol. 67, (September-October 1972), p. 360.

5. Sr. Mary Virgine Pugh, M.H.S.H., "Special Problems of the First Two Years of High School," in Gerard S. Sloyan, editor, *Modern Catechetics* (New York: Macmillan, 1964), p. 217.

6. John W. Donohue, S.J., *Catholicism and Education* (New York: Harper and Row, 1973), p. 18.

7. *The Clue to Christian Education* is actually the title of Miller's first major work on Christian education though the theological foundations for much of his religious education thought can probably be found in some of his earlier works such as *What We Can Believe* (New York: Scribner's, 1941) and *Religion Makes Sense* (New York: Wilcox & Follett, 1950). In his subsequent writings on religious education, Miller has never deviated from the position he adopts in *The Clue* on the relevance of theology for every aspect of religious education theory and practice. See Randolph Crump Miller, *The Clue to Christian Education* (New York: Scribner's, 1950).

In this present work the terms *Christian* education and *religious* education will be used interchangeably. Miller would not so use them. For him Christian education is undoubtedly religious education since Christianity is a religion. However, since Christian education derives in large part from the truths revealed in the bible, and particularly the New Testament, it is religious education with a distinctly Christian flavor. See, Randolph Crump Miller, *Education for Christian Living*, 2nd edition (New Jersey: Prentice-Hall, 1963), pp. 51–54.

8. Randolph Crump Miller, *Education for Christian Living*, p. 5. Emphasis added.

9. Ibid., p. 45.

10. Lee prefers to use the term religious *instruction* rather than religious *education* because he centers his theory mainly on one aspect of religious education, viz., the teaching-learning act. He notes that instruction is identical with teaching. Since the term *religious education* is a broader term and more widely in use it will continue to be employed in this work, even though much of what follows rather pointedly refers to teaching. However, teaching can and does go on in both formal and informal settings. The common tendency is to limit the use of the word to formal educational settings, but this may be far too restrictive. For a discussion of the terminology see James Michael Lee, *The Shape of Religious Instruction* (Notre Dame, Indiana: Religious Education Press, 1971), pp. 6–8.

11. Ibid., p. 217.

12. Ibid.

13. Whether religious education should be called a "discipline," or whether it should be called a "field," or whether it should be given some less well-defined name such as "task" is somewhat in doubt. The debate as to whether religious education is a separate discipline centers around whether religious education (1) operates at a level of abstraction consonant with its concepts, (2) has a distinct and clear-cut objective, (3) has a distinctive methodology, (4) operates within a distinctive set of moral rules. The majority opinion seems to be that while religious education contains the basis for definition as a discrete discipline it has not yet developed to the point where it can be so defined. See the symposium "Religious Education as a Discipline," *Religious Education,* Vol. 62 (September-October, 1967), pp. 387–428. See also James Michael Lee, *The Shape of Religious Instruction,* pp. 94–100.

14. Nels F. S. Ferré, *A Theology for Christian Education* (Philadelphia: Westminster Press, 1955), p. 183.

15. D. Campbell Wyckoff, *The Task of Christian Education* (Philadelphia: Westminster Press, 1955), p. 118.

16. Johannes Hofinger, *Our Message is Christ* (Notre Dame, Indiana: Fides, 1974), p. 1.

17. George Albert Coe, *A Social Theory of Religious Education* (New York: Scribner's, 1925), p. 55.

18. Iris Cully, *The Dynamics of Christian Education* (Philadelphia: Westminster Press, 1958), p. 118.

19. Lee, *The Shape of Religious Instruction,* p. 56. What Lee means by "desired religious lines" is further explained in various places. For example, on pages 24–27 he speaks about the socialization of the learner by means of religious instruction into the triple fellowship of God, the church, and of society in general.

20. Burgess, *An Invitation to Religious Education,* p. 21.

21. See, for example, James Michael Lee, *The Flow of Religious Instruction* (Notre Dame, Indiana: Religious Education Press, 1973), pp. 46, 96–97, 120, 180, 291–293.

22. Morton Kelsey, *Encounter with God* (Minneapolis: Bethany Fellowship, 1972), p. 11; see also pp. 213–240.

23. Miller, *The Clue to Christian Education*, p. 7. See also Miller, *Education for Christian Living*, p. 54.

24. Burgess, *An Invitation to Religious Education*, pp. 9–11. Particularly pertinent are the words of D. Campbell Wyckoff: "A discipline of Christian education and religious education can, and needs to be, developed that will essentially consist in a set of categories in which to organize our queries and our findings." ("Toward a Definition of Religious Education as a Discipline," *Religious Education*, Vol. 62 [September-October 1967], p. 392).

25. Burgess, *An Invitation to Religious Education*, p. 13.

26. See "Crisis and Hope in Religious Education," symposium in *Religious Education*, Vol. 67 (September-October 1972).

27. William Bedford Williamson, *Language and Concepts in Christian Education* (Philadelphia: Westminster Press, 1970).

28. T. S. Eliot, "Choruses from the Rock," in *T. S. Eliot: Complete Poems and Plays* (New York: Harcourt Brace, 1952), p. 111.

CHAPTER II

The Natural
and the Supernatural

Thus far it has been assumed that the words *natural* and *supernatural* have to do with God's relation to his creation, and more specifically, to man. It is now time to make explicit what has been assumed. The words natural and supernatural themselves tend to be rather ambiguous. They are notoriously susceptible to different nuances of meaning, and for various reasons (historical and otherwise) tend to be regarded with suspicion and uneasiness. Those familiar with the works of Lewis Carroll will remember Alice's wistful comment when she read the poem Jabberwocky: "It seems very pretty, but its *rather* hard to understand! . . . Somehow it seems to fill my head with ideas—only I don't know exactly what they are!"[1] What ideas the words natural and supernatural tend to fill one's head with and whether these words are the most appropriate ones to designate the God/man relationship will be discussed shortly. What this chapter does, first of all, is to look at the problematic and to offer some justification for retention of the terminology, particularly in the context of religious education theory. Secondly, this chapter undertakes a brief examination of the historical origin of the words "natural" and "supernatural" and the relationship between them in theological parlance. This historical survey is a preliminary to proposing a working definition particularly of supernatural which differs somewhat from the historical meaning of the word in traditional theology. The chapter concludes with a further explicitation of supernatural according to the proposed definition (and particularly in the context of religious education) and a pinpointing of the areas in which the supernatural is most evident.

WHY NATURAL AND SUPERNATURAL?

Why, it may be asked, use the terms natural and supernatural at all? Few prominent contemporary religious educationists appear to use these words in any strictly denotative sense. Particularly is this true of those in the mainstream Protestant tradition. On the Catholic side, while the terms have a certain currency it is recognized that they tend to be ambiguous and their

16

meaning misleading. The tendency of modern Roman Catholic theology, as we shall see further on, is to severely question whether a natural/supernatural dichotomy can properly express how God relates to persons in their historical, existential situation. It is worth taking some time to further pinpoint some objections to the use of the natural/supernatural terminology. The treatment will of necessity have to be brief and not in as much detail as the topic really deserves. It is a limitation we shall have to live with.

One reason for the nonuse of the terminology is that there are serious problems associated with the words themselves. It is not easy to arrive at a precise and fixed meaning for the word supernatural because it is too closely linked with its correlate *natural,* or *nature.* Not only does the prefix *super* have spatial connotations of *aboveness* and *beyondness,* but the very word natural itself has several different resonances and constantly changes its meaning according to the context in which it is used.[2] Thus, the words themselves are slippery and do not admit of sufficiently careful refinement.

A second reason that might be adduced for the suspicions attaching to the use of the terms is that historically the word supernatural is very much linked with the post-Tridentine development of Scholastic theology in the Roman Catholic tradition. The technical word supernatural is the brainchild of Scholastic theology and has suffered as a result of what some consider the wrong use to which it was put in the historical development of the theology of grace. In this theological system supernatural is used as a technical term to designate the elevation of human nature to an entitatively superior state of being, and an enhancement of the natural powers to perform acts which could not be performed without this elevation. This theological system held that, theoretically, man could exist in a state of "pure nature" in which his life would be directed to a wholly natural end in no way involving his union with and final vision of God. But, by a purely gratuitous act God elevated man to a supernatural level giving him a supernatural destiny and purpose as well as powers which would enable him to fulfill this destiny. This elevation and these powers with which man is endowed are *super*natural because they are totally beyond his natural capacity and are gratuitously given by God. Man is not, therefore, intrinsically graced by the very fact of his creation, but grace is added to him extrinsically ("from the outside"), as an embellishment, like the frosting on a cake. This position arose historically mainly as the result of the writings of two commentators on Thomas Aquinas, namely, Cardinal Cajetan (1468–1534) and Domingo Bañez (1528–1604). That theirs was a misinterpretation of the Thomistic texts and does not do full justice to the teaching of Aquinas is now generally accepted as a result of the scholarly work of Henri de Lubac and others.[3]

Extrinsicism, with which is associated the two-order conceptualization of man's relationship to God, has been criticized by many other writers besides de Lubac. Thus, for example, Gregory Baum traces such criticism back to French Catholic philosopher Maurice Blondel. Baum characterizes extrinsicism as the notion that "God is a divine being facing man from beyond history, and divine revelation is the communication of heavenly truths to men caught in their own limited earthly knowledge."[4] Thus, God cannot be conceived as a divine being who is "out there" or "over there," he can only be conceived as intrinsic to and intimately present to all of human history. "There is no human standpoint from which God is simply man's over-against."[5] There is only *one* order, the redemptive order, into which man is created and in which he is graced by the very fact of his creation; there is no supernatural realm (or order) as distinct from the natural realm (or order). The word supernatural is used simply to refer to the fact that hypothetically God could have created man in an ungraced state and that therefore man's present de facto state of communion with God in the redemptive order is purely gratuitous on God's part (*super*natural).

Catholic process philosopher Eulalio Baltazar treats the supernatural in the context of the thought of Pierre Teilhard de Chardin. He points out that the Scholastic tendency has been to think first of God creating (cosmological creation), and then redeeming through Christ (soteriological and redemptive activity). The soteriological and redemptive order is thus seen as superimposed on and distinct from the cosmological order. The natural and the supernatural thus belong to separate orders. Teilhard's vision is that of a single evolutionary order and process whose omega point is Christ—not Christ as distinct from process, but Christ within process. In such a system creation is not a distinct and autonomous order which is intelligible apart from incarnation. All things are created in and through Christ, in their beginning, their process, and their term. In this system we can posit only one world order, not two.[6]

Taking the question from the point of view of its philosophical underpinnings, Leslie Dewart calls attention to the fact that many modern philosophers have abandoned Hellenic dualism in general and the standard Aristotelian category system in particular. Dewart maintains that the nature/grace dichotomy is based largely on an Aristotelian view of nature as an intelligible necessity. If this view is abandoned in favor of one which regards nature as entirely contingent then, says Dewart, "the concept of the supernatural has lost its usefulness for Christian theism." Furthermore, "The distinction between the natural and the supernatural is a mere play on words, irrelevant to reality."[7]

The criticism of extrinsicism which has barely been outlined above, has led to the virtual abandonment by Roman Catholic theology of the "two order" system and a dissatisfaction with the terminology natural/supernatural as properly designating the true God/man relationship.[8]

Most of Protestant theology, for its part, has never accepted the extrinsicist position on the supernatural with its accompanying double order conceptualization of reality. As Protestant theologian Eugene TeSelle puts it, "Protestant writers habitually attack the Catholic distinction between the natural and the supernatural as an artificial scheme which leaves man's natural life unchristianized, makes grace an irrelevant addition to human life, and does full justice to neither."[9] Protestant theologians have, in fact, mounted an impressive attack on the supernatural both in popular and in scientific theology. Perhaps the chief architects of this attack are Rudolf Bultmann and Paul Tillich. At least it appears to be their ideas which have influenced more popular treatments of the topic such as John A. T. Robinson's Honest to God, which enjoyed such phenomenal success.[10]

One of the focal points of the attack of these theologians on the notion of the supernatural is that this notion is based on an outmoded cosmology and an outmoded worldview which postulates a three-tiered universe—heaven above, earth beneath, and Sheol or the underworld below. This view, they claim, tends to make God an object of our knowledge, a sort of superperson who dwells in a realm "out there," "above" the world in which people live. Robinson calls this a "supernaturalistic" worldview and rejects it as being out of touch with modern consciousness.[11] These notions of the nonexistence of a supernatural realm in the "beyond" seem to be strong echoes of Rudolf Bultmann's position that such a worldview is mythical. In the sense in which Bultmann uses myth, such a worldview is mythical because it is a projection of our self-understanding in our real life situation. This self-understanding speaks to us of our dependence, that we are not our own masters, and conjures up a picture of a "realm perpetually dominated and menaced by those mysterious powers which are its source and limit."[12] Paul Tillich also waged a lifelong battle against this kind of supernaturalistic consciousness which affirms "a world above the given world" in which God dwells. He denounced this as "a realm of superstitious imagination." On the other hand, avers Tillich, "If it [supernatural] means the ground of all beings, it should not be called supernatural."[13] Tillich believed that once the natural and the supernatural were separated ontologically, or even conceptually, it would be impossible to bring them together again. Because of the common tendency to reify thought, what begins as a conceptual inference, or idea, often takes on the solidity of an actual being in its own right. (Thus, for example, faith is often spoken of as though it were an actual concrete *thing* with an entitative existence of its own. Not infrequently one hears talk of "losing the faith," or "gaining more faith," or "holding on to the faith.") Even if the natural and the supernatural are separated conceptually there is danger of slipping into reification and consequently into ontological separation. For Tillich, there could be no supernatural "thing" as opposed to a natural "thing." His solution to the natural/supernatural dichotomy was to propose his theory of ecstatic naturalism. According to this theory to transcend oneself in ecstasy (that is, "standing outside oneself") is to be in touch with the very depth of nature, with the ground of all being, with the divine. In such an ecstatic state there is no distinction between natural and supernatural.[14]

To sum it up, therefore, the attack on the natural/supernatural terminology is three-pronged. (1) The words themselves present problems in that they tend to be ambiguous. (2) The dichotomy of natural and supernatural is based on the false postulate that God must supply an entitative elevation to the supernatural level in order for man to achieve his final end. Rather, creation should only be understood in terms of Christ's incarnation. Man exists in a de facto graced state which is intrinsic to him and is not an extrinsic superadded (supernatural) benefit. (3) To dichotomize the natural from the supernatural leads to the notion of an "outsider" God, spatially separated from his creation, an "object" of knowledge who dwells in a realm or order separate and distinct from the natural order occupied by his creation.

In Defense of the Terminology

Because of the problems attaching to the use of the natural/supernatural terminology, many theologians find these terms unhelpful and misleading as a means of designating the God/man relationship. Nevertheless, there are some points that can be made in defense of the terminology.

In the first place, even though it originated as a technical theological term, the word supernatural now has currency in everyday speech. In common usage it designates the consciousness of a reality other than our sense-perceptible world, a reality which transcends the space-time-energy-mass universe. As Peter Berger puts it, man understands this reality as being of ultimate significance for him and as denoting a fundamental category in religion.[15] Charles Bennett expresses the same thought: "The supernatural is a veritable factor in experience, and one which the mind can identify and grasp without being able to express."[16] In its everyday usage the word supernatural has an experiential connotation which is widely recognized and this may be one very good reason for keeping the word, or some other word which can properly express this experience. Thus, religious experience, whatever be its true nature, can serve as a basis for keeping such terms as natural and supernatural which distinguish that which is experienced in a religious context from that which is the ordinary, everyday experience of reality.

In the second place, no viable and fully acceptable alternative to the word supernatural has been produced by theologians or philosophers of religion. Eulalio Baltazar suggests that we stick to the words natural and naturalism. If, as he claims, naturalism is understood as "Christism," and if nature is understood as being totally "Christic" in the Teilhardian sense (that is, as having no meaning apart from Christ), then there is nothing wrong in dropping the word supernatural completely.[17] The difficulty with this solution is that the word supernatural is a venerable one in theological history and has now filtered into everyday speech. Many would assert that the natural/supernatural dichotomy has served well, particularly in Roman Catholic theology, in an effort to unlock some of the mystery of the God/man relationship. Furthermore, in the understanding of a great many Christians the word supernatural has always stood in some sort of opposition to the word natural as signifying the supreme otherness and transcendence of God. People tend to identify themselves with their language as they do with their other symbols. Perhaps to completely write the word out of the vocabulary, or to emasculate it, would be for many *piis auribus offensivum*. Another consideration (albeit not an overriding one), at least for Roman Catholics, is that the word supernatural is now enshrined in the documents of the magisterium.[18]

Thirdly, it appears that a strong enough case can be made that in the context of traditional theism to profess belief in God is to profess and affirm that the reality of God is different from the reality of the world. God is an ontological question and an implicit ontology is back of understanding or interpreting any theological proposition.[19] The Judaeo-Christian belief in God implies that God is a fundamentally different kind of being from the being which is immediately obvious to us in the sense-preceptible world. In other words, God is not a linguistic device for expressing some form of human consciousness, or a certain perception of reality. Some form of ontological dualism, however qualified, seems to be demanded by a theistic stance, otherwise it becomes extremely difficult to distinguish the theist from the pantheist. Herbert McCabe expresses it well:

> The issue between pantheists and traditional theists comes down to this: Can we make statements which, however much they may derive their meaning and verification from the world, are statements about God and not about the world? For traditional theology, although we can only say "God is good" because of something we know about the world and not because of some extra information we have about God, nevertheless the statement is not about the world.[20]

Ontological dualism does not mean total ontological separation (though it could) such that God becomes *a* being (albeit of a special kind) separate and distinct from the mass of other beings which make up the universe. Nevertheless, the notion must be safeguarded that "The Divine is divine only if it embodies qualities of perfection in a degree different from the human, or if it does so in a way fundamentally incapable of actualization within our natural order."[21] It is this radical distinctness of God and his creation which provides the basis for a type of terminology such as natural/supernatural. Such terminology may be looked upon as polar, that is, as referring to a distinctness which does not imply separateness. The notion of the natural does not exclude the notion of the supernatural, neither, on the other hand, are the two identical. Thus, both the notion of distinctness and the notion of relatedness are retained. God is not the world but, at the same time, remains fundamentally related to the world.

Transcendence and Immanence. The problem of keeping God and the world related while keeping them distinct is perhaps the most fundamental and ancient of all theological problems. How does one reconcile God's "separation" from the world with his creative power as the ground and sustainer of all being, and with his incarnation in Christ? Theologians have used many devices in trying to throw some light on this unsolvable dilemma. As has already been noted in the previous chapter, one such device is to speak of God's transcendence and his immanence.[22] Transcendence refers to the supreme otherness of God, to the fact that God infinitely surpasses all created and finite reality, that in him is all perfection in a supereminent degree. Immanence is the notion that stresses God's presence to and in all created reality. Created, contingent, finite reality cannot be itself without the ever-sustaining power and penetration of the divine act. Thus, the transcendence/immanence distinction is one way of looking at the natural/supernatural relationship; it is an aspect of the natural/supernatural. It is a way of viewing the God/man relationship, a way of expressing simultaneous "God-otherness" and "God-relatedness." Theology has traditionally asserted that God is fully transcendent and fully immanent, though in their explanations of the God/man relationship theologians have often tended to emphasize either transcendence or immanence. As we shall see further on, religious educationists have the same tendency and this book is concerned precisely with searching out this tendency and with assessing its role in religious education theory.

There may well be other more compelling reasons for keeping the natural/supernatural terminology than the ones outlined above. It does appear, however, that a case can be made for the retention of the terminology. In this connection one thing should be made abundantly clear. The decision to stick with these particular terms in no way implies that natural and supernatural exist as ontological entities, as individual concrete "things." Nor (and most importantly) does it mean that the religious educationists whose theories are being considered so understand natural and supernatural. The terminology is purely investigative; it is a useful tool for labeling important verities, namely, the relationship of God and his creation. Thus, the word supernatural can be use to designate the more than human dimension of experience as well being used to designate the radical distinctness but intimate relatedness of God vis-à-vis man. This usage differs somewhat from the usage common in scientific theology in that it proposes a slightly differnt thrust or focus. As will become evident when we take a look at its historical origin and development in the next section, the word supernatural gradually evolved as a means of theologically explaining the gratuity of God's gift to man, and not as an expression of experience. It is the former usage which is now severely questioned by theologians as it tends to an extrinsicist understanding of God's graciousness to man.

In any case, if the terminology is to be retained, some effort must be made to define it even though, as has already been pointed out, the words themselves make this endeavor extremely hazardous. Protestant theologian Eugene Fairweather has the truth of it when he points out that "Whatever the verbal difficulties, [however,] the idea itself is an inescapable requirement of Christian faith." The idea he is referring to is the notion of the supernatural, a notion which has its root in what Fairweather calls the real "two-sidedness" of Christian faith. This "two-sidedness" is born of a simultaneous consciousness of and belief in a human this-worldly orientation and vocation, and the recognition of a "supratemporal relation to reality which transcends all creaturely existence. "No theological task," Fairweather strongly affirms, "is more important than the clarification of the true relation of man to the supernatural."[23]

HISTORICAL BACKGROUND

In order to lay a proper foundation for clarification of the terminology it will be helpful to give a brief historical survey of the origins of the word supernatural and its correlate natural in theological usage. As has already been hinted, the word supernatural developed, but did not originate, in the theological context of the attempt by theologians to preserve and explain the gratuity of grace. Thus, in theological usage the word supernatural became practically synonymous with grace, that is, with God's gift of himself to man, but historically has a broader and perhaps much richer usage.[24]

The Origin of the Word Supernatural

The English word supernatural derives from the Latin *supernaturalis* which word first made its appearance in the 9th century through translations of the works of pseudo-Dionysius from Greek into Latin. The word supernatural is not found in the Septaugint, nor in the New Testament, nor in the early Fathers of the church. In the Latin classics one finds such expressions as *supra naturam excedens* (Seneca) or other expressions involving the prefix *supra,* or *ultra* which refer to extraordinary effects not within the scope of normal experience. The Greek Fathers similarly make use of compound words the root of which is φυσις (i.e., nature, the essence of a thing, its inner principle). De Lubac points out that pseudo-Dionysius has a whole series of expressions with the prefix ὑπερ (hyper) which suggest the transcendence of a spiritual being. De Lubac also indicates that the adjective ὑπερφυες is found in classical Greek having the sense of "that which grows out above" and, particularly in the neo-Platonist writings, the sense of "superior to," "transcending the ordinary in greatness and goodness."[25] It is this adjective ὑπερφυες which is translated into Latin by John Scotus Erigena as *supernaturalis* from which the English word *supernatural* was born. The neo-Platonists particularly tended to use the word as referring to beings, or substances, such as God, the angels, souls. The Latin usage of the prefix *super,* on the other hand, tended to refer to superior forces, or effects. Thus, from very early beginnings the two principal uses of the word supernatural were already molded, that is, as referring to superior *substances* ("Greek" usage), and to surpassing *effects,* or *acts* ("Latin" usage).

Despite the appearance of the word *supernaturalis* as early as the ninth century, it was Thomas Aquinas who effectively put the word into circulation as a technical theological term. So frequently does Aquinas use the word that, as J. P. Kenny facetiously remarks, "a complete tally would harldy be feasible without the aid of an electronic computer."[26] Aquinas uses the word in both senses, that is, as referring to superior substances, and to surpassing effects. However, the usages in the second sense are far more numerous and it is as a result of Aquinas' work that the use of supernatural as referring to acts, powers, and effects that surpass natural causes came to dominate in the theology of the succeeding centuries. Not only has the "Latin" usage dominated in theology but also in everyday speech. The word supernatural is most commonly used to refer to events which are somehow beyond full human understanding, which surpass the normal expectancies of cause and effect, which partake of the aura of the numinous. Thus, for example, the events associated with diabolic possession are frequently characterized as supernatural. The strange experiences which are referred to the activity of ghosts or poltergeists are sometimes called supernatural. Many of the saints who exhibited such extraordinary capabilities as bilocation, or the ability to work miraculous cures, were said to possess "supernatural" power.

In the course of the development of Scholastic theology a new usage of the word supernatural gradually came to the fore, much wider, and in a sense, much more technical than the original Thomistic usage. De Lubac notes that the word came to be used in such expressions as "supernatural order," "supernatural destiny," "supernatural design of the world." All of these, in one way or another, refer to the final end of man and of all creation, that is, to the final vision of God.[27] The vision of God is the supernatural par excellence. Anything which pertains specifically and intrinsically to this supernatural end of man belongs to the supernatural order. Thus the incarnation of Christ, revelation, the sacraments, miracles, and above all grace, all belong to the supernatural order, they partake of the supernatural, they are supernatural. As de Lubac pointedly remarks, "where before the older authors spoke of grace, we now constantly speak of the supernatural."[28] The history of grace in Roman Catholic theological literature has been therefore largely a history of the supernatural. Natural/supernatural has been conceived of as in many ways synonymous with nature/grace. Grace is understood as supernatural because it is God himself, a supernatural entity (uncreated grace), who produces supernatural effects (created grace) which enable man to attain his final end, which end is itself supernatural (union with the divine). As a result of the influence of commentators on the works of Thomas Aquinas, and particularly of the overarching consideration that grace must be seen as God's gift, fully gratuitous and in no way "owed" to man, nature and grace were pushed further and further apart until they came to be understood as belonging to two different orders—orders which are ontologically distinct. This then, according to Scholastic theology in the Roman Catholic tradition, is the origin of the natural order (to which man and the rest of creation belong), and the supernatural order (to which God belongs). The latter may elevate the former to its level, indeed, has to if man is to attain his supernatural destiny. This two-order conceptualization of man's relationship to God held sway in Catholic theology until, as has already been noted, the work of de Lubac and others exposed it as a less tenable position, or at least, not based on a proper reading of Thomas Aquinas.[29]

A Traditional Protestant Position on the Supernatural

As far as Protestant theology is concerned, historically there has been little discussion on the supernatural. The early Reformers, in their use of the word supernatural, stuck pretty closely to the medieval usage even though they eschewed the Scholastic doctrine on grace. Thus, for example, John Calvin is simply repeating a distinction made by all medieval theologians when he distinguishes between natural and supernatural gifts.[30] Calvin's position is that the supernatural gifts are lost by sin, but man can still function with his natural gifts even though these are so infected that they always show the effects of sin.[31] One reason for the nonevolution of the technical term supernatural in Protestant theology has to do with the separate developments in the different religious denominations of the theology of nature and grace. Great attention was given by the Roman Catholic theologians to the nature/grace relationship. In time, the natural/supernatural dichotomy came to be associated with the nature/grace dichotomy. Protestant theology, on the other hand, either totally ignored or misunderstood this fundamental Catholic distinction. Because of its almost exclusive treatment of grace in the context of man's sin and the restoring of man to his pristine capabilities, in the opinion of some writers Protestant theology has not paid sufficient attention to the Catholic emphasis on grace as God's special graciousness to man.[32] Although Christ's grace is meant for sinful man it is not exclusively liberation from sin but is also communion and personal intimacy with God. It is this graciousness of God which gives man a supernatural destiny (final union with God) and the supernatural power to perform acts consonant with this final end. However, the "supernatural" aspect of man's final end and the means of achieving it were not an issue for Protestant theology as a whole. Furthermore, the Protestant theology on grace did not grow up in the atmosphere of two-order dualism spawned by Aquinas' commentators bent on preserving, at all costs, the absolute gratuity of God's self-gift to man.

As a result of the developments mentioned above (though there may well be other reasons), the term supernatural is sparingly used in Protestant theology. Its most frequent use is probably in the context of divine revelation, that is, God's word to man which cannot be known by man's reason alone. There can be little doubt that the tremendous influence of Karl Barth has greatly strengthened this usage in modern times. Barth has been called a supernaturalist because of his insistence on the authority of the revealed word of God. This word is so supernatural as to allow virtually no questioning or confirmation by human thought and reason; the only human attitude possible and allowable is one of acceptance and obedience. The neoorthodox movement (spearheaded by Barth) in general stresses the supreme transcendence of God and those influenced by this movement have a greater tendency to use the word supernatural. The word is used in Protestant theology to designate supernatural events, miracles for example, which are understood as being beyond human power and outside the normal laws of cause and effect. The special efficacy of the Holy Spirit in giving his gifts to man is also called supernatural.[33]

NATURE AND THE NATURAL

Since *nature,* or *natural,* is the root word of supernatural and stands in some sort of polar opposition to it, before attempting a more specific statement on the supernatural it will be helpful for us to examine the word natural itself. It may be as well, however, to hang out the "warning" signs. In the first place, the word nature is dangerously ambiguous. It is ambiguous because it has a wide range of meaning, different contextual resonances, and is extremely difficult to pin down in a clear definition. In the second place, in order to define one must distinguish and separate. Something is clearly defined when it is sufficiently etched to make it distinguishable from other things which closely resemble it. In defining, it is often necessary to isolate words or concepts so that they become understandable only in a certain context. Defining, therefore, is often limited to the frame of reference in which the definition is made. When it comes to the word nature, there are several frames of reference in which the word may be defined. The frame of reference that is of most interest to religious education is a theological one, namely, the God/man relationship.

The English word *nature* derives from the Latin *natura* which itself corresponds to the Greek φύσις, the root word of ὑπερφυες.[34] Historically, the concept of nature has been used in a variety of ways consonant with the manner in which various philosophers viewed the world, its materiality or sense-perceptibleness, and the non sense-perceptible elements. What is of particular interest to religious education, however, is not so much the philosophical use of the term as its theological implications. Thus, an understanding of nature may be arrived at from an observation of the world and the metaphysical concepts which are ultimately arrived at from this observation; or an understanding of nature can stem from Christian belief in the light of revelation. Part of this revelation is that God has entered into a special relationship with man through grace in Christ. This latter view in no way negates the philosophical view of nature but rather adds a new dimension to it. Thus, the theological frame of reference in which nature may be understood builds on and is to a certain extent dependent on a particular philosophical understanding of the term. Important, also, is the historical perspective. Man is not a set of abstract attributes but exists as *this* person in a definite historical setting. Revelation is clearly concerned with man in his historical context, not with man as a philosophical abstraction—God does not relate to an abstraction.

Three stages in the growth and development of the term nature before the Tridentine period can be traced. In the early Greek period nature was used either in the individual sense of the essential reality of a being realizing itself, or in the sense of the totality of all beings in their constant evolution. This totality is seen by some Greek thinkers as either self-explanatory and responding to an inexorable inner principle of development; or it is seen as created, but by a God who has no further intimacy with nature having made it self-supporting and self-perpetuating. The second stage is represented by Augustine who, reacting to what he regarded as this pagan attitude toward nature, fell into voluntarism by which he reduced the nature of things simply to the good pleasure of God. Things are what God wants them to be.[35] Thus, for Augustine, things in and of themselves have no inner principle of autonomy apart from God's will.[36] Somewhere between the extremes represented by the two previous stages, i.e., the theory of a self-sufficient and autonomous

nature and the voluntarism of Augustine, lies the medieval Scholastic position. This is the position on which most of the theology of grace and nature is
built. Nature, in this type of thinking, is seen as simultaneously autonomous
and God-directed.[37]

Uses of the Word Nature

The word nature is used in a variety of ways. Clearly, it is a word with a
wide range of meaning and the meaning can best be determined from the
context in which it is used. Nature is hardly ever susceptible to a fixed
definition, not even, perhaps, within a single frame of reference. Also, we
should constantly keep in mind that nature is essentially an abstraction, a
concept which is built as a result of experiential observation in order to clarify
and codify experience. If we treat nature as a "thing" instead of a concept,
then the supernatural becomes a "superthing" added to, or over and above
nature.

Several writers have proposed various meanings for the word nature. One
such writer sees that in the theological context or frame of reference the term
can have four main uses. Each of these uses bears in some way on the
supernatural but not with equal intensity. They are the genetic, the abstract,
the individual, and the cosmic senses.[38] Nature in the genetic sense means that
with which one is endowed from birth, or from origin. This takes in the
historical understanding of man who is born into a historical environment. It is
in this sense that Adam's state of original justice may be said to be natural.
Secondly, nature may be looked at in the abstract sense, that is as pertaining to
a set of ontological attributes, abstract in themselves, but predicatable of all
individuals of that type or kind. In this sense one can speak of human nature as
consisting of those attributes which fit every human person, for example, the
power to reason. Sex is another such attribute, but the sexual kind (male or
female) is not. Thirdly, the word nature may be used in individual senses, that
is, as referring to *this* particular human nature as distinct from all other human
natures. Each concrete human nature is more than the individual predication
of all the essential human attributes to any particular individual. A concretely
existing human nature is built of several other factors which are not common
to each individual such as sensations, emotions, personal consciousness. Man
relates to God not in the abstract but according to each person's individual
makeup. Fourthly, the cosmic sense, which denotes the entire universe, the
created as distinct from the creator. In this sense, nature for the physicist
would mean that which is sense-perceptible; for the philosopher, or the
metaphysician, on the other hand, it could also refer to created spirits.

It may be well to note that in the Aristotelian philosophical system which
underpins much of Scholastic theology the tendency when using the word

nature is to see it as a principle of activity.[39] Thus viewed, nature would refer to the powers and faculties whereby acts are produced. Thus, for example, the intelligence is seen as a faculty which is natural to man, that is, pertaining to man's nature as a rational animal. For man, it is "natural" to intellectualize. In this connection, the *super*natural becomes that which raises these natural powers above their natural capacity and enables them to produce acts which they could not of their own "nature" produce. Thus, for example, the act of faith is spoken of as an act of supernatural knowledge of God which participates in the very act of God's own self-knowing. This is a usage of supernatural which sticks closely to the original "Latin" usage noted above. There is room, however, for the "Greek" usage as well in which nature is looked upon as an essence, that is, the principle which makes a thing to be what it is. Nature looked upon as essence would correspond to supernatural as referring to superior substances. Aquinas speaks of God as "supernatural truth" *(veritas supernaturalis)*.[40] God is also "supernatural principle" *(principium supernaturale)*,[41] and even "supernatural existence" *(supra omne existens)*,[42] if this last does not stretch the sense of Aquinas too drastically.

In conclusion, therefore, it is well to always bear in mind that even within the ambit of a theological frame of reference the word nature is rarely, if ever, susceptible to a single definition. The proper meaning of the word can only be determined from the context in which it is used. The words nature and natural have a wide, rich range of meaning and the totality of this meaning is never captured in a single phrase or sentence.

THE SUPERNATURAL

Our brief excursion into the historical development of the words natural and supernatural has shown that although the words are correlates the term supernatural did not originate as the polar opposite of natural. The meaning of supernatural as opposed to natural developed as a result of the association of these words with the theological discussion of nature and grace. A problem attendant on the dichotomizing of natural and supernatural was that, as frequently happens when concepts are distinguished, the distinction tended to become reified. In the minds of many the supernatural and the natural tended to become concrete "things" and thus their opposition and separateness became even more solidified. Let it be stated emphatically that as far as this book is concerned the treatment of natural and supernatural implies neither reification nor nonreification. If some religious educationists appear to use the terminology, or refer to the God/man relationship in a reified sense, this book makes no judgment on the theorists' use of language. If there are difficulties concerning the use of the terminology, then the treatment of natural and supernatural in this book should not be taken as an argument either for or against reification. What has been noted is that the dichotomy of the natural and the supernatural has spilled over from theological discussion into everyday speech as reflecting an experiential as well as a faith conviction that God is distinct from and other than his creation. This conviction is the basis for keeping the natural/supernatural terminology, not as mutually exclusive categories, but as indicating a polar relationship between God and his creation. The poles of this relationship always remain fully distinct but intimately related.

Let us now attempt some further clarification and definition of supernatural.

It seems obvious that the word supernatural, like its correlate natural, has a wide range of meaning and uses in popular language and literature. In general, the word supernatural is used to designate anything which is beyond the reach of empirical observation, or whatever is understood as transcending or mysterious, outside the normal operations of cause and effect. Such phenomena as spirits of one kind or another, God, miracles, magic, all bear the label supernatural. A good example of the wide range of topics to which the word supernatural may be applied in popular usage is to be found in the *Subject Headings for the Dictionary Catalogs of the Library of Congress* which gives the following cross references for supernatural: Divination, Inspiration, Miracles, Occult Sciences, Prophecies, Psychical Research, Revelation, Spirits, Spiritualism, Superstition. Even a glance at these headings will reveal that they can be roughly grouped into two general classes: supernatural substances and supernatural effects. In early Scholastic usage, as has been pointed out above, the word shared both meanings, but post-Tridentine Roman Catholic theology focused its meaning almost exclusively on supernatural effects and powers. In order to keep the richness of the word supernatural, we must not focus exclusively either on supernatural substances (God, angels, spirits), or on supernatural effects (revelation, miracles, prophecies), but must borrow from both usages.

In the proper sense of the word then, it seems best to take the term supernatural as referring to a relationship between God and his creation. Not simply the relationship of creator to created, but also a new and gratuitous relationship over and above this, a relationship of God's gracious gift of love, the covenant relationship revealed in scripture. Taken in this sense, *the essence of the supernatural is God's self-communication in love.* This communication comes to us as grace in this life and the full enjoyment of God in the next. Grace, and the beatific vision (if one prefers to refer to the afterlife with God in these terms), are supernatural in the strictest sense.

Accepting the above as a working definition of supernatural there are some things that we should note. First, the definition borrows from both the

"Greek" and "Latin" uses of the word supernatural in that it alludes to superior substances *and* to surpassing effects. If the supernatural is a means of conceptualizing God's self-communication it therefore pertains to God himself in his essence—the divine person in communication with a personal creature in knowledge and love. Only persons are capable of a mutual self-giving relationship of love. In Roman Catholic theological terminology the supernatural understood as God's self-gift is called uncreated grace. God's self-communication is manifest by certain effects in the person who receives, accepts, and responds to such a gift. These effects are said to be supernatural because they surpass any innate human capacities. Some of these effects are, for example, increased powers of perceiving the truth, discernment of good and evil, strength of purpose and courage to live virtuously, the virtues of faith, hope, and charity, the healing of man's alienation from man. He who is graced by God's gracious self-communication and presence lives *graciously*. As the poet says:

> . . . the just man justices;
> Keeps grace: that keeps all his goings graces;
> Acts in God's eye what in God's eye he is—
> Christ—for Christ plays in ten thousand places,
> Lovely in limbs, and lovely in eyes not his
> To the Father through the features of men's faces.[43]

In Roman Catholic theological terminology Hopkins' "justicing" of the just man is called created grace, that is, the gracious living out of God's self-gift.

Second, grace is not a mere theological abstraction but quite definitely has an experiential referent. As has been stated, one solid reason for keeping the natural/supernatural terminology (which is so closely associated with nature/grace) is that even though it may be a theological conceptualization it is rooted in experience. God's grace can be experienced in many ways. It can be experienced, for example, in the wonderful givenness of life which is brought home to us so forceably by the very real experience of our contingency, but particularly in those moments when we experience life as enriched and joyful. The real experience of the givenness of life and its richness is perhaps the firmest basis for religious faith, faith which is the personal gracious reply of the human person to the experience of God's graciousness: "This good life . . . man sees as God's gift or grace to him, he appreciates it, he acknowledges, confesses, and that is faith."[44] We act out our acknowledgment and appreciation of God's graciousness to us by the giving of graciousness to others: "The just man justices . . . keeps all his goings graces." God "acted out" his graciousness to us in Jesus. The experiential giving of graciousness to others, as Jesus did, is *our* expression of God's self-gift, is our expression of love. It is not a mere feeling of goodwill but a deliberate sharing of life by our active participation in the healing of persons, in the binding up of wounds. But life is not always joyful. Its givenness and the desire to share this givenness and goodness are not always compelling. The consciousness and experience of evil is as real as the experience of graciousness. The power we experience which enables us to cope with evil is the power of grace expressed as hope—hope whose final triumph is its triumph over the experience of human death. Faith, love, and hope are the experiential expression of God's gracious gift of himself to us, they are the experiential expression of the supernatural.

Third, in the context of Christian belief, God's self-communication to persons takes place in and through Christ. This self-communication implies the mystery of Christ and his church; it understands man as a sinner and in need of redemption; it includes the notion of this redemption as in some way taking place within and through the redemptive community, the church.

Fourth, in most treatises on the supernatural the topic is dealt with almost exclusively as referring to the God/man relationship. The redemption of all of the material creation, for the most part, is not treated as part of God's supernatural activity. The theology of cosmic Christology reminds us, however, that all of nature (understood in the cosmic sense) is tending towards its perfection in Christ and therefore all of nature has a supernatural end. Man is supernaturalized according to his particular nature as man, which nature is personal. All the rest of creation is supernaturalized according to each being's particular nature (understood in the genetic and individual senses), because each nature tends toward perfection and transcendence in Christ. Humankind is part of the inexorable evolutionary unfolding of the cosmos in its progress to perfection in Christ. Thus, all of nature in some way shares, through Christ, in the self-gift of God. Nature breathes the supernatural and can yield an experiential consciousness of God.[45]

RELATIONSHIPS AND THE SUPERNATURAL

In order to further clarify and etch the notion of the supernatural understood as God's self-communication which demands a response on our part, let us take a look at the question of relationships. In fairly recent times there has been a noticeable shift in emphasis in theological writing on grace and the supernatural. Instead of an ontological or metaphysical approach, the new concern is with the phenomenological and interpersonal aspects of grace—a personalist approach. This approach focuses on persons as conscious subjects rather than looking at them from the point of view of their objective nature (taken in the abstract sense). Thus, it seems, the God/man relationship can best be understood and explained by using the model of human relationships.[46]

The theme of interpersonal relationships is one that has been developed in the context of religious education mainly by Protestant religious educationists before it became an important issue in the Catholic theology of grace.[47] These educationists typically base their treatment of interpersonal relationships on the I-thou categories of Martin Buber.[48] For such thinkers, one of the main aims of religious education is to confront the learner with God in the development of a personal I-Thou relationship. Personal self-integration, self-understanding and "wholeness" are seen as the major benefits of such a relationship with God. Thus, for example, Randolph Crump Miller indicates that "Christian education is concerned with wholeness of personality. It is found in the response of the total person to the divine Person within a community of persons."[49]

Not only are relationships important when considering the God/man encounter but they are also important as pertaining to the human person/person encounter. Particularly is this aspect important when it is a question of coming in contact with God's message in scripture. Miller, for example, sees the bible as a description of relationships. The bible expresses the relationship of God with his people, and the relationships of the people among themselves as the elect of God. Thus, according to Miller, we must tease out from the bible how God and man interact and relate to one another in various life situations so that we can have a basis for interpreting out present-day experience. Biblical relationships thus provide a model of divine/human and human/human interpersonal relationships. Reuel Howe, for his part, sees a dual importance for interpersonal relationships. Like Miller, he sees relationships as basic to understanding and communicating God's message in the bible. He goes further, though, and sees God as communicating with man in and through the depth of human interpersonal relationships themselves. The experience of interpersonal relationships is a vehicle of God's self-revelation and self-gift.[50] This intimate presence of God in the heart of the human interpersonal encounter is also noted by theologians who deal with the topic in the context of the nature/grace discussion.

The issue, as has been noted, has to do with an understanding of human nature as personal. A person needs other persons for intergal growth, development, and fulfillment. Viewed as personal, human nature is never completely developed, totally stable, or fully "finished." The fashioning of the human personality goes on throughout life with lots of subtle variations, partial stops and new beginnings. Personality, therefore, must be viewed as "open" and constantly tending toward self-transcendence. This means that persons can constantly reach beyond the constricting circumstances of the historical moment in which they are situated and attain new levels of relationship with the environment—other persons, places, things. Persons develop "personally" in dialogical relationship with their total environment. More importantly, personality develops in dialogical relationship with the absolute,

mysterious ground of all reality, that is, with God.[51] The dialogical relationship is the I-Thou encounter in which God is the eternal Thou. The eternal
Thou offers himself as a continuous gift of love.[52] The human I cannot fully
become a person except through a personal relationship with another person.
The I is intrinsically structured toward the ''other,'' a thou, in a love relationship of mutual self-giving. Thus, persons are not self-sufficient, they cannot
attain their final purpose (which includes the full integration and perfection of
personal being) without God's gift of himself in love—''For thou hast made
us for Thyself and our hearts are restless till they rest in Thee.''[53]

Now, if love is of its very essence free, then it has to be gratuitous. God,
the offerer, the gift-giver, remains fully transcendent in the God/man encounter and in no way dependent on the human demand for self-integrating
personal encounter. At the same time, God as the eternal Thou is fully immanent in the God/man encounter. In order to become a person as well as to keep
on with personal development the individual must respond to God in his
self-gift. Thus, the Thou is always necessary and intrinsic to the personal
development of the I. The I cannot be thought of except in terms of the Thou;
the Thou must be immanent to the I. Thus, the supernatural understood as
personal, the supernatural as the Thou which human persons must encounter,
is immanent in the very process of the coming-to-be of the I.[54] And so, once
again, if the natural/supernatural relationship is looked at from the point of
view of transcendence and immanence there is an obvious tension. The tension is that of understanding (and subsequently living with the fruits of one's
understanding) how God can be, and must remain, fully transcendent to the
human need for personal relationship with the absolute, while at the same time
remaining immanent within the very process of that relationship. If God must
remain ''other'' in order to be the transcendent Thou toward which the human
I is structured, how can he be immanent to the I? How can God be an intimate
personal friend and at the same time be the absolute ground of being in which
all personality finds its fulfillment? The solving of this tension, or rather, the
ability to cope with it, depends on the personal metaperspective with which
each one approaches the transcendence/immanence polarity. As has already
been stated more than once, this book is concerned with the examination of
such metaperspectives and their role in religious education theory.

Some theologians, such as John W. Glaser, understand the I-Thou relationship not as ''a naked and vertical relationship with God; rather, God presents
himself to man as the infinite and absolute dimension of the encounter with
finite and created reality.'' Glaser goes on to assert, ''supernatural love of
God and genuine love of man constitute an essential unity; the fundamental
and primary arena of supernatural encounter with God is not a plane 'over' or
'beyond' my encounter with created reality, but occurs as the deepest dimension
of this encounter and in no other way.''[55] Particularly is this ''deepest

dimension'' manifested in the meeting of two human persons in the relationship of love. The development of personality which takes place in one's life is sited principally and dramatically in the investment and risking of personal freedom in a love relationship with other persons. Loving human relationships are not only the analog and exemplar of the divine/human love relationship but are, in fact, the actual focus of God's loving self-communication, his supernatural self-giving. Thus, for those who hold to this view, it is not enough to say that we cannot love God if we do not love our neighbor; for them, genuine love of neighbor *is* love of God.[56] If the supernatural is thus present in loving human relationships, then it can be said that God is revealing himself in the very depth of human encounter. Human encounter is thus one way in which God continues to reveal himself in ongoing human history.

Plausible and encouraging as the theology of relationships may appear to be, particularly as applying to religious education, let us not plunge with total abandon into the relationship waters. Rather, let us stand back, test the waters, and take account of the rocks and shoals. In the first place, those religious educationists who make extensive use of relationships in their theorizing do not always work out a clear presentation and definition of interpersonal relations themselves. In too many instances the word ''relationship'' partakes more of the sense of an emotive slogan having the sentimental and indefinable flavor of an idealistic sort of togetherness. Writers often adopt a rather romanticist approach to the question of relationships which bears little relation to the real world.[57] For example, the relationship of confrontation is rarely treated. The same can be said for the awful reality of evil in human relationships. Some religious educationists, also, tend to be ambiguous in their statements of objectives to be aimed at in promoting interpersonal relationships in the context of religious education.[58] In the second place, if theology is to be based on analogy, then the understanding of God's self-communication to man will have to be based on the analogy of human communication. We are far from having ironed out all the problems in this area.[59] Until, therefore, there is a properly worked out and scientifically verified model of human communication which can take in all the various facets of relationship, it seems only prudent to be extremely wary of too sloganesque an application of the word ''relationship.''[60] We are in fact dealing with one of those gray areas which require much more research and theorizing, both physical-scientific and theological. It is not the purpose of this book, nor within its scope, to work out such a theory.[61] Consequently, what follows on relationships and the supernatural must be considered as quite tentative.

God's self-communication to man is always supernatural. One becomes conscious of this God-communication in a variety of ways. Thus, for example, God's self-communication can become evident through his word in scripture, through prayer, through celebration in the church, through recognition of

God's gracious invitation in ordinary life-situations (the experience of his gracious giving of life and the experience of his power in overcoming evil), through the acknowledgment of an invitation to give oneself to others in love. By responding positively to these invitations we act out the grace of God's continual presence to us and the relationship established in the context of the occasion is supernatural. A positive response to God's invitation means responding in a loving fashion, that is, it means making a personal investment of our freedom for the good of the other, the "thou." The essence of the supernatural in the context of relationship, therefore, is the deep note of the personal. The note, that is, of care and value and reverence for the other person which engages us in the depth of the self as pointed toward and formed by other persons and ultimately by the divine Person. If one insists on this reverence for the personal then even situations of human confrontation can have their supernatural aspect, for confrontation does not necessarily mean evil inimicality. Finally, reverential care for the person is a perfect antidote to any manifestation of such evil inimicality.

WHAT IS SUPERNATURAL?

To conclude this chapter it will be well to pinpoint more clearly those areas in which God's self-gift to us are most evident. Pinpointing these manifestations of the divine self-communication will provide a background, marked off by some clear-cut reference points, against which to delineate different theological metaperspectives. To what, then, can we most properly apply the term "supernatural"?

First. As has already been indicated, God's grace in this life and our glory in the next are most properly termed supernatural. Grace means both God's gracious presence in Christ (realized through his Spirit) and the gracious effects this presence produces in the lived life of the recipient as expressed in faith, hope, love, and the gifts of the Spirit.

Second. Revelation is supernatural. It is supernatural whether viewed solely as God's word in scripture, or whether it is understood in the wider context of the constant unfolding of God's self-communication in each individual's personal experience and in the history of the whole world.

Third. The church is supernatural, as is its liturgy (that is, its prayer), its celebration of the eucharist and its other sacraments. In the words of Vatican II:

... Christ is always present in His Church especially in her liturgical celebrations. He is present in the sacrifice of the Mass, not only in the presence of His minister, "the same one now offering, through the ministry of priests, who formally offered himself on the cross," but especially under the Eucharistic species. By His power He is present in the sacraments, so that when a man baptizes it is really Christ himself who baptizes. He is present in His word, since it is He Himself who speaks when the holy scriptures are read in the Church. He is present, finally, when the Church prays and sings, for He promised: "Where two or three are gathered together for my sake, there am I in the midst of them" (Mt. 18:20).[62]

Fourth.   Christ himself is supernatural in that he is the source of all grace, he is the Father's self-communication to us. On the other hand, from the perspective we are adopting (that is, conceptualizing the supernatural as a relationship), the second person of the Trinity is not supernatural in essence though the supernatural "partakes" of that essence. What is supernatural is God-in-relation-to-man, a relationship which is fully expressed in Christ Jesus.[63]

Understanding the metaperspective out of which one is working will involve testing one's attitude and outlook toward these areas in which the supernatural is most evident. Reflection, for example, on how one views and personally relates to Jesus Christ will give a good indication of what brand of theological metaperspective one subscribes to. Are we more comfortable with the notion that Jesus is a constant friend and companion? Or do we find ourselves, rather, slipping into the adoration mode of reverence in the presence of the *God*-man? Delineating the metaperspectives of religious educationists in order to assess the role of such metaperspectives in religious education theory will also enable us to examine our own personal positions and to examine what effect these positions may have on our performance as religious educators.

NOTES

1. Lewis Carroll, *Through the Looking Glass* in *The Complete Works of Lewis Carroll* (New York: The Modern Library), p. 155.

2. On this point see, for example, Henri de Lubac S.J., "Remarques sur l'histoire du mot 'surnaturel,'" *Nouvelle Revue Théologique*, Vol. 61 (mars 1934), p. 249.

3. De Lubac's epoch-making book *Surnaturel: études historiques* (Paris: Aubier, 1946) was subsequently expanded into two volumes both of which have been translated into English under the titles *Augustinianism and Modern Theology* (New York: Herder and Herder, 1966) and *The Mystery of the Supernatural* (New York: Herder and Herder, 1967).

4. Gregory Baum, *Man Becoming* (New York: Herder and Herder, 1970), pp. 3–4. See also, J. P. Kenny, "Reflections on Human Nature and the Supernatural," *Theological Studies,* Vol. 14 (1953), pp. 280–287. See also

W. C. Shepherd, *Man's Condition* (New York: Herder and Herder, 1969). Shepherd equates extrinsicism with the *duplex ordo* pattern adopted by post-Tridentine Scholasticism "which sharply divides the natural from the supernatural order" (p. 32).

5. Baum, *Man Becoming* (New York: Herder and Herder, 1970), p. 170.

6. See Eulalio Baltazar, *Teilhard and the Supernatural* (Baltimore: Helicon, 1966).

7. Leslie Dewart, *The Future of Belief* (New York: Herder and Herder, 1966), pp. 209–210.

8. A pithy account of the Catholic change in thinking on the natural/ supernatural can be found in Gustavo Gutierrez, *A Theology of Liberation,* translated and edited by Sr. Caridad Inda and John Eagleson (Maryknoll, New York: Orbis Books, 1973), pp. 69–72.

9. Eugene TeSelle, "Nature and Grace in the Forum of Ecumenical Discussion," *Journal of Ecumenical Studies,* Vol. 8 (Summer 1971), p. 539.

10. John A. T. Robinson, *Honest to God* (Philadelphia: Westminster Press, 1963). This book set the record of sales for any "book of serious theology in the history of the world." See Ved Mehta, *The New Theologian* (New York: Harper and Row, 1965), p. 3. Mehta also provides an overview of the demise of the supernatural in the writings of Bultmann, Tillich, Bonhoeffer, and Robinson. See especially pp. 1–66. Further evidence of the interest this topic has evinced can be found in David L. Edwards, editor, *The Honest to God Debate* (London: SCM Press, 1963). See also, J. A. B. Holland, "The Debate About Honest to God," *Scottish Journal of Theology,* Vol. 17 (1964), pp. 257–278; Richard P. McBrien, *Do We Need the Church?* (New York: Harper and Row, 1969), pp. 38–42.

11. Robinson, *Honest to God,* pp. 32 ff.

12. Rudolf Bultmann, "New Testament and Mythology," in Hans Werner Bartsch, editor, *Kerygma and Myth* (New York: Harper Torchbooks, 1971), pp. 10–11.

13. Paul Tillich, "Vertical and Horizontal Thinking: Reply by Paul Tillich," *American Scholar,* Vol. 15 (Winter 1945–1946), p. 111.

14. For a discussion of ecstasy, see Paul Tillich, *Systematic Theology* (Chicago: University of Chicago Press, 1967), Vol. I, p. 111 ff.; Vol. II, pp. 5–8; Vol. III, pp. 112–120.

For an adequate treatment and critique of ecstatic naturalism see Larry L. Rose, "Toward a New Supernaturalism," unpublished doctoral dissertation, Claremont Graduate School (1967), pp. 178–230.

15. Peter Berger, *A Rumor of Angels* (Garden City, New York: Doubleday, 1969), p. 2.

16. Charles Bennett, *The Dilemma of Religious Knowledge* (New Haven: Yale University Press, 1931), p. 72.

17. Baltazar, *Teilhard and the Supernatural,* pp. 317–325.

18. See, for example, Henricus Denziger et Adolphus Schönmetzer, editores, *Enchiridium Symbolorum,* editio XXXII (Barcelona, España: Herder, 1963), 3004, 3005, 3006, 3008.

19. Vergilius Ferm in his discussion of "supernaturalism," which he identifies as the name of a school in Protestant theology, interestingly enough notes that the basic issue between supernaturalism and rationalism is in fact ontological and not epistemological. As he puts it, "Rationalists believe in the essential oneness of all reality, whereas supernaturalists hold that the nature of God is fundamentally different from that of the created world." Virgilius Ferm, *Encyclopedia of Religion* (New York: Philosophical Library, 1945), p. 750.

20. Herbert McCabe in David L. Edwards, editor, *Honest to God Debate*, pp. 172–173.

21. Frederick Sontag, *Divine Perfection* (New York: Harper and Brothers, 1962), pp. 18–19.

22. Eugene Fontinell makes the suggestion that perhaps it would be better to refer to God's "otherness" and his "presence" rather than to "transcendence" and "immanence" since the former terms have a more obvious experiential dimension. Fontinell's point is well taken but other philosophers of religion do not seem to have followed his suggestion in adopting this terminology. The transcendence/immanence terminology is well established and adequately serves its purpose provided that the experiential dimension is understood. See Eugene Fontinell, *Toward a Reconstruction of Religion* (Garden City, New York: Doubleday, 1970), p. 204. Gabriel Moran also discusses the use of the terminology transcendence/immanence in *The Present Revelation* (New York: Herder and Herder, 1972), pp. 180–183. He suggests that it is extremely difficult to find an experiential referent for the word "transcendence," at least from within theology.

It should be pointed out that we are viewing the problem here against the background and using the language of traditional theology with its Hellenic category system and conception of reality. The transcendence/immanence question would take on an entirely different flavor, in fact, would not be an issue at all for process theology. The ultimate reality for process theology is not being, but becoming. Change is of the essence of reality. Reality is relational. This applies to the supreme reality, God, as well as to man who is constantly becoming and is therefore never fully himself.

23. Eugene Fairweather, "Christianity and the Supernatural," in Martin E. Marty and Dean G. Peerman, editors, *New Theology No. 1* (New York: Macmillan, 1964), pp. 235–239.

24. A useful bibliography of works on the origin and theological development of the technical term supernatural can be found in J. P. Kenny, *The Supernatural* (New York: Alba House, 1972), pp. 91–93.

The principal sources for the summary given in this book are: Kenny, *The Supernatural;* de Lubac, *The Mystery of the Supernatural;* Henri de Lubac, "Remarques sur l'histoire du mot 'surnaturel.'" De Lubac admits his debt to Auguste Deneffe, S.J., "Geschichte des Wortes *supernaturalis*," *Zeitschrift für Katholische Theologie,* Vol. 46 (1922), pp. 337–360.

25. De Lubac, "Remarques sur l'histoire du mot 'surnaturel,'" p. 228.

26. Kenny, *The Supernatural,* p. 95.

27. This is in keeping with the emphasis of Thomistic theology that the final end of man consists in *knowledge,* or *vision,* of God. This in turn has led to a view of human nature which is essentially based on the Aristotelian theory of knowledge. This theory holds that knowledge involves a certain identity of knower and known. This has had repercussions on the development of the theology of nature and grace and consequently on the theology of the natural and the supernatural. See Eugene TeSelle, "Nature and Grace in the Forum of Ecumenical Discussion," p. 541.

28. De Lubac, "Remarques sur l'histoire du mot 'surnaturel,' " p. 244.

29. De Lubac remarks that though this extreme form of dualism has run its course as a position in scientific theology, it may only now be bearing its bitterest fruit. Having pushed the supernatural away from the natural for protection's sake, so to speak, it has left the field wide open to secularism. See de Lubac, *The Mystery of the Supernatural,* pp. xi–xii.

30. See John Calvin, *Institutes of the Christian Religion,* translated from the Latin by John Allen, 7th American edition (Philadelphia: Philadelphia Board of Christian Education, 1936), Vol. 1, II, ii, sections 12 & 16, pp. 292 and 297.

31. For a discussion of Calvin's use of the words nature, natural, and *ordo naturae,* see Edward A. Dowey Jr., *The Knowledge of God in Calvin's Theology* (New York: Columbia University Press, 1965), p. 65 ff.

32 See Eugene TeSelle, "The Problem of Nature and Grace," *Journal of Religion,* Vol. 45 (July 1965), p. 238.

33. See, for example, Charles Hodge, *Systematic Theology* (Grand Rapids: W. B. Eerdmans Publishing Co., 1968), Vol. I, pp. 19, 154, 623; Vol. II, p. 729; Vol. III, pp. 37, 214.

34. The root of the Latin word *natura* appears to be *nasci* (to be born). Similarly, the Greek φυσις is related to φυω (to grow). Both Greek and Latin, therefore, imply the idea of process, of becoming, of change. This gives rise to the meaning of nature as a principle of activity (that by which a being does what it does).

35. See Charles Boyer, S. J., "The Notion of Nature in St. Augustine," *Texte und Untersuchungen* (Berlin: Akademie-verlag, #64 Vol. 2, 1957), pp. 175–186.

36. Augustine was more a theologian than a philosopher. His interest was not so much in nature itself as a philosophical concept, but rather in nature related to creation, or to its final end. Thus, Aquinas notes *"Augustinus loquitur de natura humana non secundum quod consideratur in esse naturali, sed secundum quod ordinatur ad beatitudinem." (De Spiritualibus Creaturis,* a. 8, ad 1). Quoted by de Lubac, *The Mystery of the Supernatural,* p. 29.

37. Some theologians understand Aquinas as having distinguished two final ends for man, the one corresponding to man's nature as an autonomous self-directing principle—natural happiness attainable through perfection and the practice of virtue in this life; the other corresponding to God's sheer graciousness to man, which final end can only be achieved by grace—eternal

happiness and the full vision of God. Thus, see Henri Bouillard, *Conversion et Grâce chez St. Thomas d'Aquin* (Paris: Aubier, 1941), pp. 78–79. See also p. 196: "Every being has in itself a form which is the principle of its movement or of its action. But this form does not activate itself. It can only be brought into act by another being in act . . . The absolutely first mover, of both bodies and souls, is God." (Author's translation.)

38. Kenny, *The Supernatural*, pp. 100–102.

39. See note 34 above.

40. Thomas Aquinas, *Summa Theologica*, 2^a2^{ae}, q. 5, a. 1, ad 1.

41. Ibid., 2^a2^{ae}, q. 6, a. 1.

42. Ibid., 1, q. 12, a. 1, ad 3. "God is not thus said not to exist as if he did not exist at all, but because in as much as he is his own existence, he is greater *(supra)* than all that exists." (Author's translation).

43. Gerard Manley Hopkins, unnamed poem. *Poems and Prose of Gerard Manley Hopkins,* selected by W. H. Gardner, (Harmondsworth, Middlesex: Penguin Books, 1963), p. 51.

44. J. P. Mackey, "Grace," *The Furrow,* Vol. 24 (June 1973), p. 342.

45. The development of cosmic Christology as a special branch of modern theology is not a new phenomenon but carries on a tradition that goes back to the earliest church Fathers. See George A. Maloney, S.J., *The Cosmic Christ* (New York: Sheed and Ward, 1968), pp. 14–16.

46. See, for example, James P. Mackey, *Life and Grace* (Dublin: Logos Books, 1966); Peter Fransen, *The New Life of Grace* (Tournai: Desclée, 1969); Gregory Baum, *Man Becoming;* Patrick Fannon "The Changing Face of Theology: Man in Nature and Grace," *Clergy Review,* Vol. 52 (May 1967), pp. 331–336; John W. Glaser, S.J., "Man's Existence: Supernatural Partnership," *Theological Studies,* Vol. 30 (September 1969), pp. 473–488; Edward Bozzo, "The Neglected Dimension: Grace in Interpersonal Context," *Theological Studies,* Vol. 29 (September 1968), pp. 497–507; Charles R. Meyer, "A Personalist View of Grace: The Ghost of Galileo," *Chicago Studies,* Vol. 7 (Fall 1968), pp. 283–301. For a summary of trends in the theology of grace, see Francis Colborn, "The Theology of Grace: Present Trends and Future Directions," *Theological Studies,* Vol. 31 (December 1970), pp. 692–711. Only Roman Catholic theologians are mentioned here because their writings are more familiar to the present writer. Also, much more has been written by Catholics on the nature/grace relationship than by theologians of other Christian denominations.

47. Among the main exponents of interpersonal relationships in religious education are Lewis Joseph Sherrill, Randolph Crump Miller, and Reuel L. Howe. Sherrill's major work *The Gift of Power* (New York: Macmillan) was published in 1955. Miller constantly refers to relationships as a key factor in religious education and Sherrill gives him credit for seeing the importance of interacting dialogue in the context of religious education (*The Gift of Power,* p. 180). Miller's first major work on religious education, *The Clue to Christian Education* (New York: Scribners) was published in 1950. Reuel L.

Howe, though not writing strictly as a religious education theorist, has greatly influenced the thinking of some religious educationists by his two books *Man's Need and God's Action* (Greenwich, Connecticut: Seabury Press, 1953), and *The Miracle of Dialogue* (Greenwich, Connecticut: Seabury Press, 1963). Sherrill notes that though his own thought developed independently of Howe's there is a remarkable similarity. See *The Gift of Power,* p. 196.

48. Martin Buber, *I and Thou* (New York: Scribners, 1958); also, *Between Man and Man* (London: Kegan Paul, 1947).

49. Randolph Crump Miller, *Education for Christian Living,* 2nd edition (New Jersey: Prentice-Hall, 1963), p. 95.

50. Howe, *Man's Need and God's Action,* p. 23.

51. See Karl Rahner and Herbert Vorgrimler, *Theological Dictionary,* edited by Cornelius Ernst, translated by Richard Strachan (New York: Herder and Herder, 1965), p. 308. For a treatment of the dialogical relationship between persons see Howe, *The Miracle of Dialogue,* especially pages 51–83.

52. While it may be true that God is always supernaturally present to all persons by the very fact of his gracious gift of life, God's gift is always an *offering* in the sense that his supernatural presence does not coerce but respects our freedom to respond.

53. *The Confessions of St. Augustine,* translated by F. J. Sheed, (New York: Sheed and Ward, 1950), I, 1, p. 3. See also, Thomas Aquinas, *Summa Theologica,* $1^{a}2^{ae}$, q. 2, a. 8.

54. For a fuller treatment of the I-Thou encounter in the context of grace and the supernatural see Baltazar, *Teilhard and the Supernatural,* pp. 213–246. See also Charles R. Mayer, "A Personalist View of Grace: The Ghost of Galileo." Mayer develops the theme of grace in the context of love as seen through existentialist philosophy.

55. Glaser, "Man's Existence: Supernatural Partnership," p. 478.

56. For a different opinion which says that love of neighbor is *not* always love of God, see Marcel van Caster, "On Loving God by Loving Men," *Lumen Vitae,* Vol. 28 (December 1973), pp. 637–648.

57. For a critique of the way in which religious educationists use the word "relationship" see William Bedford Williamson, *Language and Concepts in Christian Education* (Philadelphia: Westminster Press, 1970), especially pages 77–87.

In discussing the use of interpersonal relationships as a model for understanding such theological concepts as grace, the sacraments, morals, and particularly faith, James P. Mackey sounds this warning note. We must realize, he points out, "that our use of the model of interpersonal relationships is likely to be as culturally restrictive as it is enlightening, since in fact we base the model almost exclusively on the type of interpersonal relationship that has become characteristic of late Western romantic art and literature." Mackey, "The Theology of Faith: A Bibliographical Survey (and More)" *Horizons,* Vol. 2 (Autumn 1975), p. 226.

58. See Joseph D. Glass, "Objectives in Religious Education," unpub-

lished doctoral dissertation, Yale University (1966), pp. 281–282, 283–284.

59. For a treatment of the state of research and theory in human communication, see C. David Mortensen, *Communication: The Study of Human Interaction* (New York: McGraw-Hill, 1972).

60. As William Bedford Williamson indicates, slogans are words or short phrases with emotional overtones. They are capable of arousing interest and enthusiasm, but are conveniently incapable of strict definition. They are prescriptive rather than descriptive and often tend to be vague and ambiguous. See Williamson, *Language and Concepts in Christian Education*, p. 41–42.

61. For a review of the criticism attaching to an attempt by theologians to base a theology of grace entirely on a personalist, phenomenological approach, see Colborn, "The Theology of Grace: Present Trends and Future Directions," pp. 701–704.

For an examination of some of the notions involved in setting up a model of human communication in order to better understand God's communication to man in revelation, see Gabriel Moran, "Revelation in All Our Relationships," *New Catholic World,* Vol. 216 (May–June 1973), pp. 100–103.

62. Walter M. Abbott, editor, *The Documents of Vatican II* (New York: Guild Press, 1966), pp. 140–141.

63. On this point see Kenny, *The Supernatural,* p. 14. See also Herbert McCabe in David L. Edwards, editor, *Honest to God Debate,* p. 174. The four areas in which the supernatural are most evident have been selected and adapted from Kenny, *The Supernatural,* pp. 11–14.

CHAPTER III

Theological
Metaperspectives

One of the many bizzare experiences of Lewis Carroll's Alice was that of alternately being nine feet tall and three inches tall.[1] As Alice discovered, things can be extremely awkward if one is nine feet tall in a world built for rather small people. On the other hand, being three inches tall means that one has to cope with such unexpected happenings as coming face to face (literally) with a caterpillar! Alice discovered that from nine feet up one has quite a different perspective on things than if one were not much taller than a mushroom. As the Duchess might have pointed out with relish, the moral of all this is: The meaning one grasps from experience and the resulting output of energy in reaction to that experience will in large measure depend on the perspective one brings to experience. Everyone acts out of a personal metaperspective which makes sense of experience and enables one to cope with it. That religious education theorists adopt a particular theological stance with respect to the natural/supernatural relationship seems evident from a reading of their works. These metaperspectives will be amplified and analyzed in the succeeding chapters, but it will be helpful to first provide a more general overview before specifically applying the metaperspectives to religious education theory. This chapter aims at providing such an overview.

As with any of the great religious themes, it is seldom possible to clearly indicate unvarying or hardline positions taken by theologians and others with respect to these themes. What generally happens is that in the course of history, and particularly in the history of theological expression, a dialogue tends to develop between seemingly irreconcilable religious realities. H. Richard Niebuhr, for example, notes this dialogue phenomenon in connection with the two complex realities of Christ and culture.[2] In a certain sense, the culture/Christ dichotomy is simply another expression of the natural/supernatural, nature/grace, God's immanence/God's transcendence dichotomies. Basically they are all facets of the same phenomenon—our simultaneous experience of a this-worldly and an other-worldly reality. It may well be that this consciousness of seemingly irreconcilable realities is a reflection of a seemingly irreconcilable reality deep within ourselves. Life is a tension of apparent contradictions because within ourselves we embody the most

44

fundamental of all contradictions. In us, God makes something of nothing, and something and nothing are the two most mutual of opposites.[3] Be that as it may, Niebuhr notes that it may be possible to "stop" the dialogue from time to time and indicate partial answers which have been given to this perennial problem. That the answers will always be partial is only to be expected from any human enquiry into the divine. Likewise, metaperspectives are partial in that they rarely supply full answers or dictate fully adequate responses to experience. They are partial also in that one scarcely ever embraces a certain metaperspective so completely as to be totally free of all ambiguity. As Niebuhr puts it (referring to Paul and to Martin Luther) people are "too complex to permit neat identification of a historic individual with a stylized pattern."[4] And, the metaperspectives delineated in this book *are* stylized patterns. They are conceptual constructs arising from a research analysis. In view of the complexity of the problem itself (i.e., the natural/supernatural relationship) and the many factors that may influence judgment and personal expression, it is hardly surprising that religious educationists exhibit some inconsistencies. While they may give strong indications of substantively working out of a certain metaperspective, they sometimes appear to slip into another. Nevertheless, the positions that will be described are substantially representative of the religious educationists' stance on the natural/supernatural relationship—substantial enough, that is, to allow identification of congruences and correlations that may exist between their particular theological overview and their religious education theory.

The bringing to light of different theological metaperspectives requires that we keep three things in mind. First, one of the aims of this book is to encourage religious educators to reexamine and bring to specific awareness the metaperspective out of which they themselves work, with which they are comfortable, and which makes their work purposeful and rewarding. In the descriptions which follow, therefore, the reader should keep asking: Where do I fit in? Do I see myself in any of these descriptions? Can I offer any reasons for my particular outlook? How does my particular metaperspective work itself out or reflect itself in the attitude and in the choice of practical skills I bring to my work as a religious educator?

Second, what is being attempted is an examination of theoretical positions and not the theorists themselves. The endeavor is to identify different theoretical stances and the major theorists are used as illustrative of these positions. What is important, therefore, is the theological metaperspective itself and its affinity to and congruence with a certain religious education theory, not so much the particular theorist whose metaperspective it is.

Third, and most important, the differences that may be detected in the theological outlooks of various religious educationists *are due more to differences of emphasis than to differences of hard-core theological conceptuali-*

zation. What a metaperspective does is to add a certain color, a certain tone, a certain fragrance to theological reality. A biologist who studies a flower, while being aware of all aspects of the flower, may be more inclined to call attention to and to emphasize the reproductive apparatus, or the way the flower is fitted to receive insect visitors, or the relationship of the parts of the flower to one another. An artist or a poet, on the other hand, looking at the same flower may tend to emphasize the color, or the scent, or the beauty of the symmetrical whole. Similarly, religious educationists may look at the same theological reality but tend to emphasize different aspects of that reality. Thus, for example, while religious educationists may be in basic agreement that revelation consists both in God's special revelation in scripture and in his continuing revelation in historical human experience, they tend to emphasize one or another of these aspects as being of greater importance in the religious education context. Again, religious educationists may agree that grace is a free gift which enables one to act in a manner pleasing to God. However, some may tend to see grace as coming from above by God's gracious condescension and giving added impulse to human acts. Others tend to emphasize that grace acts through and within the very perfection of the human acts themselves. A third example is that of the church. There are many images that fit the reality which is the church, such as that of the people of God, or that of the servant church, or that of the church as institution or as sacrament. While accepting the full multifaceted reality, according to their own particular metaperspective religious educationists may tend to emphasize one or other of these images and their view of the church will be colored by that particular image. As we shall see, analysis of the works of major religious education theorists indicates that for the most part particular theological emphases espoused by the theorists are closely related to their respective religious education theories.

There appear to be two quite clear-cut metaperspectives with respect to the natural/supernatural relationship out of which religious educationists operate.

1. The Supernatural Above the Natural[5]

This is a metaperspective which tends to see the natural and the supernatural as belonging to two separate realms or orders, the latter "above," "superior to," "beyond" the former. Pushed to its extreme this position represents a full ontological dualism, though not all who hold it would wish to view it in metaphysical terms. According to this viewpoint, the supernatural enters the natural from above as gift—a healing, saving, elevating gift. This elevation bestows on the natural a supernatural dimension as well as a new value, an eternal value. The natural is not substantially changed by this gift but rather is radically redimensioned and redirected. By this supernatural "invasion" the natural is endowed with supernatural powers so that it now is capable of performing acts on a supernatural level, that is, acts which are specifically related to the supernatural end of created humanity.

This metaperspective, therefore, tends to emphasize the otherness and transcendence of God vis-à-vis man. God is primarily he who is to be adored and served, he who has complete dominion over his creatures. Though God may be the Father of all who gives good things to his children, the tendency is to look upon him as a dispenser of favors who still exacts obedience to his transcendent word. This word the Father has graciously condescended to reveal in his son Jesus. From his supernatural and unseen world God breaks into the human world giving it meaning and purpose by his revelation in Jesus, but ever remaining distinct from this world and transcendent to it. Christ the redeemer who unites in himself God and man, is above all himself God who is to be reverenced and adored. Persons must direct their lives in accordance with God's world revealed in Christ as recorded in the scriptures and lived out in the community of the church. Thus, human life has a dualistic flavor—a natural life and a supernatural life. Natural life has a certain value and can achieve a natural end, but its proper spirit, intention, and direction to man's supernatural end can only come from God's special and gracious gift of grace. In fine, the relationship of the natural and the supernatural is a "vertical" one. This metaperspective looks first to God, his essence, his will, his word, his gift, and relates man to these. The movement of union (if it can be conceived as a movement) is from God to man and back to God.

Because of its insistence on the transcendent otherness of the supernatural this metaperspective may best be termed *transcendist*.

2. The Supernatural Within the Natural[6]

This metaperspective is more or less the polar opposite of the previous one, though opposite should not be understood as meaning mutually exclusive. According to this second position there are not two orders or realms (natural and supernatural) but only one.[7] There is no ontological separation between natural and supernatural but merely a conceptual distinction. The stress is strongly on the immanence of the supernatural, so much so that those who hold to this metaperspective sometimes find it necessary to defend themselves against the charge of pantheism and Pelagianism.[8] What this position seeks to emphasize, however, is not the identity of the natural and the supernatural but that God is within all reality in the most intimate degree possible. All things are supernatural according to their very nature, and the more perfectly they realize and are true to their nature, the more supernatural they are.

God is immanent in man by his creative power, his indwelling power, and by his permeation of man's being in Jesus Christ. God's message and revelation come through every avenue of experience in man's historical situation. Man has power to grasp and appreciate the revelation of God in all of his (man's) experience.

In this type of thinking there is little if any distinction between the supernatural and the world, between the sacred and the secular, between the workings of divine grace and human effort. All human activity which is truly loving and deeply personal is intrinsically grace-filled and grace-bearing, graced and gracious, supernatural. Christians, instead of separating themselves from the world, should be in it and of it in the fullest possible way. In their work for a better world they are thereby participating with Christ in bringing about the realization of the kingdom of God. Thus, for this position a very close link, if not a perfect unity, exists

> between human values and relations with God; between man's planning and God's salvific plan as manifested in Christ; between the human community and the Church; between human history and the history of salvation; between human experience and God's revelation; between the progressive growth of Christianity in our time, and its eschatological consummation.[9]

Seen from the point of view of this metaperspective, the relationship of the natural and the supernatural is a "horizontal" one. This position looks first to man and the human condition and sees the promotion of human values and virtues as totally God-imbued. There is no movement of union between the natural and the supernatural because they were never, nor are ever, separated.

Because of its insistence on the immanence of the divine in all human process, and on the supernaturality of the natural, this metaperspective may fittingly be called *immanentist.*

3. An Integrationist Metaperspective?

If the transcendist and the immanentist metaperspectives represent polar positions with respect to the natural/supernatural relationship, it might be logical to expect that there is some intermediate position, or rather several such positions. Is it possible to identify a third metaperspective which represents the stance of those who do not fully subscribe to either of the other two positions? Such a third metaperspective would not so much be an intermediate or middle-of-the-road position as it would be an attempt to achieve a working synthesis or integration of the transcendist and immanentist metaperspectives. It would be a position which attempts to incorporate the strengths and eliminate the weaknesses of the transcendist and the immanentist stances and to hold them in some sort of productive dialectic. At the same time, it would try to strike a balance between the seemingly opposite emphases of transcendence and immanence, between a thoroughly transcendist approach and a thoroughly immanentist one. If it indeed exists, then, because it attempts to integrate the transcendist and immanentist metaperspectives one might call it the *integrationist* metaperspective.

Reading the religious education literature one gets the distinct impression that there are some major religious educationists who, consciously or unconsciously, appear to be attempting some form of productive integration of transcendentism and immanentism. They maintain an essential separation between the natural and the supernatural but not in as radical a form as the transcendists. While maintaining the overriding and prior importance of the supernatural they also have every indication of wishing to give due consideration to the natural. As one writer sees it, for example, man is a creature who stands in a relationship of total dependence on God, but "his selfhood is not swallowed up or obliterated in God, but he stands as it were facing God his creator."[10] The tendency of the integrationists is to focus attention on man, his situation and his experience. Not that they see in man the intrinsic expression of the supernatural (as perhaps the immanentists might hold) but rather that man is the " 'space' within which the Mystery of God, and all things connected with it, must be heard and understood."[11] Focusing attention on man and on human values (which the integrationists understand as distinct from divine values) does not necessarily lead to an understanding of human experience as fully revelational (as some immanentists would hold). There are certain things about man that can only be known by God's direct revelation. For the integrationists, the word of God is still seen as *given;* the notion of God's special self-disclosure from outside of human experience is still emphasized. Thus, the integrationist position still "distinctly maintains a dualism, a polarity between the Word of God and human conscience. . . God's word must be *expected,* otherwise it would not be heard (and this is where it integrates human experience), and *unexpected,* otherwise it would simply be an echo of ourselves."[12] Those who appear to attempt an integrationist stance see grace as an external given (as in the transcendist perspective) but also as intrinsic to and working in full concert with the scientific laws that govern nature as God's creation (as in the immanentist perspective). Man must pray as though everything depended on God but also work as though everything depended on himself. As far as the church is concerned the integrationists simultaneously assert (a) that the church is a redemptive fellowship community in Christ where the supernatural can be experienced within the very experience of Christian *koinonia* (redemption has to do with the natural as well as the supernatural), and (b) that the church is essentially a mystery and so Spirit-imbued and supernatural as to be always more than the members who comprise it. If the transcendists tend to look to Jesus Christ first as God and the immanentists tend to look to him first as man, the integrationists attempt to emphasize the "whole" Christ whose divinity can only be appreciated through his human self-expression.

Those who attempt an integrationist stance appear to see man as caught in the crossfire of two opposing value systems, supernatural values and natural values. While due weight and consideration must be given to both sets of values, an attempt must be made to integrate human values with sacred values, the former being subordinate to the latter. One is torn between a sense of the Absolute (the supernatural), which seems to call in one direction, and one's experience of the relative (the natural), which demands that one live in the real world and conform to its values. As one writer puts it, "In his [man's] daily life he is naturalistic, rationalistic, and empiricistic; on Sundays he is idealistic, transcendental, and supernatural."[13] In fine, the integrationists appear to see the relationship of the natural and the supernatural as "vertical," as do the transcendists, but with a different starting point. The integrationist metaperspective looks first to the human condition and to human experience, and from there it reaches out to God as savior and teacher and author of the supernatural life. The movement of union between the natural and the supernatural is from man to God and back to man.

Ideally, one might expect that the correct thing to do would be to attempt some form of integration of the transcendist and immanentist metaperspectives. If while being a unified whole truth is multifaceted, then perhaps the emphases of transcendentism and immanentism only capture certain nuances of what is a complex (from our point of view, that is) reality. The question that must be asked is: How well do the religious educationists who attempt an integrationist stance succeed? Is their metaperspective clear-cut enough to be called a valid and distinct third position? Is it even possible that such a third position can exist? Does it not perhaps represent an alternate sliding from transcendentism into immanentism and vice versa? The only way these questions can be answered is by applying the same test criteria as will be applied to the other two metaperspectives. And this is the next item on the agenda.

In chapters 4, 5, and 6 the metaperspectives outlined above will be examined in more detail. First, each metaperspective will be more clearly delineated by reference to the four basic areas to which the term supernatural may be especially applied, namely, revelation, grace, the church, and Jesus Christ. Next will follow a brief sketch of some of the major religious educationists who appear to be representative of the metaperspective in question. Finally, the religious education theories of these religious educationists will be analyzed in the light of the theorists' metaperspective. Religious education theory will be considered as relating to the six areas noted in chapter 1, namely, the aim, the content, the teacher, the student, the environment, and evaluation.

NOTES

1. Lewis Carroll, *Alice's Adventures in Wonderland* in *The Complete Works of Lewis Carroll* (New York: The Modern Library).

2. H. Richard Niebuhr, *Christ and Culture* (New York: Harper Torchbooks, 1951), p. 39 ff.

3. On this point see F. J. Sheed, *Theology and Sanity* (London: Sheed and Ward, 1953), pp. 17–18.

4. Niebuhr, *Christ and Culture,* p. 170.

5. Use of the word *above* implies no spatial connotations. The use of height metaphors to represent superiority and greatness is well known and accepted in ordinary speech. Preference for such metaphors when referring to the divine may possibly derive to some extent from the recognition by simple people of the infinite height of the sky, which is therefore associated with power and transcendence. See Mircea Eliade, *Patterns of Comparative Religion* (New York: Sheed and Ward, 1958), p. 99 ff.; see also Edwyn Bevan, *Symbolism and Belief* (London: George Allen and Unwin, Ltd., 1938), pp. 11–81.

6. Again, the use of the word *within* does not connote spatial withinness. Other words and expressions such as *suffuse, penetrate, form one with* are also used to express the idea of God's intimate association with his creation. All expressions, however, tend to have mechanistic connotations. God *is* where he *acts*. He acts in creation by his power, his presence, and his essence.

7. Those who adopt this stance have difficulty in finding a word which can suitably describe this single order of reality. Thus, for example, while some, like Baltazar, would prefer to say that everything is *natural* (Baltazar, *Teilhard and the Supernatural* [Baltimore: Helicon, 1966], pp. 317–325), others, like James Michael Lee, would prefer to say that everything is *supernatural* according to its nature (*The Shape of Religious Instruction* [Notre Dame, Indiana: Religious Education Press, 1971], pp. 291–293).

8. See, for example, Lee, *The Flow of Religious Instruction* (Notre Dame, Indiana: Religious Education Press, 1973), pp. 291–293.

9. The General Conclusions of the International Study Week on Catechetics at Medillin, Columbia (1968), No. 12, quoted by Luis Erdozain, S.J., "The Evolution of Catechetics," *Lumen Vitae,* Vol. 25 (March 1970), p. 25.

10. Lewis Joseph Sherrill, *The Gift of Power* (New York: Macmillan, 1963), p. 24.

11. Joseph Bournique, "The Word of God and Anthropology," *Teaching All Nations,* Vol. 4 (July 1967), p. 371.

12. Ibid., p. 375.

13. Baltazar, *Teilhard and the Supernatural,* p. 265.

CHAPTER IV

The Supernatural
Above the Natural

God transcends all things seen and unseen. God is God and man is man. The two stand in a most intimate relation, so that all of man's life is determined by his relation with God and God's with him. But it is a relation between Creator and creature that is confused and destroyed when the creature begins to think of himself as in some way divine by nature, or when he conceives his God as residing somewhere within creation itself.[1]

This passage from a major religious education thinker neatly encapsulates the main thrust and emphasis of the transcendist metaperspective. God is God and man is man, and though there is a close relation between them the basis of that relationship is not the nearness and the similarity of creator and creature but rather their fundamental dissimilarity. Any attempt to bridge the yawning chasm between creator and creature is in fact an attempt to dissolve the relationship between them. Thus, while the transcendists accept the presence of God in all of creation, especially through his son Jesus, they very definitely emphasize not God within all process, but God outside of process controlling, directing, sustaining. The emphasis is on God who is "above" creation, "above" all nature, totally "other" and transcendent even in his nearness to us in Christ. The God-language of the transcendists is liberally sprinkled with such expressions as "the almighty Father," "the holy Lawgiver," "the adorable Majesty," "the unseen One who reigns over all," "the Master of creation." The foundational Christian attitude and the basis of all Christian education is this: God is he who is to be adored, reverenced, loved, and served. First among "the minimum essentials of a Christian economy of salvation," is "the awareness of the immensity and the dominion of God, the orientation of ourselves to life hereafter according to his will."[2] Human life, for the transcendist emphasis, derives its significance and momentum from its being consciously shaped and directed toward supernatural other-worldliness, not natural this-worldliness. The secular is only sacred when it is consciously directed to God and caught up in a divine value.

Now to some further etching of the transcendist metaperspective as revealed by an analysis of the works of religious educationists.

52

DELINEATION OF THE TRANSCENDIST
METAPERSPECTIVE

1. Revelation

What it is.   Religious educationists who appear to work out of a transcendist metaperspective *typically emphasize the firm and fixed content of revelation.* Revelation is an unchanging body of truth. It is the supernatural word of God to man (with emphasis on *word*). This message is the good news of man's salvation in Jesus Christ, the great and joyful tidings that we have been called to a new life in Christ. Jesus Christ *is* God's supreme revelation to man; in Christ God has said it all. The content of the message, which is in the form of a history of salvation (a history of God's salvific dealings with man), is to be found principally in the bible.[3] The bible is the book of books, a unique book in which God himself speaks authoritatively through the instrumentality of the inspired authors. The bible is a compendium of Christian truth, which truth is salvational. The bible contains the words of life, thus, it is *the* great book of Christian spirituality. Not only must we use the bible to learn and be inspired by the history of our salvation, but we must learn to find in the bible answers to our present day human problems. The bible speaks to us in our here and now existential situation. The message of the bible is *normative* for the whole of life.

The tendency of the transcendist theorists, therefore, is to focus on revelation as a rather static body of truth. This truth, guaranteed by the divine inspiration such that it is God's truth, must be handed on safely and integrally from generation to generation. Although some transcendists may well accept the concept of a continuing revelation, this aspect is clearly not in the forefront of their thought. The picture that they paint in bold splashes of color is that of the omnipotent God sending down to earth his supernatural word in Jesus whose authoritative message must be heard. The God of the transcendists is he who speaks from the cloud, "This is my Son, the Beloved. Listen to him" (Mk. 9:8).

Why it is.   The main purpose of revelation according to the transcendist-minded religious educationists is to herald the great glad tidings of our salvation, our call to a new supernatural life in Christ. Revelation is also the story of all that God has done for us and all that he will do in order that we may reach our supernatural destiny. Thus, one theorist states ". . . divine revelation certainly is, of its own essential nature, the revelation of the divine love that chooses, calls, and enriches us in Christ. Therefore the Christian life must be considered as the response of our love to the divine love."[4] God's message calls us to a new supernatural life. God's message calls us to break out of the confining and death-dealing cast of a purely secular, earth-bound existence. We are invited to respond to God's call.

How it is.   How do we come to grasp and respond to God's revelation? The transcendists insist that this is only possible by faith which is itself a free gift of God and to which, in the final analysis, we can intrinsically contribute nothing. The initiative is always completely on God's side. God's message is transmitted through such means as the written word of the bible, or through teaching, preaching, missions, the church's liturgy, in such fashion that we are confronted with God's call and invitation. Our response to this invitation is faith, faith which is not merely a belief in the truths of revelation but a "truly committed acceptance of this invitation, an acceptance which produces its fruit in life."[5] The clarity and insistence of God's call may be muffled (or intensified) by the manner in which the message is presented by those teachers charged with its transmission. Nevertheless—and here is a crucial transcendist maxim—our response is in no way determined by the expertise of the teacher but solely by God's grace. Nor can Christians be educated according to the strict meaning of the term *educate* (from the Latin *e-ducare,* to lead out or draw out). Christian truth can never be "drawn out" of a student by teaching techniques however skillful they may be. Revelation is not something that arises from within one's own thought processes or deep in the human psyche. Rather it is something which is presented to one from without, something with which one is confronted and which demands a living response of faith.[6]

Adding it all up, religious educationists representative of the transcendist school of thought typically emphasize the thoroughly transcendent and otherworldly character of revelation as God's word to man. This message, which is woven into the history of salvation, is handed down by God through his inspired human instruments the sacred scripture writers. To the invitation to a nonearthly and supernatural life contained in God's message, man responds by faith which expresses itself as a commitment to God by a Christian way of life. Such faith is a *gift of God;* in no way can it be caused or induced by human techniques. Finally, Jesus Christ *is* God's message; we only know the message insofar as we know him.

2. Grace

What it is.   Religious educationists tend to adopt different attitudes or stances on grace depending on whether they adopt the traditional Roman Catholic or the traditional Protestant emphasis. The Protestant stance tends to view grace primarily in relation to sin and points to grace as bringing reconciliation and forgiveness. Grace brings conversion from sinfulness to a life in God, whether this is understood as a forensic nonimputation of guilt or an actual intrinsic change in the person. Grace establishes a new relationship

with God because of the redemption wrought by Christ. Grace is God's offer
of forgiveness to which we respond by faith.

By way of contrast, the traditional Roman Catholic emphasis is on the
enabling power of grace, that is, grace enables us to act in a God-like manner
and provides a union and personal intimacy with him. Grace is understood as
a real but created sharing of the divine life which enables us to overcome the
effects of a nature wounded by sin. One Roman Catholic religious
educationist in fact warns against viewing grace in such a fashion that its only
function will be seen as an overcoming of the effects of sin. This, he claims,
would be to reduce grace "to the plane of nature" and make it a mere "help in
our moral struggle" instead of a supernatural elevation to a new life which
totally permeates all our being and activity.[7]

At all events, as far as the transcendist emphasis among most major religious educationists both Protestant and Roman Catholic is concerned, the
following should be noted. First, grace is conceptualized as a free and supernatural gift of God which, in the most unqualified sense, is beyond the
achievement of all human striving. Thus, grace-directed acts are understood
as fundamentally and generically different from merely human acts. Second,
human freedom is not impugned or taken away by grace but enhanced by it in
that we are elevated to a radically different plane of living and enjoy the
freedom of the sons of God. Grace saves us from the self-destructive tenden-
cies of our own freedom by extricating us from the mire of our own con-
tingencies. Third, grace brings healing from the disrupting and corrupting
influence of sin, particularly as a deep-rooted enhancement of human personality in its relationship to God and to other persons.

How it works.   According to the transcendist emphasis God's gift of himself has its effect through faith, a living faith which includes hope and love.
Such faith determines all our judgments and actions and so expresses our
living relationship with God in Jesus Christ. As one theorist puts it, grace
gives us "the possibility of approaching God with confidence, and of offering
him worthy service in the community of the Church. Grace includes the
ability to offer worship: God the Father allows mankind to approach his
throne."[8] Grace acts in human nature to fulfill it, not annihilate it. Nevertheless, grace is conceptualized by most transcendists as irrupting (i.e., as
"breaking in") from without and radically redimensioning and recapacitating
the human person. The dramatic picture projected by the transcendist emphasis is that of the divine power "seizing" the human person and producing
within that person God-like acts totally beyond purely human capability. The
transcendists point to *God who acts in man.* The Christian who acts under the
influence of grace in observing the moral law, for example, is in fact observing a supernatural morality which is immeasurably more important than the
natural morality proposed by the commandments and by which all are bound

Christian and non-Christian alike.[9] An act of supernatural faith made under the impulsion of grace is so unequivocally different from a mere human act of belief that the latter can never become the former without God's special intervention. Precisely what the difference is between a natural act and a supernatural one transcendist-minded religious educationists never attempt to clearly state, except perhaps that it lies in the realm of intentionality—a grace-filled Christian *intentionally* acts out of love of God. In any case, the essence of the act is beyond the reach of scientific observation because it is supernatural.

The Holy Spirit.   For the transcendist theorists, grace is the gift of the Holy Spirit personally present within us. Thus, with the Holy Spirit are associated all the works of grace, such as illumination of the mind, strengthening of the will, persuasion to do good, forgiveness and reconciliation, and the spread of Christian belief and fellowship. With all of this almost any Christian religious educationist would agree. However, those who habitually work out of a transcendist metaperspective conceptualize the action of the Holy Spirit in exactly the way they do for grace. They tend to visualize the human person as being "seized" and permeated by the Spirit and radically transformed. The Holy Spirit is understood as acting in us almost as though the human person were "ghosting" the acts of God. It is the Spirit who comes, the Spirit who initiates, the Spirit who takes possession, the Spirit who strengthens, the Spirit who moves us to respond. "We cannot come to him [God] except he first come to us. Our coming is wholly response and is possible only as the same God who speaks to us in his Word takes possession of our hearts by the power of his Spirit and moves us to yield ourselves to him."[10] The presence of the Holy Spirit confers on the human person a divine transcendence which lifts us beyond ourselves and enables us to do things we could not do before.

3. The Church

What it is.   The key idea which seems to shape the thinking of the transcendist theorists on the church is that it is the body of Christ.[11] The preferred image of the church is that of Christ, the word of God to man, actively carrying on his work of redemption and sanctification in the world. The transcendist theorists also point to the church as a people, a community, a society. They use such expressions as "the People of God," "a redemptive community," "the sum total of all those called by God." Nevertheless, always the emphasis is on the supernatural and otherworldly character of the church where the grace and power of Christ operate. The church is in the world but not of it. The church is a community which transcends human community both in its being and in its community action. The body of Christ acts supernaturally in the world.

Because it is in and through the fellowship of the church that Christians are in closest contact with the redeeming Christ, the church is the specially favored locus of revelation and salvation.

The tendency of the transcendist theorists is to regard the church as an inward-looking, self-sufficient fraternity which, because it is the body of Christ, possesses the full divine truth. Consequently, Christians should aim to bring as many as possible into its redemptive fellowship. Some Roman Catholic theorists tend to emphasize that the hierarchical structure of authority in the church is also instituted by Christ and therefore has a special claim to the presence and guidance of the Holy Spirit in its teaching and governing function. The theorists also note that the church is both a human and a divine reality (in the same way that Christ is both human and divine), and that its humanness is also a sinful humanness and in need of redemption. Nevertheless (and again the point must be made), the main transcendist emphasis is on the church as the otherworldly, grace-filled manifestation of Christ's presence on earth—the church animated by the Holy Spirit, God's word to man, the one ark of salvation.[12]

Worship. All transcendist-minded religious educationists agree that the principal function of the church is its prayer, its worship, its liturgy, which is the heart of the fellowship or *koinonia* which is the church.[13] The function of *diakonia*, that is, the function of service to the world and its political institutions, though acknowledged, is not emphasized by those who favor the transcendist perspective. The church's worship is the privileged locus of God's encounter with his faithful people. The transcendist focus is illustrated by such statements as these: "liturgical prayer is preeminently filled with a sense of the majesty of the infinite God";[14] "in divine worship . . . our own encounter with this superterrestrial world is accomplished."[15] In worship we are engulfed by the otherworldly dimension of the presence of the mysterious and unseen God. His greatness, and our sense of dependence, are dramatically borne in on us. Our worship is a looking "up" to God who "dwells in the heavens," who totally transcends all things of earth but who "looks down" to us and takes us into personal union with himself through his son Jesus. For the transcendists, worship is thus removed from the ordinary, mundane, run-of-the-mill human activity and raised to a plane infinitely surpassing the merely secular. If ordinary human work can be looked upon as a form of worship then it is indirect worship. Direct worship (that is, the purer and more perfect form) requires a certain withdrawal from the world for the world tends to impede and contaminate our union with the divine in prayer.[16] Prayer and action, it seems, belong to separate and distinct realms.

The transcendists also see worship as a perfect expression of God's message to man. For this reason they extol Christian worship as being of capital educational importance. Not only does it teach Christ who is God's salvific word to us, but it also accomplishes what it teaches. Our contact with the supernatural in worship enables us to live our Christian life in "gratitude, love, and obedience" to God—a terrestrial life elevated to God's level.

The Church and Revelation. All transcendist religious educationists hold that the church has a key role to play in the interpretation of divine revelation. The clue to the transcendist viewpoint is their understanding of the function of the Holy Spirit. They understand the Spirit of God as being more active in the church than elsewhere. For them this means that the Spirit conveys a meaning and an interpretation for scripture which we could not arrive at by our own unaided efforts. The transcendists push to its literal extreme the adage that "only the Spirit of God can interpret the word of God." Protestant religious educationists tend to look more to an internal authority which is due to the intrusive working of the Spirit in each individual, albeit mediated and helped by the Christian community. The typical Roman Catholic stance is to look more to the authority of the institutional church since the Spirit of God is understood as informing the very institution itself, i.e., the particular offices of the institution. The point to be made is that the transcendists emphasize the church as "mediating" the direct action of the Spirit who "possesses" the church as its very soul. Scriptural interpretation is a divine, not a human work.

4. Jesus Christ

In speaking of Jesus Christ the transcendist theorists' preferred perspective is evident in their use of such expressions as God's mercy "descending" to us in Christ, and through Christ the creature "mounts back" to its source.[17] They see in Christ an "awe-inspiring greatness," an "adorable majesty";[18] Christ *is* God's unique word.[19] It is out of this framework and perspective and with this characteristic other-worldly orientation that the transcendists interpret how Christ is the focus and the turning point of history, the unique and absolute norm for grasping and understanding God's self-communication for he *is* God's self-communication. Even though Christ unites in himself the human and the divine the transcendists are always acutely conscious of his Godhead, his distinctness, and, in a sense, even his remoteness from the human scene. Jesus, while being fully human, is worthy of adoration and it is this adoration mode which is so distinctive of the transcendist approach.

Like all religious educationists the transcendist theorists are agreed that the essence of the Christian life consists in a personal union with God in Jesus Christ, what one theorist calls a "wordless intimacy."[20] The type of union they envisage here is of the "vertical" kind. In its existential expression this union bears a definite relation to the Christian community and to the world just as Jesus' own "vertical" relationship with his Father was expressed in the perfection of his human relationships. Nevertheless, the important component of the union is that which takes place with an eternal Thou who ever remains "other." In other words, love of God is prior to as well as separable from love of neighbor.

REPRESENTATIVE RELIGIOUS ✗ EDUCATIONISTS

Of all the Roman Catholic scholars (and there have not been many) whose theorizing has profoundly affected religious education in this century Josef Andreas Jungmann is probably the most influential. An Austrian Jesuit, Jungmann is not primarily a religious educationist. His major field of interest and brilliant scholarship is that of pastoral and liturgical studies. For many years he held the chair of pastoral theology at the University of Innsbruck and lectured in catechetics and homiletics. For Jungmann, religion teaching is an essential part of the church's pastoral ministry and must rank in importance alongside the pastoral preaching of the word of God. In fact, he says in many places in his writings that catechetics is the sister of homiletics; they both belong to the same genre, that is, the ministerial proclamation of the word of God to man as revealed in Jesus Christ.[21] His epoch-making book *Die Frohbotschaft und Unsere Glaubensverkündigung*[22] (which translated means The Good News and Our Proclamation of the Faith), first published in 1936, was initially regarded in some quarters with profound suspicion as being too innovative. In fact, it had to be withdrawn from circulation by order of Rome although it was never openly condemned. However, in time this book and other writings by Jungmann became the basis for the kerygmatic and salvation history movements which greatly influenced Roman Catholic religion teaching in the 1950s and early 1960s.

Jungmann's theological metaperspective seems markedly transcendist. His position on the relationship of the natural and the supernatural is that it envisages two world orders, the supernatural and the natural. The two orders are ontologically distinct and separable. The reality of God stands over against nature. God totally transcends his creation and it is this transcendence which Jungmann emphasizes and which, for him, appears to specify all else. God and his creation stand in a "vertical" relationship. In Christ God has given man a message of salvation which is supernatural in character. The message is transmitted and handed down to man, as it were, from above. The instrument of this transmission is the teacher who, in turn, is the instrument of the Church to whom the message is really given. The message must be handed on in its entirety and in a spirit of joyful proclamation. Although not writing in English, Jungmann's influence in English-speaking religious education circles has been assured as his major works have all been translated into English. He has also written articles for such journals as *Lumen Vitae* and *Worship*. By any standard of judgment he must take his place among the major religious educationists of this century.

Another very important and influential Roman Catholic figure in religious education whose theological metaperspective appears to be characteristically transcendist is Johannes Hofinger. Hofinger, like Jungmann an Austrian Jesuit priest, studied under Jungmann at Innsbruck at about the time that Jungmann was writing *Die Frohbotschaft und Unsere Glaubensverkündigung* (1932–1936). The influence of the master is quite apparent and Hofinger has been among the most active and effective disseminators of the ideas first proposed by Jungmann, to whom he (Hofinger) readily acknowledges his debt.

Since 1949 Johannes Hofinger has been a member of the East Asian Pastoral Institute in Manila, Phillipines, and he served as the Institute's director from 1957 to 1965. He has written and lectured indefatigably on religious education conducting courses and seminars on the Kerygmatic approach to religion teaching in many parts of the world.[23] Much of his work has been in mission catechesis, that is, the teaching of religion to Christian neophytes and those still being evangelized. Not only has he lectured and taught in English-speaking countries, but, like Jungmann, his major works have been translated into English, and journals such as *Lumen Vitae* and the *Catholic School Journal* have carried his articles. Perhaps the best summary of his position is contained in the very title of his book *Our Message Is Christ* (1974). The transcendent God, the Father in heaven, has given man a message, has spoken his word for man's salvation in Jesus Christ. This message is handed down and transmitted through the instrumentality of the ministers of the church so that man, upon receiving and responding to the message, may "rise" to God again. Grace gives man a share in the divine nature and elevates him to the supernatural level, pointed and proportioned to his final end, the supernatural vision of God. The message is all-important for Hofinger, all religious education revolves around this. And the message is Christ who must therefore permeate every facet of the religious education enterprise.

A third religious education theorist whose theological metaperspective betrays the telltale transcendist signs is James D. Smart. Smart, a very distingusihed Presbyterian pastor, scholar, and teacher is, like Jungmann, primarily a theologian. Nevertheless his pastoral and ministerial interests have led him to write and lecture on religious education and he has exerted considerable influence in this field. He served for many years as editor-in-chief of curriculum publications for the Board of Christian Education of the Presbyterian Church of America. His extensive writings and works on religious education have been widely reviewed and discussed and his influence has been extended by his teaching at such important centers as the University of Toronto and at Union Theological Seminary in New York (1957–1971). Because his theoretical approach to religious education is rooted in theology he is generally closely linked with such writers as Lewis Joseph Sherrill and Randolph Crump Miller.[24] However, as far as the natural/supernatural relationship is concerned Smart gives every appearance of being far more transcendist than either Sherrill or Miller.

As do Jungmann and Hofinger, Smart sets religious education squarely within the pastoral ministry of the church. Preaching and teaching, he says, though perhaps different in form, have the same content and the same objective. For Smart, the major task of religious education is the proclamation of the word.[25] This means the handing on and the handing "down" of the divine message pronounced from on high in the coming of Jesus Christ. The word is Christ, present in the church and evident principally in the written scriptures. Proclamation of the word and its reception by those who hear it should lead to true Christian living within the church, it should lead to the making of true disciples who give committed witness to the word. True it is that the word is communicated by persons to persons, but it is more the power of the word itself than the interpersonal communication which is important. God's mighty and transcendent power expressed in his word creates its own dynamic. Because of the all-powerful, intrinsic energy of the word the task of the religious educator is merely to serve as a conduit for the message. It is the word itself which will affect the minds and hearts of the students, will stir up faith and bring about a commitment. The focus, therefore, is on God who "breaks in" from above, from beyond, who "hands down" his message of salvation, and who, from his unseen world, exerts his power and his presence in this world through his word, Christ.

Having examined the transcendist metaperspective and indicated some major religious educationists who appear to be working out of this metaperspective, it is time to analyze in detail the six major areas of concern for religious education from the viewpoint of the representative transcendist theorists.

THE AIM

The clue to the thinking of the transcendist theorists of religious education is their singleminded insistence on the absolute and unqualified primacy of God's message to man, his word of salvation given in Jesus Christ. As Johannes Hofinger puts it, this message is "the incomparable good news of the eternal love of God, who, through his only-begotten Son, has called us to Himself and enables us to reach our true home."[26] Their constant highlighting of this basic Christian tenet affects their theorizing with respect to all areas of major concern to religious education. It is the leitmotif, the constantly recurring thematic element in all their thinking on religious education. Thus, for the transcendists, *the overriding aim of religious education becomes the faithful handing down of this divine message in such fashion that it calls forth a response of faith.* The comprehensive aim of religious education can be nothing less than God's own aim, his own plan of salvation in sending his Son Jesus. Such an aim is thoroughly transcendent and supernatural; in no sense can it be accomplished by mere human effort, but only by God's grace. According to the transcendists there are two main aspects to the aim of religious education, (1) personal knowledge of and union and reconciliation with God in Christ, and (2) discipleship within the church for the continuance and spread of the Christian message. The position is well summarized by James Smart: "The goal of Christian teaching is that there may be Christians on this earth today and tomorrow, in fellowship with God and with each other as the Church of God, and offering themselves to Jesus Christ as a body through which he may continue his invasion of the world."[27]

Personal Union with God

In order to achieve such a union, claim the transcendists, the student must first know and understand God's message in Jesus Christ. Thus, the message must be proclaimed and presented to the student just as Jesus Christ proclaimed and presented it in his own teaching on earth. As Josef Jungmann puts it, "an effective catechesis must be bent on producing in the listeners a striking picture of the entire content of Christian doctrine and on making them aware that Christian doctrine is truly a joyful message."[28] Jungmann's use of the term "listeners" here is instructive. The message is *proclaimed* whether in preaching or in teaching); we *listen.* The message is proclaimed in just the way that the apostles proclaimed the message in their preaching—the *kerygma*—the joyful announcement of the good news of salvation.[29] Knowledge of God through the proclamation of the word, awareness and understanding of his bounteous salvation in Christ, will produce in the student a desire for union with Christ. Also, this knowledge will bring about a response of reconciling faith that expresses itself as a commitment to the Christian life. What this seems to be saying is that for the transcendists knowledge automatically leads to desire and subsequently to action. Such a position comes out of their understanding of the message of God as containing a supernatural dynamic, a Spirit-imbued power, the grace of God which works in those who hear the word.

In what does a living commitment to the Christian life consist? In the broadest possible terms it means a participation in the mystery of Christ. More specifically it means uniting oneself with the living Christ. This union is understood by the transcendists primarily as a vertical and intentional referring of all one's actions to the Christ-God who dwells in heaven. While the horizontal component of union with Christ through love of neighbor is also understood as important, the transcendists tend to think first in vertical terms. Johannes Hofinger catches the transcendist nuance well when he writes, "As man is composed of body and soul, Christian life is composed of prayer and action.... Prayer is like the soul; action is like the body which needs to be animated by prayer."[30] This dichotomizing of prayer and action is a reflection of the transcendist dichotomizing of the supernatural and the natural. Prayer belongs to the supernatural dimension, action to the natural dimension. The former must "animate" the latter, raise it to a new and supernatural level. Thus, helping the students to pray and involving them in prayer is an important aim of religious education. Prayer means worship of God which is a reverential expression of our dependence on him, an interior and humble turning to our Father in heaven in obedience to his will. Animated and strengthened by such prayer the Christian carries a worshipful attitude into daily life. He lives the grace he has received by observing the commandments, summed up in love of neighbor for God's sake. Such a love is supernatural because it is specified by the grace-inspired intention of pleasing God.

Discipleship in the Church

The second aspect of the aim of religious education for the transcendist theorists is that union with God and living the Christian life also means membership in the Christian community and discipleship for the spread of that community—Christian witness to the world. Training for discipleship is what James Smart calls "deepening the human channel of communication" whereby the life of Christ who came into the world may reach out to others. And so, an important feature of the aim of religious education for these theorists is training to be the church. Training, therefore, not only in doctrine and in a knowledge of the historical and biblical roots of the church, but training in the Christian way of life with its accent on the fellowship of union among church members. But the transcendists leave us in no doubt as to the true roots of this Christian way of life. "The Christian standard of conduct is not a natural possibility for any person; it is a supernatural possibility, to be realized only through the redemptive power of Jesus Christ working in human persons through the gospel."[31] The final objective of Christian education, it seems, *is strictly beyond the reach of the educator since it is thoroughly supernatural.* All that the teacher can do is to provide the channel through which God's action may occur.

In conclusion, therefore, religious educationists whose metaperspective is characteristically transcendist propose aims for religious education which are supernatural and transcendent, that is, pertaining directly to God and dependent solely on him for their accomplishment. The human channel for the communication of God's message is just that, a channel. It is an instrument through which God's Spirit works, an instrument which can but prepare the ground for the bestowal of grace. Transcendist theorists do speak, albeit somewhat guardedly and without enthusiasm, of such seemingly tangible objectives as personality development and producing a mature, intelligent Christian. For all that, the impression one gets is that even these human factors are largely the work of (or at least very definitely subordinate to) God's supernatural grace. On account, also, of their transcendist bent these theorists have difficulty in proposing specific and tangible religious education practices which would be calcualted to achieve the aims they set. If God's grace is ultimately going to achieve the objectives then little is required beyond, perhaps, a refinement in the manner in which the divine word is proclaimed and heralded.

The true aroma and flavor of the transcendist emphasis seems to have been convincingly captured by James Smart to whom may be left the final word. If the aim of Christian education is to produce Christians and the Christian character, then, he observes, we must beware of too much trust in educational methodology. The Christian, he declares, "is not just a person with certain superior qualities of character . . . but a person who in confrontation with Jesus Christ has come to know God in his judgment and mercy and whose graces and gifts of character are all of them the fruits of God's Spirit." And, Smart flatly states, "There are no scientific techniques for producing that kind of human being."[32]

THE CONTENT

As far as the transcendist theorists are concerned, the heart and core of the content of religious education can be expressed in one pithy sentence: *The content of religious education is a dynamic and authoritative divine message, the major source of which is the bible.* The emphasis, therefore, is on a divine message given from on high by the creator and Father of all out of love for his wayward children. The content is a message, but the message is a person—Christ. Christ speaks to us through the church he founded so that the content of the message cannot ever be dissociated from its luminous setting in the church. Furthermore, since the content of religious education is God's authoritative word, there follows a crucially important principle for religious education: To a large extent the content will determine the very form and process of religious education which consists in transmitting that word. The message must be transmitted with absolute fidelity and in the same manner as God proclaimed it, that is, as incarneted in Christ. The message must be transmitted as an integrated whole, not fragmented into over-rationalized and irrelevant detail. Finally, of its very nature the content is divine truth (from whence comes its power and authority) and is not in any sense man-made; it is supernatural.

The Content Is Christ

For the transcendists, the "unfathomable riches of Christ" form the core content of religion teaching. These riches are most clearly manifest in the history of salvation contained in the scriptures, which are therefore the basic source of our knowledge of Jesus. It is most essential that exactly the same message that was pronounced by Christ himself be taught, and in such manner that the entire theme of the message be seen to revolve around him. The teacher is, as it were, a sounding board who faithfully resonates the full content of the divine communication. Every aspect of doctrine, every facet of teaching must refer to and be brought into relation with Christ so that the central theme of God's revelation will become more evident and compelling. Proclaiming the message, however, does not simply mean transmitting information about the biblical corpus. The content of religious education is not mere knowledge, but knowledge as a motivation for a Christian lifestyle. Therefore, the content of religious education is Christ in a living and active relationship with the students, whose lives will continually witness to their commitment by prayer and Christian action.[33]

The content of religious education is Christ, and Christ is the church. Consequently, for these theorists the proclaimed message of Christianity is intimately linked to and inseparable from its church context. Therefore, part of the subject matter content of religious education is any material which will enable the students to better know the church, affirm their allegiance to it, and be better disciples of the Christian message. Such subjects as church history and the lives of holy Christians should form an indispensable part of a complete religious education curriculum. Church history and hagiography give clear evidence of Christ's presence in the world. The grace of Christ is seen as irrupting in history, and in the personal lives of Christians, to change the course of natural events. But, let it be noted, the transcendists do not advocate that such material be taught for its own sake but only that the students may know the church and so confirm their Christian loyalty and commitment and improve their Christian witness. The teaching of such content will also contribute to the growth of the students as mature persons.[34]

The Arrangement of Content

Some transcendist theorists set great store by the proper arrangement of the subject matter content of any given curriculum. They inveigh against a fragmented, rationally-developed presentation of doctrine because this, they claim, tends to destroy the integralness of the mystery of salvation in Christ. Religion, they assert, is an organic unit, not a discrete series of "do" or "don't" practices. The general principle for the arrangement of content is this: To "strikingly set forth the Christocentricity of the Gospel message and its character of Joyful Tidings."[35] Such an arrangement follows the "dynamic of God's revelation." In effect, this means that content is presented with an integral and Christ-centered arrangement. In other words, content is presented in the very manner in which God graciously revealed himself in the history of salvation—a manner calculated to highlight his fatherly care for us in Christ.[36] The theorists further point out that the primacy of divine truth over mere moral considerations must always be upheld. God's in-breaking word in revelation is divine truth. It is this truth which when received and accepted works its own inner dynamic and brings about a personal transformation. Religion teaching, therefore, must never develop into a forum for dealing with moral problems. Teachers must beware of the danger of choosing content merely on the basis of the students' psychological needs.[37] While not insisting as much as the Roman Catholics do on a specific Christ-centered arrangement of content, James Smart also sees content as probably the most important determining factor in religious education. Thus, his starting point for a religion program is the doctrine of the Trinity for he sees the Trinity as "a description of how God comes to man, to sinful man, and yet remains the God that he is."[38] The Trinity is but the human-language expression of the ineffable experience of a God who dramatically breaks into human history in the person of Jesus Christ. God-centered revelatory content, therefore, is basic to religious education. Because this content is divine and supernatural truth containing the power of the Spirit, it must take precedence over method which is man-conceived and man-influenced.

Method, the Handmaiden of the Message (Content)

Though they generally advocate a "harmonious synthesis" of content and method, the transcendist theorists tend to divide one from the other and see them as separate, if interlocking, entities. Methods of teaching are the instruments or servants with which to inculcate content. The key principle is: The method must always be subservient to the message. Why? This must be so because the content, being God's divine word, has an inner dynamic all its own which both informs and challenges. Such a position correlates well with the sharp distinction the transcendists make between natural and supernatural. God's word is supernatural; in no way can it be adulterated. The captivating insistence of God's message must not be minimized or rendered sterile by human methodology. The most that the teacher might strive to do is to make the divine content "revelant" to the students and leave God's word to work its mysterious power through grace and the Holy Spirit.[39] By "relevant" the theorists mean that the word of God must be presented in such a way that it is made interesting and captivating. It must be presented in such a way that the students will be stimulated to make further investigations of their own and personally penetrate more deeply the inexhaustible riches of the divine message. The word must be shown to have meaning for the concrete circumstances of the present-day lives of the students. But—and this is an important but—making the message "relevant" cannot be taken to mean that the method does anything more than prepare the ground for the work of grace which in no way depends on the teacher.

Content and Religious Experience

As we shall see in the following chapters, several prominent religious educationists claim that the principal content of religious education is experience, which (depending on their point of view) is either itself religious experience or leading thereto. Theorists who favor a transcendist metaperspective are extremely chary about asserting any such thing. They agree that Christian doctrine and the Christian message can and should be made exciting and moving so that it captures the imagination of the students and generates tremendous enthusiasm for the Christian life. Furthermore, particularly in worship, holy affections may be aroused by the otherworldly atmosphere that should prevail in such celebrations. Nevertheless, transcendist theorists in general tend to look upon religious experience as something quite out of the ordinary, dramatic, and esoteric, akin to the conversion of Paul on the Damascus road, or the ecstasies of the saints. Jungmann, for example, makes a distinction between "personal experiences" (which for him means an active involvement of the person's faculties and emotions) and "religious experience." For him, personal experience is an "awakening of the soul" and is not, though it may lead to, religious experience.[40] Much as the teacher should aim at achieving "an elevated and dignified mood . . . so that not only the intellect but also our feelings, our hearts should be touched," extraordinary experience of God (i.e., religious experience) "is not the stuff of everyday life, and we could never hope to provoke one for ourselves or for someone else."[41] Adding a touch of vehemence, James Smart sternly calls the attempt by some teachers to give children an experience of God "blasphemy." He sedulously warns against the danger of letting students get the impression that thrilling and memorable experiences, or the moving effect of a religious service, constitutes a Christian experience of God.[42]

Thus, leading transcendist theorists of religious education tend to reserve the meaning of religious experience for some very extraordinary and ineffable personally-involving event which can positively be linked with the divine. The point to be made is that the transcendists have a very elevated, sublime, and even esoteric view of religious experience which goes well with their emphasis on the transcendence and otherness of the supernatural. As the transcendists see it, the true content of religious education is God's divine word. This word may, if it is the divine good pleasure, "break in" by its Spirit-pervaded power and produce a genuine religious experience.

THE TEACHER

According to major transcendist theorists *religion teachers are before all else ministers of the word—God's saving word to man in Christ.* Teachers are God's instruments for transmitting the good news of salvation. Teachers are the faithful servants of God's word such that the power and efficacy of the teachers' words derive solely from the supernatural power and efficacy of the message they proclaim. Teachers may therefore be likened to messengers who deliver the exact content of revelation to the students, just as Christ was God's supremely faithful messenger to man. As to method, this is largely determined by the very message itself. The method of delivering the message flows from and is but an echo of the very manner in which the message was first given by Jesus Christ and his early disciples.[43]

Teachers are Ministers of the Word and of the Church

The church is the body of Christ, and Christ is God's revelation to his people; therefore, argue the transcendist theorists, God's message reaches out to the world through the church by the preaching and teaching of the church's ministers.[44] Christian religion teachers are no ordinary run-of-the-mill individuals. They are the special representatives of Jesus Christ; they should perceive themselves as such and be so respected by the students. They have been called and hold their commission to teach from Christ, through the church. For the transcendists, teachers are ministers of the word and authoritative heralds of a supernatural message. They speak with the authority of Christ because the power of their words is the Spirit-imbued power of the message they proclaim. The God who "dwells in heaven" speaks to his creation through the faithful instrumentality of his chosen ministers, preachers and teachers.

While theoretically, according to the transcendists, the power of God's word cannot be weakened by the obtuseness of his human instruments (grace is not under human control and the Spirit blows where he wills), all agree that the Christian witness of the teacher is of capital importance. For the transcendists, only a committed Christian can teach Christianity. Christ taught as much by the example of his lifestyle as by his words, and teachers must be for their students examples of the very life of Christ. The quality of the teachers' attachment to the ideals of the Christian life will shine through in their teaching to enhance the message they proclaim. Teachers must not only be outstanding witnesses to Christianity but also apostles whose enthusiasm for the spread of the word and the promotion of the church is contagious. Consequently, the teachers' attitude toward the church is all-important. This attitude will become evident in the teachers' manner of speech, general demeanor of reverence, and lifestyle of prayer and Christian social action. In their teachers the students should be able to identify with Christ.[45]

What the transcendists are saying is, as one of them puts it, that forming the image of Christ in students "is ultimately a matter of divine grace, but it must employ human resources."[46] Not that grace is dependent on human resources—God's arm is not foreshortened by the feebleness of his human instruments. Nevertheless, one cannot help being left with the impression that here is one of the unsolved (and probably unsolvable) problems of the transcendist emphasis. If grace is not in any way subject to human interference how can it "employ human resources"? Does the teacher's method, manner, and demeanor affect the intrinsic and grace-filled power of the Christian message? As we shall see, the immanentists have their own particular problem of explaining how grace can so work within and according to nature that God does not become pantheistically identified with man.

The Teacher's Method

As has already been noted, transcendist-minded theorists typically separate method and content though they understand the former as being largely determined by the latter. The content determines the method because the content is supernaturally given. The teachers' main task is to present the Christian message in such a way as to open up its meaning and significance for the students. The basic principle always is: The teachers should be more concerned with the message than with the method. Method is but a means to an end and it should never become so important as to be an end in itself.[47]

In their treatment of religion teaching, transcendist-oriented religious educationists frequently use such terms as "description," "narrative," "presentation," "transmission," "heralding," "explanation." Their very language conveys the notion that they are envisioning a very teacher-centered methodology. Such a conceptualization of the teaching process can only come from the notion that the overarching consideration in all of religion teaching is this: Be faithful harbingers of God's word. Although some of them would claim that teaching religion does not mean lecturing,[48] the emphasis of these theorists appears very definitely to be on an authoritative pouring of the good news into fairly passive receptacles, viz., the students. As described by some religious educationists, teaching seems closely to resemble preaching, and it is not easy to distinguish between the two. The teaching techniques suggested by some theorists such as the narrative technique (telling the story of salvation), or the text-development technique (presenting, explaining, and applying to life biblical and church-related texts), ultimately hark back to the principle that the message must be taught as it was revealed by God in Jesus. Teachers are to follow God's method as he proclaims the good news of salvation—to teach as Jesus did.[49]

All of religion teaching, maintain the majority of the transcendists, should take place in an atmosphere of prayer, of worship of God, and in an interior spirit of union with him. The "atmosphere" that is envisaged here is one which conveys a reverential sensitivity to the awesome presence of the unseen God. While all theorists state that such an atmosphere can and should be accomplished in the classroom, all agree that it is far more easily achieved in the context of liturgical worship. The Roman Catholic theorists particularly, affirm that the actual mysteries of salvation in Christ's life, death, and resurrection are reenacted in the liturgy. Consequently, active involvement in the liturgy (preparation for the service, singing, communal prayers, sacramental participation) is the "classic" way to teach God's message. They also note that this was par excellence the method used in the early church. The liturgy provides (1) a certain knowledge of and actual involvement with the mysteries of salvation, (2) a sense of active union with Christ present in the world, (3) an atmosphere of reverence and worship which emphasizes the supernatural character of God's invitation.[50]

In fine, as Johannes Hofinger reminds us, according to transcendist-minded religious educationists there are many *techniques* for teaching religion but only one *method*. The method is God's method as revealed to us in Christ; there is no possibility of an adequate man-made method to deal with so supernatural a message. God's method is the method which "proclaims 'the wonderful works of God,' which show forth the truth and especially the love contained in them, moving the heart and inspiring the whole of life."[51] It is a method which ensures that God's call will ring in the hearts of the students but a call which, when all comes to all, teachers cannot control.

Again, we may well leave the final word to James Smart who convincingly captures the transcendist flavor and neatly encapsulates the transcendist theorists' approach to the teacher. The making of a Christian, Smart contends, is a mystery—a mystery of grace beyond human control and interference. Consequently, teachers may never delude themselves into thinking that by sheer technique they can "produce a development in human beings that, according to the New Testament, is the work of the Holy Spirit through the Gospel of Jesus Christ."[52]

THE STUDENT

For the transcendist theorists, in the context of religious education *there can be no other view of man (the student) than that which is revealed by God.* It is this theological approach which provides the key to their theorizing about the student.

James Smart expresses it this way: "[Man] is God's creature and the structure of his life [is] determined by his creaturely relation to God. But this relation is so concealed that it fails to register on the charts of psychologists and sociologists except as a puzzling vacancy. Who man is can only be known by revelation and faith."[53] Revelation tells us that man is created by God and destined for an eternal life of perfect fellowship with him, but also that man is a sinner and in need of redemption. Man is a complex of natural and supernatural elements, the relationship which does not appear on the scientists' charts. The transcendists make a clear and sharp distinction between man in his natural and observable state and the invisible (i.e., unobservable) configuration of his personal relationship with God. This relationship, which man already possesses in germ by the very fact of his creation and baptism, is activated and brought to fruition by the supernatural power of God's message which man receives in religious education within the church.

The Student and Learning

The overriding principle adhered to by the transcendists is well expressed in the saying: It is God who educates.[54] However, clinging to such a principle ensures that the transcendists will set very little store by scientific learning theory. Not only do they not attempt any careful definition of what learning is, but they take refuge in rather imprecise formulae such as "laying open to us a new relationship" with God,[55] or "the formation of human hearts and minds."[56] Transcendists can offer no strict definition of religious learning because they consider it to be essentially a mystery, the ineffable mystery of God in his relationship with a human person. In other words, religious learning is the work of God's grace not man's efforts, and therefore, it is not open to scientific examination and definition. Nonetheless, despite their supernaturalist outlook the transcendist theorists do attempt to pay some homage to scientific learning theory. Thus Johannes Hofinger, for example, states that teaching procedure must be adapted to the "psychology of learning." He recommends the three-stage teaching process of perception, assimilation, and response, which correspond to the three stages of learning, viz., concrete experience, reflection, and understanding, acting out of the knowledge assimilated. In this way revelatory truth is transformed into a living relationship with God.[57] Similarly, James Smart recognizes that personal experience is the best form of learning. He notes that unless students can relate the biblical message to their own life-experiences and thereby arrive at some personal meaningful synthesis, then hearing God's word will not have a fruitful outcome in terms of Christian life.[58]

But, when all is said and done, the gaze of the transcendist school of thought reaches beyond the best and most skillful endeavors to bring about learning. So far as they are concerned religious learning is to be had only in an encounter with God. The supernatural message received by the students finds a deep echo within them, makes them conscious of who they are in the eyes of God, makes them understand their dignity and their destiny, and induces them to respond by a life of prayer and Christian discipleship. Thus, the transcendists seem to propose that conscious attention to the message on the part of the students will *of itself* produce a desire for an active life of Christian commitment. If the message is convincingly presented, Christian action will follow automatically. Knowledge unerringly leads to action. The powerful interior dynamic of God's word cannot be denied and will inevitably have its effect. In the living faith-response to God's word a true relationship of love is established with God, and concrete learning of God's message takes place. But all this is the work of grace given in the Spirit; it is supernatural. The human preparation of the student by the teacher to respond to God's word is just that—a human preparation.[59]

In sum, the transcendist theorists' emphasis on the primacy of the supernatural and its sharp distinction from the natural correlates well with their theorizing on the student in a religious education setting. It is the student considered from the point of view of a grace-caused supernatural relationship with God who is of interest to these theorists. The student is not a complex of personality variables and behavior patterns but a creature of God called to a supernatural destiny, learning of this call and responding to it by God's grace.

THE ENVIRONMENT

By the term *environment* here is meant the entire field of experience, that is, all the elements, whether remote or proximate, which may affect students in the religious education setting and influence religious learning. For example, such factors as home situation, type of school, teacher behavior, instructional aids, physical conditions, may all affect the student and hence all belong to the learning environment. Some of these environmental elements are more remote than others, that is, they form the background for rather than immediately determine student behavior. Such elements belong to what may be called the general environment and are often not under the direct control of the teacher but nevertheless do interact to affect student behavior. The environmental elements which are more directly related to the immediate teaching act belong to what may be called the instructional environment and are more readily controlled by the teacher.

Transcendist-minded religious educationists typically do not see the environment as an element or factor which merits great attention in the religious education process. Some theorists do admit that the environment can contribute to the success or failure of religious education. On the other hand, others give the impression that they are more intent on *saving* students from the environment than positively using environmental variables to aid religious learning. In general, transcendist theorists tend to regard the majority of experiences which engage the students in the normal course of life as hostile or inimical to the best interests of religion. Ordinary experiences such as newspapers, films, posters, the influence of the peer group, the example of adults, are regarded by some theorists as belonging to "the world." "The world," these theorists tend to agree, is thoroughly "secularized" and therefore divorced from the supernatural. Not in these "worldly" experiences is God to be found. In modern times we have lost the general environmental influence of a strong Christian life such as existed in earlier periods of the history of the church. This being so, the educational agencies (school, church groups, religion classes, liturgical settings) should aim at creating conditions in which the supernatural is "welcome," in which there is an atmosphere of reverence and prayerful adoration. According to one theorist "the catechist and the educator must resist the influence of the hostile world; they must create in the true sense of the word, another kind of world, out of the school class itself and out of the liturgical life which is so essential to the school."[60]

Therefore, the transcendist theorists do not see the environment as an important factor in religious education because, for them, the environment reeks of the secular, the unsupernatural. This attitude corresponds perfectly to their insistence on the dichotomizing of natural and supernatural. Transcendist theorists do not emphasize the supernatural dimension of all of experience but tend to see God-experiences as special, infrequent, and out of the ordinary. For them, the environment bears the markings of the natural rather than the supernatural and of itself does not contribute to the thoroughly supernatural ends of religious education.

EVALUATION

The purpose of any evaluative procedure is to determine whether the aims and desired outcomes of a project have or have not been achieved. One can thus assess the efficiency of the operation and collect data which may assist in future planning. Evaluation procedures do not consist only in a terminal assessment of achieved outcomes. Evaluation can proceed throughout the entire process and thus act after the fashion of a regulatory mechanism by way of cybernetic feedback.[61] *Since for the transcendist school of thought, the aims of religious education are supernatural and transcendent, the question of evaluation plays an entirely insignificant part in their religious education theory.* The transcendists insist that scientific mechanisms having to do with the assessment of human behavior cannot touch the core of the grace-produced relationship with God which is the principal aim of religious education. Strict application of scientific evaluative principles would be to deal with man, as one transcendist has it, "not as a child of God but as a complex of animal impulses and reflexes." Against this brand of frankensteinian horror "a Christian educator . . . has to protest with all his strength."[62]

It would be a mistake to think that religious educationists who favor a transcendist metaperspective entirely eschew all forms of evaluative procedure. They admit the usefulness of such evaluative measures as tests and quizzes but see them more as aids to memorization than as anything else. Now, sheer knowledge of doctrine, bible history and the like, while being important and useful, is not necessarily an indication of a religious attitude which leads to proper religious conduct. And so, memory tests do not really evaluate the true aim of religious education. The only true evaluative criterion that the transcendists will accept is a theological one in which the entire religious education enterprise is continually reveiwed against the background of Christian revelation. As James Smart expresses it, "The real need is for an ongoing process, a constantly renewed critique, in which all the phenomena that appear in the field of the Church's education will be examined in the light of the essential Christian revelation, in order to discern at each point what is Christian and what is not."[63] What these theorists see as a need, therefore, is not so much an evaluation of the specifics of student behavior, but rather a critique of overall trends and practices. The evaluative criterion is: Are these trends and practices Christian? Such a criterion can only be derived from an interpretation of special revelation. It must necessarily be rather vague and unspecific. Further, such a criterion is more frequently applied to the teacher as a minister of the divine message than to the student. It is more frequently applied to teaching practices and to the content of religious education than to an assessment of aim-achievement from the student's point of view.[64]

The attitude of representative transcendist theorists toward specific evaluation of student learning outcomes in religious education is well in keeping with their transcendist metaperspective. (1) Christian behavior is the result of God's grace and supernatural effects cannot be assessed by natural agencies; (2) only theological criteria derived from revelation (which of their nature lack specificity) can be used to evaluate the Christian configuration of the religious education enterprise; (3) the teacher (and particularly the content of teaching) rather than the student should be the object of evaluation in order to ascertain whether the true Christian message is being transmitted.

NOTES

1. James D. Smart, *The Creed in Christian Teaching* (Philadelphia: Westminster Press, 1962), p. 71.

2. Josef Andreas Jungmann, *Handing on the Faith: A Manual of Catechetics,* translated and revised by A. N. Fuerst (New York: Herder and Herder, 1964), p. 166.

3. Some Protestant theorists hold that God's message is to be found exclusively in the bible and that all revelation strictly so called ceased at the ascension of Christ. (See Smart, *The Creed in Christian Teaching,* p. 167 ff.). Other theorists would consider this a rather restrictive view of revelation. The Roman Catholics, particularly, would see revelation as continuing and extending historically through apostolic tradition. But even these latter transcendist theorists tend to focus more exclusively on the bible as the sure and authentic source of God's revelatory message.

4. Johannes Hofinger, S.J., in collaboration with Francis J. Buckley, S.J., *The Good News and Its Proclamation: Post Vatican II Edition of The Art of Teaching Christian Doctrine* (Notre Dame, Indiana: University of Notre Dame Press, 1968), p. 200.

5. Johannes Hofinger, S.J., *Our Message Is Christ* (Notre Dame, Indiana: Fides, 1974), p. 4.

6. Jungmann, *Handing on the Faith,* p. 28.

7. Josef Andreas Jungmann, S.J., *The Good News Yesterday and Today,* translated (abridged) and edited by William A. Huesman, S.J. (New York: W. H. Sadlier, 1962), p. 53.

8. Josef Jungmann, *Announcing the Word of God,* translated by Ronald Walls (New York: Herder and Herder, 1967), p. 106. See also James Smart, *The Teaching Ministry of the Church* (Philadelphia: Westminster Press, 1954), pp. 28–29.

9. Jungmann, *Handing on the Faith,* p. 373.

10. Smart, *The Teaching Ministry of the Church,* p. 29.

11. See, for example, Jungmann, *The Good News Yesterday and Today,* p. 92; Hofinger, *The Good News and Its Proclamation,* p. 20; Smart, *The Teaching Ministry of the Church,* p. 109. See also James D. Smart, *The Rebirth of Ministry* (Philadelphia: Westminster Press, 1960), p. 176.

12. Jungmann, *The Good News Yesterday and Today,* p. 92.

13. While Protestant religious educationists generally use the word "worship" Roman Catholics prefer to speak of the "liturgy," which is worship performed by the church as a body and presided over by a properly designated minister. Liturgy is thus distinguished from purely private individual or group worship.

The Greek word *koinonia,* which means communion, fellowship, common sharing and participation, is sometimes used by religious educationists to designate the community which is the Christian church. As used in the New Testament *koinonia* designates a special relationship of the Christian to God, an intimate sharing and union with him. When applied to the church, therefore, it means more than common fellowship. Added to this common fellowship and sharing is that God in Christ is intimately present within every relationship in the church community such that the *community* becomes a *communion.*

14. Jungmann, *The Good News Yesterday and Today,* p. 114.

15. Ibid., p. 155.

16. Hofinger, *The Good News and Its Proclamation,* pp. 205–211.

17. Jungmann, *The Good News Yesterday and Today,* p. 9.

18. Hofinger, *The Good News and Its Proclamation,* p. 49.

19. Smart, *The Creed in Christian Teaching,* p. 164.

20. Jungmann, *The Good News Yesterday and Today,* p. 145.

21. See, for example, Josef Jungmann, "Theology and Kerygmatic Teaching," *Lumen Vitae,* Vol. 5 (1950), pp. 258–263; Jungmann, *Handing on the Faith,* pp. xii, 73; Jungmann, *Announcing the Word of God,* pp. 59–65.

Many Roman Catholic religious educationists prefer to use the word "catechesis" or "catechetics" in lieu of "religious education," or "religious instruction." As some writers have pointed out this may be a less accurate use of the word "catechesis." For a discussion of this point see James Michael Lee, *The Shape of Religious Instruction* (Notre Dame, Indiana: Religious Education Press, 1971), pp. 6, 28–30.

22. This book, abridged and edited, appeared in English translation under the title *The Good News Yesterday and Today* (New York: W. H. Sadlier, 1962). For an assessment of the impact of *Die Frobotschaft und Unsere Glaubensverdikündigung* see *The Good News Yesterday and Today,* pp. 169–228.

23. Francis J. Buckley, calls Hofinger the "great apostle of Kerygmatic renewal." See the preface to Hofinger, *Our Message is Christ.*

24. See, for example, Harold William Burgess, *An Invitation to Religious Education* (Notre Dame, Indiana: Religious Education Press, 1975); George M. Schreyer, *Christian Education in Theological Focus* (Philadelphia: Christian Education Press, 1962); J. Gordon Chamberlain, *Freedom and Faith* (Philadelphia: Westminster Press, 1965); Sara Little, *The Role of the Bible in Contemporary Christian Education* (Richmond: John Knox Press, 1966).

25. Smart habitually uses the upper case *W* when writing the "Word" as referring to God's Word, i.e., his message to us in Christ.

26. Hofinger, *The Good News and Its Proclamation,* p. 9.

27. Smart, *The Creed in Christian Teaching,* p. 194.

28. Jungmann, *Handing on the Faith,* p. 36.

29. For a discussion of the meaning of *kerygma* see Lee, *The Shape of Religious Instruction,* pp. 28–34. Gabriel Moran also discusses kerygma and kerygmatic theology in *Catechesis of Revelation* (New York: Herder and Herder, 1966), pp. 20–29. See also Vincent M. Novak, "The Kerygma in Religious Education," *Catholic School Journal,* Vol. 60 (April 1960); Francis Somerville, "What does Kerygmatic Mean?" *Guide,* Vol. 46 (October 1961); Hofinger, *The Good News and Its Proclamation,* pp. 8, 78, 279–315.

30. Hofinger, *Our Message Is Christ,* p. 94.

31. Smart, *The Teaching Ministry of the Church,* p. 79.

32. Smart, *The Rebirth of Ministry,* p. 103.

33. Hofinger, *The Good News and Its Proclamation,* pp. 250, 268, 270; Jungmann, *The Good News Yesterday and Today,* pp. 79, 33; Smart, *The Teaching Ministry of the Church,* pp. 118–119, 152–153.

34. For example, see Smart, *The Teaching Ministry of the Church,* pp. 116–119, 125–129; Jungmann, *Handing on the Faith,* pp. 106–108; Hofinger, *The Good News and Its Proclamation,* pp. 73–84.

35. Hofinger, "The Place of the Good News in Modern Catechetics," in Jungmann, *The Good News Yesterday and Today,* p. 175.

36. Hofinger, *The Good News and Its Proclamation,* pp. 73–84.

37. Jungmann, *Handing on the Faith,* p. 137 footnote 55; see also pp. 139–140. By "psychological needs" Jungmann appears to mean the solving of moral problems which may arise at particular stages of a student's development, at puberty, for example.

38. Smart, *The Teaching Ministry of the Church,* p. 89; see pp. 88–92 generally.

39. See Hofinger, "The Place of the Good News in Modern Catechetics," pp. 171–179; Hofinger, *The Good News and Its Proclamation,* pp. 6–11, 13.

40. Jungmann, *Handing on the Faith,* p. 206; see pp. 204–212 generally.

41. Ibid., p. 206.

42. Smart, *The Rebirth of Ministry,* p. 104.

43. See Jungmann, *Handing on the Fatih,* p. xii. Dealing with James Smart's approach to the bible in Christian education Sara Little in *The Role of the Bible in Contemporary Christian Education,* (Richmond, Virginia: John Knox Press, 1961), p. 68, expresses it well when she writes: "Christian education is determined by the very essence of that with which it deals . . . the 'content' of revelation 'imposes itself as such' upon the form and process of Christian education. . . [Christian education] centers around and is empowered by the continuing creative activity of the Word of God. Its sphere of activity is the Church. And its purpose is to be a 'servant of revelation.' *Thus man's role as educator is to be understood only in the light of God's role as revealer."* (Emphasis added)

44. Transcendist theorists are not fully agreed on the difference or distinction between preaching and teaching. One theorist, for example, sees preach-

ing as pertaining to the proclamation of the gospel to unbelievers or those new to the faith, and teaching as a fuller explanation of the content of revelation and a training of Christians to a more committed and active participation in Christian discipleship (Smart, *The Rebirth of Ministry*, p. 92, and chapter 4 generally). The minister of the church is both preacher and teacher. All teaching should to some extent partake of the preaching mode as preaching tends of its very nature to be more emotive and stirring than plain teaching. Lack of precision notwithstanding, all representative transcendist theorists are agreed that both preaching and teaching belong to the total ministry of the word and must go hand in hand. Catechetics and homiletics are sisters.

45. See Hofinger, *The Good News and Its Proclamation*, pp. 26–27, 166, 248; Jungmann, *Handing on the Faith*, pp. 75–76; Smart, *The Creed in Christian Teaching*, pp. 13, 31.

46. Jungmann, *Handing on the Faith*, p. 71.

47. Hofinger, *The Good News and Its Proclamation*, pp. 13, 85–86.

48. For example, Johannes Hofinger, S.J., in collaboration with William J. Reedy, *The ABCs of Modern Catechetics* (New York: W. H. Sadlier, 1962), p. 70.

49. Hofinger, *The Good News and Its Proclamation*, pp. 86–88. See also Johannes Hofinger, S.J., editor, *Teaching All Nations*, English version revised and partly translated by Clifford Howell, S.J., (New York: Herder and Herder, 1962), p. 398.

50. Jungmann, *The Good News Yesterday and Today*, pp. 114–116; Jungmann, *Handing on the Faith*, pp. 97–100; Hofinger, *The Good News and Its Proclamation*, pp. 53–56.

51. Johannes Hofinger quoting from The Program of the Catechetical Apostolate drawn up by the International Study Week on Mission Apologetics, Eichstätt, July, 1960. See *The Good News and Its Proclamation*, pp. 86, 327.

52. Smart, *The Rebirth of Ministry*, pp. 100–101.

53. Ibid., p. 102.

54. The expression is used by James Smart, *The Teaching Ministry of the Church*, p. 168.

55. Ibid., p. 91.

56. Hofinger, *The ABCs of Modern Catechetics*, p. 62.

57. Hofinger, *The Good News and Its Proclamation*, pp. 89–91; *The ABCs of Modern Catechetics*, pp. 62–63.

58. Smart, *The Teaching Ministry of the Church*, pp. 118, 168; *The Creed in Christian Teaching*, p. 189.

59. Smart, *The Teaching Ministry of the Church*, pp. 168–169; Jungmann, *Handing on the Faith*, pp. 244–261; Hofinger, *The ABCs of Modern Catechetics*, pp. 59–71 passim.

60. Jungmann, *Handing on the Faith*, pp. 77; see also pp. 97, 124–125, 137–138.

61. For a treatment of the use of cybernetic theory in teaching see C. Kyle Packer and Toni Packer, ''Cybernetics, Information Theory and the Educative

Process," *Teachers College Record,* Vol. 61 (December 1959), pp. 134–142.

62. Smart, *The Rebirth of Ministry,* p. 103; see also Smart, *The Teaching Ministry of the Church,* p. 42.

63. Smart, *The Teaching Ministry of the Church,* p. 70. It is the opinion of James Edward Thorness that the evaluation function of theology "is probably the most important point, the thesis, of Smart's theory of religious education." See "Analysis of the Function of Theology in Selected Theories of Religious Education," unpublished doctoral dissertation, Syracuse University (1966), pp. 162–163.

64. Hofinger, *The Good News and Its Proclamation,* pp. 247–252.

CHAPTER V

The Supernatural
Within the Natural

Much of the older Christian thought represented God and the world as two separate realities, as though the world of nature were distinct from another world called the supernatural. But any such distinction as between natural and divine is no longer tenable.[1]

These words, written by George Albert Coe in the year 1911, represent one of the basic theological tenets of the liberal Protestant religious educationists of the pre-World War II era.[2] What Coe considered to be "older" Christian thought surfaced again in rather dramatic fashion with the neo-orthodox movement of the late 1930s and 1940s. In time, this "return-to-orthodoxy" trend made its influence felt in the theorizing of major religious educationists. As far as Roman Catholic religious educationists are concerned, theological liberalism was scarcely an issue until the Vatican II era of the early 1960s. Coe continues:

Christian thought does not think of God as superior to the world in the same sense as that in which a thinker is superior to any one of his own thoughts or to the entire combination of them. But a thinker does not exist apart from his thoughts but only in them . . . . Just so we have come to think of God as living his life in the process of the world, not apart from it.[3]

The theological stance or metaperspective evinced by this statement may fittingly be called *immanentist*. It is a metaperspective which focuses on the divine as deeply involved in and inextricably woven into every aspect of natural process. It is a metaperspective which views things not in terms of an existential separation of natural and supernatural, but as God acting so totally within all things human that there is nothing human which is not also divine. God is not man's over-against; every statement about God is simultaneously a statement about man.

The immanentist stance is characteristic of several religious educationists. To call them immanentists, however, does not necessarily mean that these theorists deny the transcendence of God vis-à-vis his creation. What it does mean is that they emphasize very strongly God's *withinness* to the processes of the world and particularly to all aspects of human relationships. To put it

80

another way, these theorists' preferred outlook is immanentist, and it is this immanentist flavor which seems most evident in their religious education theory.

As will become evident, there is much less agreement among religious educationists who espouse the immanentist position than among the transcendists. While the transcendists show remarkable similarily of views with regard to the various areas of critical concern to religious education, the same cannot be said for the immanentists. Immanentist theorists tend to adopt different theological and epistemological stances within the general immanentist framework. One possible reason for this is that transcendists, far more than the immanentists, allow theology and theological principles to enter into their religious education theorizing. On the other hand, other factors, such as epistemological considerations, may be more determinative of the theorizing of the immanentists. Be that as it may, the crucial issue as far as this book is concerned is the agreed immanentist stance of many religious educationists. It is on the basis of their immanentist emphasis that they are grouped together in this chapter.

DELINEATION OF THE IMMANENTIST METAPERSPECTIVE

1. Revelation

What it is.   Representative immanentist religious educationists typically emphasize that *revelation is a continuous personal experience.* Since God is immanent in all worldly and human processes, then he participates intimately in the very depth of human experience, all of which is potentially revelatory. Some theorists would admit that revelation consists both of a set of doctrinal propositions and of experience in event and encounter (one does not exclude the other).[4] Nevertheless, as far as religious education is concerned their preferred emphasis is that of revelation as ongoing human experience.

The views of theorists who appear to favor an immanentist outlook on the place of the bible in revelation vary rather widely. Some whould hold that the bible is the inspired word of God and that it provides cognitive data about God not elsewhere available. For these theorists the bible, together with the teaching of the church, is the most important normative source for the interpretation of the rest of experience as revelatory.[5] Others would hold that scripture is only a partial expression of God's word and that therefore it cannot be normative for interpreting human experience as revelatory. As one theorist states, "anything that is truly personal and humanizing can be used to bring out the sense of God's revelation."[6] Others again, adopting a very liberal stance, would hold that the bible is little more than a body of social literature, albeit of a very powerful kind, which can help us to cope with the problems we have to face. In the thinking of this latter group the bible does provide us with a story of the development of religious consciousness in man, but is only one of many such books. Therefore, the bible can in no way be normative for interpreting experience as revelatory because the very interpretation of the bible itself is a human process. To use such an interpretation as normative for other human experience would mean giving human opinion the force of a divine command. Such a situation would mean a denigration of human freedom and a denial of the immanence of God within the very process of that freedom.[7]

Why it is.   Representative immanentist theorists intimate that the purpose of revelation is that man may enter into personal communication and union with God. As one of them puts it, "The subjective aspect of revelation, then, constitutes an existential introduction of the individual into the blessedness of God's own life, and in so doing effects an inner transformation in that individual."[8] Other theorists would prefer to focus far less on the individual. They tend to emphasize that union with God and personal transformation can only take place in the context of loving interpersonal relationships. According to some, there can be no personal union with God except within a social context. There can be no question of the "me-and-God-alone" type of "vertical" union. What is most noble on earth, what most intimately reveals God is his immanence in the coming to be of the person. And persons cannot be except in relationship to other persons.[9]

How it is.   In their treatment of how we come to grasp and respond to God's revelation immanentist theorists typically downplay any direct divine action through a special gift of faith. For them, the emphasis is on God the Holy Spirit working within the very process of experience and according to the laws and principles which govern how that experience is to be interpreted. Some theorists totally discard any notion of a special and direct divine intervention through faith. We can discern the divine presence, they aver, simply by discovering love among people.[10] Other theorists, while not fully discarding the notion of faith as a special divine intervention see faith as a component in the revelational process itself, which process is coextensive with the totality of experience. Thus, declares one theorist, "Faith is directed not toward revelation but toward people and the universe. Revelation is not the answer to faith but the underlying reality which gives sense to faith as an open-ended search."[11] Still others, while affirming a distinctive divine action in the faith-recognition of experience as revelatory, strongly underscore that the divine action takes place according to and in concert with the laws of nature.[12]

Representative religious educationists whose metaperspective is characteristically immanentist either completely deny or drastically minimize any purely supernatural element in revelation. If God's action is to be conceived of as distinctive, then it is distinctive only in the sense of being so totally enmeshed in human process that the perfection of this very process makes it distinctive. If revelation is to be thought of as salvational, then salvation will come largely through the "humanization" of human relationships. The supernatural is within the natural, at the very core of the human condition; there is no separateness or separableness of natural and supernatural realm or order.

2. Grace

What it is.   As far as the immanentists are concerned, the characteristic differences of opinion among Roman Catholics and Protestants relative to grace are not of great significance. The reason for this is that Protestant religious educationists who espouse the immanentist position are also generally of a very liberal bent. They are not comfortable with such hard-core theological notions as grace, even in relation to sin, or salvation. For them, sin and salvation are meaningless concepts if taken as referring to the individual removed from the social context. Grace is regarded as some form of rather indefinable "social cement" which helps bring about the creation of an ideal human society. It is only within such a society that we are "saved" for it is in such a society that God "participates" with us. In the liberal view there can be no question of grace referring to any form of individualized union with God.[13]

Some Roman Catholic immanentist theorists see grace as God's free and unmerited gift of himself by which he (God) is personally present to us as known, loved, and possessed. Such a position differs little, if at all, from the transcendist position. However, the immanentists tend to emphasize that the clearest manifestation of the working of divine grace is to be found in charity among people. In fact, all acts of charity, all manifestations of love, are grace-inspired and grace-bearing. Revelation, also, is grace since it is God's gift of himself. Since the immanentist theorists for the most part equate revelation with human experience, then to a certain extent all human activity which is truly human may be said to be graced.[14]

How it works.   While possibly not wishing to totally identify the workings of grace with human action, many immanentist theorists tend to sail very close to the wind in this regard. Their strongly immanentist accent on God working in and through human process leads them to emphasize that grace works strictly within and according to the ordinary laws of nature. Thus, remarks one theorist, "grace and the divine-human encounter tend to be rendered most operative in terrestrial situations which are most true to themselves."[15] It is impossible to discern any distinctive divine action which is not also human. The whole of nature, the whole of human existence and social organization is graced and Spirit-imbued. If the transcendists tend to emphasize God who acts in man, the immanentists tend to emphasize man who acts in concert with God. A God-inspired and God-induced act of supernatural faith for the transcendists is for the immanentists a human act of belief or existential assent in which God intimately participates. Thus, for example, take the case of two students one of whom finds it much easier to believe and to make an act of faith than the other. The transcendists might be inclined to say that in the mysteriousness of God's designs he gave more grace to one than to the other. The immanentists, on the other hand, would tend to emphasize that the first student, because of a number of human factors (home background, personality traits, greater diligence and application) was more disposed to believe, that is, the human process of believing was more active. The immanentists would see God as working within all these human factors and according to their own particular mode. There is no divine act which is not also human, and vice versa.

The Holy Spirit.   As do the transcendists, Roman Catholic immanentist religious educationists understand grace as being the gift of the Holy Spirit personally present within us. Nevertheless, the immanentists stress that the Spirit works strictly in accord with the laws of created nature and not in some quasi-magical, totally "spiritual" or supernatural manner. One theorist summarizes it well when he observes that to say that the Spirit "blows where he wills" means in fact to say that the Spirit wills what he has made. If the Spirit is continually creating all things, then, say the immanentists, he is most intimately present and most revealed in the perfection of the very process of creation. We can facilitate the action of the Spirit by perfecting, as far as possible, the human conditions through which the Spirit works.[16]

3. The Church

What it is.   By and large, the immanentist theorists tend to draw attention to the church as a community and make this the major focus of their concern. It is through and in proper human community that salvation takes place; the church community radiates this salvation to the rest of the world. The church, therefore, is an outward-looking community concerned with the humanization of man and with social improvement. The church is a community searching for the divine in human experience. When we ask the question, "In what way is this community different from other bodies of like-minded people gathered together for philanthropic purposes?" the answers given by the immanentists vary. The very liberal-minded among them would claim that the church is unique only in that it is more radical and closer in its orientation to the social ideal of Jesus than are other groups.[17] In no way, therefore, is the church a new and special creation of Christ. God is not any more present in the church than he is in any other mutually loving and caring group dedicated to the ideal of the humanization of man. (Except, perhaps, in the sense that the Christian is more conscious of being intimately involved in the redemptive mystery of Christ operative everywhere in the world.) In such a conception of the church there is little room for institutional structure. If institution is necessary then it is for purely practical purposes. Some less liberally inclined theorists while insisting on the community aspect of the church, and also insisting that the church cannot be identified with any particular institutionalized structure, continue to see the need for institution. Church structure and community are, for them, a form of codification of God's incarnational presence in the world. Consequently, participation in church community *and* institution, with its specialized behaviors and distinctive lifestyle, serves as "a unique God-to-man mediational channel" and enables the individual to better enter a personal relationship with God.[18] Other theorists would tend to be more chary of church institution and church-related lifestyle as special divine mediational channels. They tend to see church-adopted bureaucratic institutional patterns as destructive of true community which is the proper locus of revelation, and hence of the manifestation of God's presence.[19] In any event, some immanentist theorists tend to accept the notion that the church (whether as community, or as institution, or as both) is a special and more clearly visible example of God's presence in the world. In spite of this, and here is the point, in their theorizing on religious education what they tend to focus their attention on is the immanence of the church within the very fabric of the human community. If the supernaturality, or the "special creation" view of the church is accepted, it is not emphasized. In fact, for these theorists the church is "supernatural" because it is so thoroughly human.

The Church and Revelation.   As we have seen, the immanentists cling to the notion that the main thrust of revelation is to be found in ongoing experience. God continually reveals himself by participating in the very depth of all experience. Now, the most truly human experiences take place in community; therefore, insofar as the church reaches the ideal of human community in that precise measure is it the special and favored locus of revelation. While most immanentist theorists would agree on this point, the Roman Catholics differ from the liberal Protestants, and among themselves, on the relationship of the hierarchical institutional structure of the church to revelation. For the liberal Protestants there is no problem because they do not hold for a hierarchical institutional structure. Some Roman Catholic theorists, on the other hand, would claim that the church magisterium[20] has a special Spirit-guided role to play in the interpretation of revelation.[21] Other theorists would claim that such a role is necessary only if we understand revelation as some*thing* which is *given* to the church; some*thing* which the church must have, and hold, and guard from contamination, and dispense to its members and to the world. If, on the other hand, we view revelation primarily as experience in community and church as dedicated to promoting such community experience, then our view of institution (and, of necessity, magisterium) will have to change.[22]

Thus, among the selected immanentist religious educationists, the notion of the church community as a specially favored locus of revelation seems to be generally accepted. There is less agreement—in fact, hardly any at all—on the special divinely-instituted structure of the church with a prior claim on the inspiring aid of the indwelling Spirit. As far as obtaining a consensus among the immanentists is concerned, the role of the institutional church plainly tends to raise the specter of Babel. The point to be made, however, is that the immanentists as a group are far more concerned with the notion of church as a revelatory community than they are with any other aspect of church. The concept of revelation rather than the concept of church is the key factor in their thinking. The church very definitely exists for revelation, not the other way round.

Worship. All immanentist theorists recognize the great educational possibilities of church worship but they approach the question from different standpoints while remaining within the general immanentist framework. The liberal Protestants see the socializing process as the main aim of religious education. They maintain that church worship is best expressed as an affirmation of oneness among the worshiping group. Such an affirmation of togetherness will strengthen the resolve of the group in their efforts to improve the whole social condition. Worship is a fostering of the human communion, which communion is divine precisely because it is so human. God is affirmed in the social process of communal togetherness, but not in any "vertical" or transcendent sense. Worship is the place where growth in personality takes place and where God is most clearly manifest in the coming-to-be of the person.[23]

While these notions of communal togetherness, celebration, *koinonia,* are all high on the immanentists' list of priorities, some theorists, particularly the Roman Catholics, would not push their immanentist stance as far as the liberal Protestants. The less liberal immanentists see the worship of the church, the liturgy, as the high point of the divine-human encounter, the special and specialized locus of ongoing revelation. The experience of God in liturgical participation is tied in with the fact that the sacraments and other liturgical forms are specially structured and highly enriched means of encounter with God.[24] While God is immanent in all experience, his immanence is more readily experienced as divine in some processes than in others. Particularly is this true of those symbolic acts instituted by Christ and propagated through the church which constitute the acts of the Christian liturgy. Roman Catholic theorists, particularly, affirm both the social and the individual aspects of communion with God through the liturgy. In general, their stance does not differ greatly from that of the representative transcendists. In fact, it is in the context of liturgical worship that the immanentists come closest to maintaining a sharp distinction between natural and supernatural.

4. Jesus Christ

In considering the question of Christ in the writings of immanentist religious educationists we are again faced with a wide variety of views ranging from extremely liberal to more traditional and orthodox. According to the extreme liberal position, to state that Jesus Christ is God and Savior is "utterly dogmatic and authoritarian."[25] Liberals of this extreme persuasion make no clear connection between the person of Jesus, God, and the Holy Spirit. For them Jesus is a social leader whose spirit and example we should follow. Of particular value is his ethical teaching which is epitomized in his love for persons and the supreme value he placed on persons. Jesus gives no "final notion of the divine," rather, he ensures that our notion of God will change with changing appreciation and re-creation of social conditions.[26] For these theorists, relationship with Jesus can in no sense be taken "in the abstract," that is, apart from relationship with the rest of society. Consequently, there is no vertical component in our relationship with God, we relate to him in and through ethical regard for persons and in no other way.

While not all immanentist theorists would wish to pitch their tents in the camp of the far left, echoes of the liberalist emphasis can be heard in more orthodox quarters. Some, for example, see the incarnation of God in Jesus as a continuing process throughout history and not as a static once-for-all constitution of the divine personality of Christ. Jesus is in process within the universe and is thus a constant reminder that the whole universe contains the divine and is revelatory. If the transcendist theorists are prepared to make the blunt statement that Jesus *is* God, is the enfleshed divine, and is to be adored, some immanentists seem less commited to such direct language. Their preference is for more oblique expressions such as "he is the chosen one who affirms the historical character of revelation," he "exemplifies in his person the logic that all flesh mediates the divine-human interaction," and "in Jesus, the receptivity of the human for the divine reached a high point."[27]

Still other immanentists present a picture of Jesus Christ which differs little from that presented by the transcendists. However, the immanentists place far greater emphasis on the process incarnation of God in Jesus such that nothing in the world is purely secular. Thus, the immanence of God is in fact an immanence of the incarnated Christ such that all reality contains a divine element. That is, all reality contains a divine pole of revelation through Jesus. As a result, the revelatory aspect of all reality and all experience can lead to a personal union with Jesus. Such a personal union with Christ in the lives of students is one of the principal focuses of religious education.[28] Perhaps the particular nuance this emphasis is trying to catch is captured by Patrick as he sang:

> Christ with me, Christ before me,
> Christ behind me, Christ within me,
> Christ beneath me, Christ above me,
> Christ at my right, Christ at my left,
> Christ in the fort,
> Christ in the chariot seat,
> Christ in the poop:
> Christ in the heart of every man who thinks of me,
> Christ in the mouth of every man who speaks to me,
> Christ in every eye that sees me,
> Christ in every ear that hears me—[29]

Three things appear to be common to the somewhat diverse emphases of the immanentist religious educationists with respect to Jesus Christ. First, there is a common tendency to focus on the humanity of Jesus. It is only through Jesus' expression of what is perfectly human that the divine can be appreciated and related to. Second, Christ is incarnated in all human process and experience. Christ filters through experience. Third, personal relationship with Christ is viewed primarily (though for some theorists not exclusively) as a horizontal relationship with other persons.

Conclusion

From the evidence adduced above, it is obvious that the religious educationists who favor an immanentist metaperspective present a broad spectrum of views with respect to the four locuses where the supernatural may specially be found. In fact, the views are so diverse that in concluding this section it may be well to restate why they have been grouped together in this book. *The central point of agreement among them is their highlighting of the divine incarnation at the heart of all human process.* This particular guiding principle leads to the equally important axiom that *all experience is potentially revelatory, can yield a consciousness of the divine.* As we shall see, it is this latter axiom that appears to be the leitmotif of the immanentists' theorizing on religious education. Thus, if all reality contains the divine and has a revelatory dimension (albeit to different degrees) then all human activity which is truly human is graced. The church is a revelatory community where the intimate meeting of the divine and the human is more intense and more visible. Jesus is incarnated in all of experience and is revealed therein.

It cannot be too often or too insistently stated that what we are dealing with here are not so much hard-core theological conceptualizations as they are modes of emphasis which give a particular theological "flavor." The fact, for example, that the transcendist theorists do not emphasize the processional view of the divine incarnation does not mean that this aspect is totally excluded from their thinking. Similarly, representative immanentist theorists downplay, but do not necessarily exclude (except, perhaps, for the very liberal among them), the transcendent pole of the natural/supernatural relationship. Some immanentist religious educationists may build their immanentist emphasis into an already existing framework of quite traditional Christian theology. Others may push their immanentist emphasis to its logical extreme and end up with what some might call a very atheological stance— atheological, that is, when measured against traditional Christian theology. In every case, particular concepts, however diverse, emerge tinged with immanentist color. It is these coloring tints and hues which spread across the entire mosaic of their religious education theory and make it recognizably immanentist.

REPRESENTATIVE RELIGIOUS EDUCATIONISTS

There is little question that of the liberal Protestant religious educationists representative of the immanentist position George Albert Coe is the outstanding example. In the first half of this century his influence in liberal Protestant religious education was pervasive. In the judgment of one commentator he was the "father of religious education in America."[30] Coe exerted much of his influence on future religious educators by his teaching at Northwestern University in Chicago, at Union Theological Seminary in New York, and for the last five years of his teaching career, at Teachers' College of Columbia University. He was one of the founding fathers of the Religious Education Association and remained actively involved with the Association until his death in 1951. One only has to browse through the pages of the Association's journal *Religious Education* to appreciate the extent to which liberalist views such as Coe's pervaded the pre-World War II religious education scene. Coe himself wrote many of his 260 published articles for *Religious Education*.

Coe would probably have taken umbrage at being called a theologian, and, in fact, his approach to religious education does not make use of very many technical theological notions. The dominant theological concept in most of his writing is what he calls the divine-human democracy of God. By this he means that God is immanent in all of social process and is a co-worker with man. Into the other foundational concepts of his religious education theory, viz., the scientific process, personality, and the social process, Coe worked his immanentist metaperspective. Thus, he sees God at the heart of all scientific process. As man enters into the scientific process he is sharing with God

in the evolution of the moral order. Proper scientific enquiry contributes to the
growth of human personality, which growth, for Coe, is the clearest manifestation of the withinness of God to all human enterprise. For Coe, personality
is sacred. Since the coming-to-be of persons is a social process then clearly,
social process and social reconstruction should be the focal point of education.
Thus, all *true* education is, in fact, *religious* education because the coming-
to-be of persons (with which education should be chiefly concerned) is the
essence of religion. To what extent Coe himself was committed to a personal
God, and not to a God who is a sort of social personality, is not at all clear.
His emphasis is clearly on God within social process and social interaction, on
God within evolution and an ever-changing world, on God within personality
growth. He does not admit to any person-to-person relationship with God in
the mystical sense and apart from social interaction.[31] Finally—and what is of
major interest to this book—Coe sees no sharp distinction between natural and
supernatural. As William Clayton Bower puts it, referring to Coe's theory of
the revaluation of values, his theory "... makes it possible to cloes the gap
that has historically arisen from the dichotomy between the 'natural' and the
'supernatural,' between the 'religious' and the 'secular,' between the 'temporal' and the 'eternal'."[32]

A second religious educationist whose theological stance seems characteristic of the immanentist approach is Gabriel Moran. Moran, a member of the
Institute of the Brothers of the Christian Schools, would probably prefer to be
known as a theologian with an interest in religious education rather than as a
religious educationist in the strict definition of that term. However, ever since
the publication of his first major work on religious education *The Catechesis
of Revelation* (1966) Moran has been an important figure in the contemporary
religious education scene. His extensive writing, lecturing, and teaching,
have put him squarely in the forefront of the religious education field—a field
which he is inclined to deny exists at all.[33] He attempts to redefine and
re-create religious education in the light of his own broad definition of revelation. The meaning of revelation, he claims, cannot be established solely by
scripture, or by Christian theology, or by ecclesiastical definition. It can only
be established by the consensus of a community fully immersed in the search
for the divine at the heart of all experience. He describes his search for a new
field as "ecumenical" because it covers the broad spectrum of experience out
of which comes an appreciation of revelation.[34] This is in contrast to his
earlier writings on the subject which are perhaps less innovative and are
recognizable as in keeping with more traditional Roman Catholic theological
and religious educational thinking. In his contending that the true meaning of
revelation only emerges from the unfolding of all human relationships in the
context of true community, Moran reveals his immanentist emphasis. God is
at the heart of all natural process. The more than human, the divine, emerges

in the experiential appreciation of all that is human because God is intimately present to all that is human. As to the terms natural and supernatural, Moran finds them unhelpful as descriptive of revelation, and he reacts against the extrinsicist tendency of the transcendist position.[35]

His primary educational focus is that students should be brought to a conscious awareness of the self-revealing God at the heart of the broad scope of all experience. Such a conscious awareness will enable students to make free religious decisions in the light of revelation. Moran quite definitely stresses the prior importance of the intelligent encountering and wrestling with reality. This does not mean, according to him, that education becomes purely cognitive and ratiocinative. Intelligence is an activity of the whole person and as far as religious education is concerned includes the ability to probe even beyond the bounds of reason in response to the more than human dimension of experience.[36]

A third religious educationist whose theological metaperspective is clearly immanentist is James Michael Lee. Lee, a Roman Catholic, is the initiator and major proponent of the social science approach to religious instruction.[37] This approach made its first clearly-focused appearance in *Toward a Future for Religious Education* (1970) which was edited by Lee and by Patrick C. Rooney.[38] The social science approach was further refined into a thoroughgoing system of religious instruction with the writing of Lee's trilogy, *The Shape of Religious Instruction* (1971), *The Flow of Religious Instruction* (1973), and *The Content of Religious Instruction* (in press). The significance of this trilogy is that it is intended to construct, for the first time, a comprehensive and systematic theory of religious instruction. The development of the social science approach has stirred up much discussion and critical comment in religious education circles, and Lee must rank among the major religious education thinkers of the present time.[39]

The social science approach to religious instruction is centered in the teaching-learning act and has as its chief aim the facilitation of religious behavior in the student. The whole enterprise is based on empirically verifiable and tested a posteriori data. The approach, therefore, is scientifically oriented and eschews educational decisions made on a priori, speculative, or merely authoritative grounds. Following the canons of social science, Lee contends that the social science approach to religious instruction is value free, that is, the actual process of religious instruction is not affected by any theological or confessional position. A social science approach can work just as well with and be adapted to any theological position. Lee notes that the proper content of religious instruction is the religious instruction act itself. The act is, in fact, a harmonious blend of structural content and substantive content. The structural content (which is the actual process of teaching-learning) is strictly nontheological and follows the ordinary scientific laws of human behavior. However, the substantive content (which is, in fact, *religion* and is a blend of many subcontents) encompasses a particular theological and confessional stance. Therefore, as Lee points out, the social science approach never operates in a vacuum, it is always *someone's* social science approach because it contains *someone's* theology, and *someone's* confessional stance, and *someone's* epistemological presuppositions.[40] The approach presented in Lee's writings is his own version of the social science approach and contains his own stated preference for the immanentist emphasis;[41] his own position that there is no ontological distinction between natural and supernatural;[42] his own position that nature is always graced nature and so "God-soaked" that it is most supernatural when it is most truly itself.[43] Lee's emphasis on the immanence of God within all natural process leads him to hazard an opinion that "To use the social science approach to make religion teaching more effective is to be more true to God, since it is more in harmony with the natural rhythm of the facilitation of learning in which the power of God flows as initiation, enablement, fruition, and completion."[44] Finally, it may be well to remark that Lee's pervasively immanentist position vis-à-vis the natural/supernatural relationship seems to be joined to a general theological outlook which is very much that of the traditional and orthodox Roman Catholic.

THE AIM

Broad or General Aim

Common to all religious educationists who show preference for an immanentist metaperspective is their proposal that *the broad aim of religious education is concerned with some form of socialization of students into community relationships which are considered to be religious.* This socialization into community relationships also includes socialization into some form of Christian lifestyle. The form and purpose of this socialization, however, are nuanced differently by different individual theorists. Thus, the liberal Protestants who equate Christian living with properly ethical practices also equate the general aim of education with religious education. If, as George Coe puts it, the general aim of education is to "bring society and the individual child together,"[45] then this, also, is the general aim of religious education. Hence, what has to be taught is "humane and just living in the various relationships, and also active, well directed labor that contributes to the common life of the present and likewise to the improvement of it."[46] What is the rationale for this aim? "The social issues of the present," declares Coe, "must be taken as the call of God to our pupils, and as the sphere of entire consecration to the will of God."[47] God is at the heart of social involvement and social reconstruction, immanently re-creating society and manifesting himself in the process. The aim of religious education is to teach the students to cooperate with God in building a new democratic order in society. Such an aim is eminently Christian since, as Coe states, "the redemptive mission of the Christ is nothing less than that of transforming the social order itself into a brotherhood or family of God."[48]

Gabriel Moran also sees that openness to the wider community of mankind and the re-creation and humanization of society is ultimately the goal of religious education. He more specifically brings this aim under his own theological umbrella of revelation as the totality of experience. God is revealed in the depth of experience and therefore the main aim of religious education should be an awakening in the students of a conscious awareness of experience. This process of awakening, Moran contends, is social in the best sense of the word as it provides a person with a religious outlook from which to relate to all other persons who also share in experience. Furthermore, awakening awareness expands a person's freedom and intelligence to join in re-creating the world, which re-creation is a specifically Christian endeavor.[49] Moran is sceptical of attempts made by religious educators to directly socialize students into a specific form of belief and practice. Such religion teaching smacks of too directive an indoctrination, does not sufficiently respect the students' freedom to make their own faith decisions, and is therefore antieducational. Such a position, Moran claims, possibly derives from the belief that revelation is a *thing* given to the church to be handed on to students instead of an unfolding encounter with the divine through experienced relationships. Thus, he says, "The reason for studying religion is to understand it so that when one does choose to live by it or not to live by it, his choice will be an intelligent one."[50]

While flavoring the issue with his own particular nuances, James Michael Lee more clearly perhaps than any other immanentist theorists lays the general socializing aim of religious education on the line. One of the major focuses of religious education, he declares, "is to consciously facilitate the socialization of the individual into the church community in particular, and into the Christian fellowship-community in general, and finally into God's special fellowship."[51] In this statement Lee pinpoints the threefold source of the relationships a Christian may be expected to experience and engage in—God, the church, and the world. Thus, though Lee, in concert with other immanentists, accepts all of experience as revelational, he also indicates that "God truly encounters man in a very special and unique way through the church society."[52] Furthermore, although these three aspects of experiential relationships are interconnected and interwoven, they *are* nevertheless clearly distinguishable. Unlike some other immanentists, therefore, Lee does see a place for an individual personal relationship with God, although such a relationship may well be enhanced through the social context. According to Lee, Christianity as a specific set of behaviors, cognitive, affective, and lifestyle, *can be taught*. Social process and the re-creation of the world are not the sole aim of religious education.

Proximate and Immediate Aim

As they do for the general aim, immanentist religious educationists evince differently nuanced conceptualizations of the proximate aim of religious education. Common to these various conceptualizations is that teaching should aim at some form of personality growth in the students. Such a growth is religious and is evidenced by behavioral change; that is, learning.[53] For very liberal immanentists, such as George Albert Coe, the aims of religious education, though not *primarily* individualistic, must include the personality growth of the student. For Coe, the coming-to-be of the person is *the* ultimate value; it is the "core meaning of existence"; it is the clearest and most immediate mainfestation of the divine in our midst. Such a growth in personality is brought about in and through social relationships. More specifically, personality growth is achieved by teaching students how to revaluate their values and integrate all values into a unified value system. Such revaluation of values makes for personal self-realization through "moral creativity" which, for Coe, is the closest a person can get to mystical experience. Hence his oft-quoted statement, "the aim of Christian education becomes this: Growth of the young toward and into mature and efficient devotion to the democracy of God, and happy self-realization therein."[54]

Personality growth which involves learning and leads to maturity is conceived by Gabriel Moran primarily as the stimulation of personal consciousness and awareness and the development of intelligence. Moran defines intelligence as "the ability to deal with experience in a way that leads to understanding."[55] Intelligence, therefore, enables one to react in an appropriate manner to the general experience of the total environment. Dealing with experience in such a way that it leads to appropriate action within one's total environment is not, claims Moran, a purely cognitive or "cerebral" affair. Such action involves the whole person intellectually and emotionally. In fact, distinguishing between intelligence and emotions may be very misleading because these are not two separate and discrete facets of human personality such that one can work without the other.[56] The direct aim of religious education is to train the students to be self-directive and free. The aim is that the students reach understanding and freedom, not that their emotions be manipulated. The aim, therefore, is not to make the students religious but to lead them to make free decisions as to whether they want to be religious or not.[57]

This is in keeping with Moran's frequent assertion that religion ultimately means meeting and relating to the immanent God who comes to us as the divine dimension of all of experience. Our highest capacity to relate to the God of experience is our intellectual ability to grasp the meaning of God's experiential self-revelation. Consequently, the prime and immediate focus of religious education should be the expansion of the students' intellectual ability in the religious context of experience.

In the thinking of a third representative immanentist, James Michael Lee, personality growth and socialization into proper relationship with God, the church, and society in general can and should be brought about by a planned process of behavior modification. Christian living (i.e., the religious dimension of life), which is the ultimate aim of religious education, consists, according to Lee, of a definable set of observable behaviors. Consequently, religious instruction "consists in facilitating the modification of the learner's behavior along desired religious lines."[58] The word *behavior,* as used by Lee and by social scientists in general, is an all-inclusive term. It involves a balanced and integrated modification of the cognitive, affective, and lifestyle elements of the learners' total religious commitment. Such a clear-cut and definitive proximate aim is, according to Lee, very necessary for the proper planning of religion teaching. It is also necessary for fruitful teaching in that it serves as a means of continuous evaluative feedback. Also, and here is the crux, such a precise and behaviorally-stated aim is also eminently religious. Learning is a human process and follows all the scientific laws that govern the operation of human behavior. (Lee holds that there is nothing mystical or mysterious about religious learning; it is not different from other human learning). Lee's immanentism leads him to assert that God is deeply involved in the midst of the process of learning. In fact, the more humanly perfect is the whole teaching-learning process and the more perfectly it manifests its true nature, the more revelatory and supernatural it is.[59]

In sum, the major religious educationists discussed above nuance their presentation of the aims of religious education somewhat differently. Nevertheless, in spite of the patchwork quilt effect that their theories present, it is clear that in each case the way that aims are stated corresponds to the particular theorist's immanentist viewpoint. The immanentist metaperspective is like a common skein which links together the differently patterned patches. Thus, the aim of religious education has been conceptualized (1) primarily as growth and social change, (2) primarily as an awakening of personal awareness to the depth dimension of experience and a development of intelligence, and (3) primarily as specified behavior modification for Christian living. In each case the overarching immanentist principle is applicable. The theorists view their own particular statement of aim as primary because they understand this as being the best way to bring about a relationship with God who is immanent within and at the very core of human process. The supernatural is intimately bound up with the natural such that all experience is potentially revelatory.

THE CONTENT

Noncontent

One thing that immanentist theorists are agreed on is that, substantively at least, the content of religious education does *not* consist of cognitive religious truths and propositions authoritatively handed on in a transmissive manner. They appear to be in specific opposition to the transcendists on this point. Some immanentists do admit that there is an important place for such content but it is never the substantive content.[60] Others would have grave suspicions as to whether such content serves any valid educational objective.[61] The major point at issue is that all agree that doctrinally formulated religious truth does not constitute the entire content or even the major part of revelation. If God is revealed in the totality of experience, then teaching only formulated truths is narrow and restrictive of the total experience in and through which God reveals himself. Furthermore, such a conceptualization of content tends to lead to a transmissionist mode of teaching, that is, the teacher faithfully transmits to the students certain facts and doctrines. For the immanentist theorists, transmissive teaching is the epitome of noneducation in that it tends to supply answers instead of expanding the students' capacity for freedom and inquiry. George Albert Coe would add that it also brings students into subjection to others in that they become slaves to the authoritative pronouncements of the teacher. Any such eventuality would be against the ideal of the divine-human democracy which Coe sees as one of the chief focuses of religious education.[62]

All immanentist theorists are further agreed that there can be no content/method dichotomy or duality. Again, this position is in clear contrast to the opinion of major transcendist theorists who hold that method is a means of conveying content and that the supernatural character of the content of religious education demands that it take precedence over mere human method. For the immanentists, content and method must blend harmoniously into one teaching act, together they must produce a unified experience. The unified experience is, in fact, lived religion. As Gabriel Moran puts it "[But] concentration upon content is also an inadequate approach. It is based upon the misconception that there is a content to Christianity which is separable from a way of living and communicating with others."[63] It is important to point out that, apart from educational and epistemological considerations, one of the assumptions underlying this contention that there is no content/method dichotomy is the theological one that God is immanent in and through all human process. If God is thus present in all process, then there is no such thing as a "supernatural" content which is transmitted by a "natural" or human method. Method-content is a unified experience which is itself the religious education act. It is the revelation of God in which the students should be immersed.

Content

When one boils it all down there can be little doubt that, *for the immanentist theorists, the content of religious education is experience*. Since the immanentist emphasis highlights God as present in all experience, then all of experience is potentially revelatory and can be called religious. At bottom, religious education is in fact religious experience. To this basic point of agreement, various religious educationists add their own particular nuances.

For religious educationists such as George Albert Coe, social process and social reconstruction are paramount. Although they consider religious education content to consist of all of life's experiences, their attention is riveted to "present relations and interactions between persons." The context is life, that is, life lived according to the Christian ideal that ethical regard for persons is the most exalted of all ideals. Coe's "ethical regard" is in many ways a sort of euphemism for love. Anything that will make students realize and act on the love ideal is suitable material for the religion lesson, be it scripture, art, history, science, or current life-experiences.[64] In point of fact, the more that students can be actually immersed in social process in accord with the Christian ideal, the more will the experiential content of religious education become actualized in them as religious experience. It follows that the more the school experience can duplicate the life-experiences of the students the more effective it will be from a religious point of view. Thus, theorists such as Coe tend to emphasize the operational aspect of religion. Religion is really a pattern of observable behaviors, more particularly those behaviors which pertain to ethical love.[65] Coe tends to oppose the assumption that reality is first grasped intellectually and then reacted to. He espouses the Deweyesque notion that we only learn by doing. Thus, we can only say we love God if we truly act out love for others. Thinking and saying are not enough, the only thing that really counts is doing. Religious experience is precisely tied to this active religion. It is this form of experience in which students should be thoroughly immersed.

James Michael Lee's approach to religious experience is similar to Coe's in that he too opts for an operational definition of religion.[66] The experience of God comes about in the doing of religious acts, the living of a religious lifestyle. Consequently, the focus of the content-experiences of religious education is, for Lee, strongly behavioral.

Lee's treatment is detailed and extensive but can, in fact, be summed up in a single sentence: The content of religious instruction is the religious instruction act itself. "Religion is . . . the substantive content; instructional practice is the structural content. The substantive content plus the structural content as they are existentially formed and fused in the religious instruction act itself comprise the proper content of religious instruction."[67] The substantive content (which itself is a harmonious blend of several subcontents such as cognitive content, affective content, lifestyle content) provides valenced forms of experience. For Lee, content is the form which experience takes. "Thus," he affirms, "the task of the religion curriculum or religion lesson is to provide structured units of experience which enable learners to interact in a living fashion with the various substantive contents of religious instruction."[68] The religion lesson should be an experience in lived religion, it should be a "laboratory for Christian living." In his structured content-experiences Lee would find a place for every aspect of the students' lives as pertaining to their threefold relationship to God, the church, and all of society. Some experiences will be more revelatory than others (such as, for example, the experience of liturgical prayer which more directly relates to the divine) because revelation is at once objective and subjective. It is objective in that because God interpenetrates all of reality, all of reality is therefore revelatory. It is subjective because at various times and circumstances we grasp this revelation more fully than at other times and circumstances. Consequently, some experience-contents (both objectively and subjectively) can be more religious than others. Nevertheless, God is in all of process and in every experience such that the whole religious instruction act is religious experience—no matter with what specific content a particular instruction act is concerned.

While in basic agreement with Lee and Coe that all of life's experiences furnish the content of religious education, Gabriel Moran flavors his considerations with a slightly different epistemological approach. His approach is less behavioral and less act-oriented than that of the other immanentists. He is more concerned with awakening intelligent awareness of experience by a reflective process. Thus, reality *must* first be grasped intellectually before it can be reacted to (cf. Coe above). Such an awareness is necessary if the students are to fruitfully orient their behavior toward the more than human aspect of experience.[69]

Since all of experience is revelatory and contains a more than human dimension, Moran notes, as do Coe and Lee, that any material from the arts or sciences can be used as a starting point for religion teaching. Thus, the aesthetic experience born of art in all its forms is particularly apt to produce an awareness of the more than human dimension. Another starting point for religion teaching could be the questions of ultimate concern to human life that people have asked and still do ask. In this context, Christian doctrine has a legitimate if peripheral role. Doctrine can be understood as providing evidence of how some people have answered the major questions of life. By studying these doctrinal "answers," students might come to their own particular religious expression.[70] Moran's position seems well stated when he affirms that Christianity's mission is "the affirming of all human values and the taking up of all that is human to push the human beyond itself."[71]

Briefly, therefore, let it be reiterated that for the selected immanentist religious educationists the content of religious education is all of experience. God permeates all of experience. All of experience contains a more than human dimension, it bespeaks God in his self-gift to man. Variations on this theme are offered by different theorists, yet, despite the apparent discord, there is no mistaking the dominant immanentist motif. Thus, some focus on a variety of contents as offering different modes of experience; others insist on the lived aspect of social experience; others again emphasize a conscious awareness of the intimate nature of any experience as it yields the more than human. Finally, some immanentists accentuate as basic the behavioral and lived aspect of religion while others tend to accentuate the conscious awareness of religious experience as being prior to and necessary for proper direction of religious living.

THE TEACHER

Some immanentist theorists consider "teacher" to be a narrow and confining category and they see the wider community as being the main agent of education.[72] Thus, teaching and education are not necessarily interdependent. Teaching is only one specialized facet of education. Granted, however, that teachers are an integral part of the whole system by which a society educates, the immanentist theorists have a strong tendency to regard them as *functional experts*. While the theorists would admit that the witness of the teachers' lifestyle, their personality, and the ability to relate to students are important factors in teaching, by and large their primary emphasis is on the teachers' pedagogical skills. It is an emphasis which correlates well with these theorists' process-revelational metaperspective. Thus, the careful arrangement of the teaching environment, the attention to effective teaching skills in fact point up that God works in and through nature and that things are most divine when they are most human. In this way, the teaching of religion is no different from the teaching of any other learning outcome. All of experience is potentially revelatory. Once again it must be noted that the representative immanentist theorists tend to add their own particular nuances to the main theme.

Perhaps of all major religious educationists James Michael Lee has come out most strongly in favor of a detailed and carefully planned approach and strategy for teaching religion.[73] In fact, to understand Lee is to understand the teacher. Lee insists that learning is a construct and can only be inferred by observing performance. Thus, the only way we can be sure someone has learned religion is by observing them perform religious acts. The teachers' job is precisely to facilitate observable religious behavior in the students. This focus on observable religious behavior[74] is in keeping with Lee's performative definition of religion, but, most importantly, it is also in keeping with his immanentist theological emphasis. God is immanent in all human process, therefore, the more perfect the skill of human behavioral facilitation the more intimately and inherently it is revelatory. "Wherever teaching and learning take place" notes Lee, "God is intimately and existentially present in every zone of the process."[75] Consequently, one of the major tasks of the teacher is "to so structure the learning situation that the God dwelling in all the aspects of the instructional environment will be actualized for the student."[76] The teacher, therefore, is not so much the instrument of a remote and transcendent God as a literal extension of the immanent divine and an active coparticipator with the student in God's self-revelatory acts. Lee's insistence on the teachers' role as "pure function" means that theoretically the teachers' own religious beliefs and personal lifestyle should not affect the behavioral change they plan to bring about in the students—provided, that is, that the teachers can fruitfully deploy their personalities and teaching skills.[77] What this appears to be saying is extraordinarily well in keeping with the whole immanentist emphasis, namely, that the teaching act is religious and revelatory in and of itself and through its own very perfection. Grace is intimately linked with and intrinsic to the perfection of all things human.

George Albert Coe's treatment of the teacher and teaching revolves around his particular insistence on the emergence of personality as the most sacred and ultimate of all values. Thus, the teacher-pupil relationship is a matter of partnership in shared experience, through which sharing personality grows and develops. The sharing must take place in the social context. Consequently, teachers must provide those conditions which most closely duplicate in a very practical and "doing" way a real life of shared love. Teachers are leaders who must encourage students (according to their particular stage of development) to make "experiments in social living." For this, teachers must plan carefully and exhibit every technical skill as would any craftsman bent on proficiency; no less can be required of an efficient "co-worker with God."[78] Coe insists, as does Lee, that religion teachers are no mere instruments or tools of the divine but that rather teaching is in fact the acting out of religion. The emergence of personality through teaching within the social context is verily the emergence of the divine in our midst. Teacher-directed personality emergence is an example of the creative inworking of the divine at the core of the educational process.[79]

Another aspect of the immanentist outlook is expressed by Gabriel Moran. His claim is that only the total community can educate according to the full meaning of the word educate. Teaching is a restricted part of education which, at the highest levels of the educative process, should aim principally at what Moran calls "the honing of an adequate language" which is properly expressive of experience.[80] Language honing is based on teacher-student mutuality, a process in which teacher and student are engaged in a joint search for a language which can convey the depth-meaning of shared experience. At the heart of all experience is the more than human dimension. Relatedness to this more than human dimension constitutes religion. The ability to put one's experience into words which are fully expressive itself adds to the richness of experience and to a further plumbing of and relatedness to the divine depth of all that is human. An allied benefit of this whole process is that the students become freer and more self-directed. Thus, as Moran declares, "The teacher's job is not to provide the information so much as to give a way of handling it."[81] There seems little doubt that, in accord with all immanentist theorists, Moran's core concern is that teacher and student together participate in present revelation through teaching-learning mutuality. Teachers are not so much agents of the authoritative teaching church which possesses revealed truth as they are members of a religious community which is "struggling toward a truth which no one possesses but all can share."[82]

In fine, *representative immanentist theorists perceive the teacher to be a functional specialist who facilitates participation in revelatory experience.* The teaching of religion differs not at all from teaching for any other learning outcome. Whether the main thrust of teaching is directed toward the facilitation of religious behavior, or toward the shaping of conscious experience through the honing of language skills, or toward the growth of personality in the social milieu, all these focuses are but modes of participating in revelatory experience. The more skillful the teacher, the more is relationship to the divine depth of all experience facilitated.

THE STUDENT

Representative immanentist religious educationists propose no dichotomy between natural and supernatural elements in the student.[83] These theorists are less interested in a theological assessment of students than in their personality structure, psychological and scientific makeup, and socio-economic background. Some theorists, such as George Albert Coe, reject the notion of original sin, the need for individual salvation, and that man is moving toward an "eternally predetermined goal."[84] Other theorists, while not denying the reality of original sin and the need for redemption, do not focus on these theological notions as intrinsically related to the students' behavior and ability to learn. The strong tendency of the immanentist theorists is to consider the students as they presently are, that is, in their own peculiar scientific existential situation. Typically, these theorists do not view religious and moral development as something special and "supernatural" (that is, directly given by God as a special unmerited gift). Rather, they understand this development as taking place "within the normal interactive growth patterns of human maturation and learning."[85] Thus, the principle of immanence is always operative in that the very scientific behavioral process of character development is "supernaturalized." The supernatural potency of all of reality is realized to the extent that reality is true to its own scientific laws. Student personality development and growth is no mysterious and "spiritual" process belonging to a grace dimension beyond the reach of human observation and even manipulation (as the transcendists would have it). Immanentist theorists insist on the importance of students as integral persons and not entities dichotomized into body and soul. The development of personality is one of the main aims of religious education because this very process of personality development is a religious process. The coming-to-be of the person is the coming-to-be of divine revelation at the core of the educative process.

It is perhaps important to indicate that different immanentist theorists emphasize different aspects of personality growth and the way to bring it about. Thus, some theorists (as for example George Coe) stress the importance of the community and social influences as being vital to personality development. Others (as for example Gabriel Moran) tend to emphasize the importance of the development of a mature intelligence. Others again (such as James Michael Lee) emphasize the inculcation of specified behaviors and the immersion of students in a stimulus-rich environment. From the point of view of this present book, what is important is not so much the different views on, or advocated methods of personality development. What is important is that the immanentist theorists see the human and scientific development of personality as itself religious and revelatory.

Student Learning

In marked contrast to the transcendist position, the majority of immanentist theorists will not admit to any mysterious or supernatural element in the learning of religion. There is nothing in the learning process which is exclusively the work of the Holy Spirit and consequently outside of and beyond human control. There is no such thing as "Christian" learning which is Spirit-induced and therefore different from any other kind of learning. The Holy Spirit works only within and according to the ordinary scientific laws of learning.[86] Thus, as Gabriel Moran remarks, the Spirit does not make up for bad instruction on the part of the teacher. "The formula is not instruction plus Spirit equals formation, but instruction 'in the Spirit'—which does not magically lead anywhere but which may contribute to the eventual emergence of the adult believer."[87] The more that teachers direct their teaching according to the scientifically discovered laws of learning the more "Spirit-filled" will the teaching be. Also, and of vital importance, the more will the students be brought into contact with the self-revealing God immanent in the very teaching-learning act according to the perfection of that act. If the immanentist theorists insist that the teaching of religion should be fully adapted to the developmental and existential state of the particular students, it is not merely because this is sound pedagogical practice but also because it is sound religious practice. If the divine is immanent in nature according to the very mode of that nature, then students are far more likely to encounter the self-revealing God when the process of that encounter is in accordance with the God-created laws of learning and personality development.

One of the scientific laws of learning frequently referred to by the immanentists is that "present experience is the best teacher." The richer, the more direct, the more immediate is the experience of the learner, the easier and longer-lasting is the learning. Among the most important duties of teachers, therefore, is the preparation of learning situations which are as experientially rich as possible. The more meaningful the experience is to the students the more intimate is their contact with God who is not external to experience, but who is present as the more than human dimension of all experience. As James Michael Lee puts it "[Now] revelation is had most deeply in the encounter of the learner with meaningful aspects of his environment. . . . There is an essential and existential connection between revelation and that which is significant to the learner."[88] It is for this reason that many immanentist theorists see participation and involvement in liturgical prayer as a rich learning experience and why so much care and preparation should go into the making of such rich experiences.

Student Freedom

All representative immanentist religious educationists insist on the need for preserving and fostering the core freedom of the student. On account of their immanentist viewpoint they make little or no distinction between freedom as a natural human quality on the one hand, and "supernatural" or religious freedom (that is, freedom to accept or reject God who reveals himself) on the other. All exercise of freedom is, for these theorists, cooperation with the divine creative process. God will only reveal himself within the free choices of the students as they react to their own existential situation. Thus, for religious educationists such as George Albert Coe, freedom is at the heart of the process of the coming-to-be of persons, that is, within the core of the most perfect of divine manifestations.[89] Gabriel Moran insists, as does Coe, that religious education should not be over-directive in the sense that it supplies ready-made answers to religious questions. Religious education is both truly religious and educatory when it fosters free and open reflection on experience. By conscious awareness of the revelatory aspect of experience students may make free decisions as to the religious direction of life.[90] With his insistence on the facilitation and inculcation of specified religious behavior, James Michael Lee appears to some to advocate a process which is more directive and more restrictive of student freedom than that advocated by other immanentist theorists. Lee claims, however, that the more that teachers are *aware* of their own pedagogical behavior and of the consequences of that behavior the more do they become capable of giving students their freedom. He further insists (1) that teachers and students should together preplan the desired learning outcome, (2) that teachers should be careful that on no account should they be the only variable in the learning situation (as they would tend to be in a transmissionist mode of teaching), and (3) that teachers should be as sparing as possible in their use of teacher-centered teaching devices. The learners (students), Lee maintains, are always free to react creatively to the entire learning situation and (most importantly) to the revealing God immanently and intimately present in the very teaching-learning act itself.[91]

THE ENVIRONMENT

While no immanentist theorist denies the importance of the environment, only James Michael Lee regards the environment as a critical factor in the religious education process. Lee advocates careful control of the instructional environment in order to achieve the planned and behaviorally-stated goals of the religion lesson. Whether their interest in the environment as a factor in religious education is broad and ill-defined, or very specific, the immanentist theorists relate the environment to the total experience of the student. Thus, for example, George Albert Coe would advocate a controlled social environment as best contributing to the aims of religious education. He is appreciative of the influence of the natural habitat of the students, inheritance factors, social conditions, home influence, the sights and sounds of the world.[92]

Gabriel Moran, likewise, indicates that education should take place in a controlled environment and places considerable emphasis upon the community aspect of this environment. Without a community influence and a community dimension he doubts whether there can be any true religious education. It would neither be religious (an awareness of and response to revelation), nor education (a teacher can teach, but only a community can educate). Hence Moran's preferred definition of religious education is: "The whole religious community educates the whole religious community to make free and intelligent decisions vis-à-vis the whole world."[93] Despite, however, their acknowledgement of the importance of the environment in religious education, the interest of most immanentist religious educationists in the environment is too broad to be of here-and-now practical value to the religion teacher.

James Michael Lee, on the other hand, insists on careful structuring of the learning environment as an integral and necessary part of any fruitful religion teaching.[94] His reason for this insistence is in perfect harmony with his immanentist metaperspective. If, as Lee maintains, the Holy Spirit works strictly within and according to the mode of all things human, then encounter with God will be facilitated by structuring the environment in such a way as to make this encounter more probable. Thus, Lee advocates purposive and careful structuring of all the elements of the instructional environment (physical environment, teaching technique, teacher personality, affective climate, state of readiness of the student, materials of teaching), and as many elements of the general environment (home situation, school climate, peer group, community influences) as possible. The aim is to bring about the desired learning outcome, that is, some form of religious behavior. All this sounds very directive, behavioristic, and even mechanical, however it is well in keeping with the immanentist perspective. Structuring the environment, according to Lee, is not an effort to control the working of the Holy Spirit, rather it is an effort to give the Spirit easier conditions in which to work—the teaching process is primarily facilitational. What is being facilitated is an encounter with God. Thus, insists Lee, "Religious instruction is the deliberative planning of that environment in which the learning Christian encounters Jesus . . ."[95] who is present as the divine dimension of all experience. As do other immanentists, Lee appreciates the great importance of the social and community milieu in the religious education process. His conceptualization of the religion class as a "laboratory for Christian living" highlights Lee's contention that education takes place best in a "personalized interactive milieu," a "lived and living learning situation." There can be little doubt that the accent here is on new experience, on first-hand lived experience, as the best way to learn. And (one keeps coming back to this basic immanentist dictum) it is also the best way to be confronted and engaged by revelation. The "laboratory for Christian living" works in such a way that the revelation experience becomes integrated into the lifestyle behavior of the students. Students become religious by living religion in and through the learning experience.[96]

Thus, briefly, as far as the immanentist theorists are concerned, whether their interest in the environment as a factor in religious education is broad and general, or whether it is very pointed and specific, their theological focus is the same. The environment contributes to the general experience of the student; the God of ongoing creation is at the heart of all experience; the richer and more meaningful the learning experience the more revelational it becomes; the more revelational it becomes the more conducive it is to true religion, that is, encounter with God and response to that encounter by a religious lifestyle.

EVALUATION

The practicability of any evaluative process will hinge on (1) how specific and recognizable are the aims and goals the achievement of which one wishes to evaluate, and (2) whether adequate criteria can be set up by which to make the evaluation. As has already been noted, the tendency of the immanentist theorists is to adopt an operational definition of religion and to state religious education goals in performance terms.[97] Thus, according to the immanentists, whether or not the students are religious, or whether teachers have succeeded in teaching religion, can only be properly determined if the students exhibit behaviors which are considered to be religious. The immanentists constantly emphasize that God works in and through all natural and human process. Consequently, religious learning outcomes can and should be scientifically assessed. It is not difficult to recognize that such a position is diametrically opposed to the transcendist stance which claims that the aims of religious education are supernatural and therefore beyond the reach of scientific measurement—how can one measure faith? If, argue the immanentists, religious outcomes are not measurable (and this means even faith) then there is no possible way of telling whether someone is religious or not. More to the point, there is no way of testing whether religious teaching has or has not been successful—no way, therefore, of improving such teaching and correcting mistakes. The same immanentist principle is at work here, viz., God is creatively present in all human process, even a scientific evaluative process. Scientific measurement of religion is not a question of desecrating a holy domain or "treading where humans should not venture." Rather, it is cooperation with God in his ongoing self-revelation in and through his creation.

And so, theorists such as George Albert Coe insist on continual tests for efficiency as to whether the set goals of religious education are being achieved. With his particular insistence on the emergence and growth of personality as being the core of revelation and religion, Coe calls for scientific measurement of moral conduct. He has no doubt that we can and should assess such "inner" factors as motives and attitudes by the moral quality of the observable goals for which a person strives. One can only conclude that people have an attitude of justice when they are seen to act justly. Coe scoffs at the adage "religion canot be taught it can only be caught" because, according to him, the social and moral outcomes at which religious education should aim can be scientifically assessed and measured.[98]

As was the case for the environment, of the representative immanentist theorists James Michael Lee stands out as being the one most insistent on the scientific application of evaluative principles as an integral part of the religious education process. For Lee, evaluation is integral to the teaching-learning act. Further, evaluation should be continuous throughout the teaching process, it should not be merely a terminal assessment of goal achievement. Thus, Lee sees the evaluative process as properly built into any adequate theory of religious education—after the fashion of cybernetic theory.[99] The purpose of such a process-integrated procedure is to help the students to achieve clearly and empirically assessable religious goals. Not only will continuous evaluation aid the students in the achievement of desired religious goals, but it will also serve as a monitoring device for the teachers to assess their own pedagogical efficiency.[100]

Clearly, in their treatment of evaluation (those of them that do treat of it, that is) the immanentist theorists run true to form. Their immanentist focus correlates well with their statements on evaluation in religious education. Evaluation makes for efficiency in teaching and according to the immanentist principle the more thoroughly scientific, human, and efficient one is in achieving the goals of religious education the more does one participate in the divine revelatory process. Religion *can* be measured; to say anything else is utter nonsense. Religious goals do not belong to the sphere of the unmeasurable supernatural so much as they belong to the sphere of the observable natural. To belong to one is to belong to the other. People are just because they act justly, good because they bear witness to goodness, possess faith because they give evidence of their faithfulness, are Christians because they live the Christian life. Hard-core immanentists see and understand religion in performative terms: "You will be able to tell them by their fruits" (Mt. 7:16).

NOTES

1. George Albert Coe, "The Idea of God," *Religious Education*, Vol. 6 (June 1911), p. 178.
2. Sydney Ahlstrom describes theological liberalism as "any movement that seeks to moderate orthodox doctrines by an individualistic emphasis on

man's rational and moral powers." Sydney E. Ahlstrom, editor, *Theology in America* (Indianapolis: Bobbs, Merrill, 1967), p. 58.

For a description of theological liberalism in the context of religious education, see Adelaide Teague Case, *Liberal Christianity and Religious Education* (New York: Macmillan, 1924). See also Major J. Jones, "The Place of God in the Educative Process According to George A. Coe, William C. Bower, and Harrison S. Elliot," unpublished doctoral dissertation, Boston University School of Theology (1957), pp. 21–103. See also, "Liberalism," *The Westminster Dictionary of Christian Education* (Philadelphia: Westminster Press, 1963), pp. 389–392.

In theological writing the terms *liberal* and *liberalism* are frequently set in opposition to *orthodox*. This latter term is used to designate a form of traditional Christian theology with its emphasis on such things as original sin (man is born with a strong propensity to evil); Jesus Christ the Son of God (Christianity is a revealed religion, Christ is the full expression of that revelation); the word of God (which is directly given and claims man's attention and obedience); the Holy Spirit (who is the soul of the church and the inspirer of man's actions); salvation (which is of God, man cannot save himself); and many other concepts such as church, kingdom of God. In this book the terms liberal and orthodox will be used in the sense outlined above.

3. Coe, "The Idea of God," p. 178.

4. For an example of one theorist who holds this, see James Michael Lee, *The Flow of Religious Instruction* (Notre Dame, Indiana: Religious Education Press, 1973), p. 22; also James Michael Lee, *The Content of Religious Instruction* (in press), chapter 3. Some other immanentist theorists would not admit that there is any such thing as a revealed body of truth. For example, George Albert Coe, "The Assault Upon Liberalism," *Religious Education*, Vol. 34 (April-June 1939), p. 88.

5. For an example of a theorist who holds this, see Lee, *The Content of Religious Instruction*, chapters 2 and 3.

6. Gabriel Moran, *Catechesis of Revelation* (New York: Herder and Herder, 1966), pp. 81–82. In his more recent writing, Moran seems to indicate that whether scripture should be normative for interpreting the revelatory aspect of human experience is part of the more all-encompassing question of whether Christianity can be the norm by which one judges all religious expression. To understand Christianity as having a position which becomes normative for interpreting all the rest of human experience is, for Moran, an example of a nonrelational and individualized concept of truth which he opposes. For him, the notion "true religion" is an unintelligible one. Truth goes beyond all religion and all experience. Christianity is but one expression of that truth. Though, for some, it may be the best expression, it cannot be taken as normative for explaining all truth. See Gabriel Moran, *The Present Revelation* (New York: Herder and Herder, 1972), pp. 309–312 and all of chapter 4 generally. See also Gabriel Moran, *Design for Religion* (New York: Herder and Herder, 1970), pp. 44–48.

7. For an example of this opinion see George Albert Coe, *A Social Theory of Religious Education* (New York: Scribner's, 1925), pp. 115, 335. See also George Albert Coe, *What is Christian Education?* (New York: Scribner's, 1929), pp. 56, 194–195. In this regard Coe probably represents an extremely liberal Protestant position. For a less liberal view on the use of the bible but still within the ambit of immanentism, see William Clayton Bower, *Christ and Christian Education* (New York: Abingdon-Cokesbury Press, 1943), pp. 74–99.

8. James Michael Lee, *The Shape of Religious Instruction* (Notre Dame, Indiana: Religious Education Press, 1971), p. 232.

9. See, for example, George Albert Coe in Edwin E. Aubrey "A Theology Relevant to Religious Education," *Religious Education,* Vol. 34 (October-December 1939), p. 197.

10. Coe, *A Social Theory of Religious Education*, p. 334.

11. Moran, *The Present Revelation*, p. 45.

12. Lee, *The Shape of Religious Instruction*, p. 233. See also pp. 230–234 generally, and pp. 283–284.

13. For example, see Case, *Liberal Christianity and Religious Education*, pp. 25–33. It is interesting to note that while George Albert Coe strongly exposed the liberal position during the most significant and productive years of his career as a religious educationist, in his earlier writings his theological position was far more orthodox. Thus, for example, in *Education in Religion and Morals* (Chicago: Fleming H. Revell, 1904), he writes: "In every genuine utterance of the religious impulse there is manifested 'prevenient grace,' the divine empowering and inspiration that 'come before' our human acts and give them effect" (p. 38. See also pp. 54, 61).

14. On the whole, religious educationists seem to steer clear of a precise and clear definition of what is meant by "human" and what influences are "humanizing." In general, they seem to see those behaviors and attitudes as human and humanizing which promote justice, peace, freedom, and love and which "dramatically reform[s] society as a whole in the direction of redistributing the means to live." (Gabriel Moran, *Religious Body: Design for a New Reformation* [New York: Seabury Press, 1974], p. 38.)

15. Lee, *The Flow of Religious Instruction*, pp. 46–47; see also p. 293.

16. Lee, *The Shape of Religious Instruction*, p. 235; see also *The Flow of Religious Instruction*, pp. 141, 145, 148.

17. See, for example, Coe, *A Social Theory of Religious Education*, pp. 89–92.

18. Lee, *The Shape of Religious Instruction*, p. 26.

19. Moran, *The Present Revelation*, pp. 299–300.

20. The "magisterium" is the official teaching authority of the church. In the Roman Catholic hierarchical institutional structure the magisterium comprises the pope and bishops.

21. For an example of this see Lee, *The Shape of Religious Instruction*, pp. 104–105, 114.

22. Thus Moran, *The Present Revelation*, pp. 304–308. Moran does not clearly spell out what institutional pattern would best fit the community-oriented notion of revelation. He claims that although some structure is necessary for community there is always a tension between true community life and the institutional structures which always threaten to destroy it.

23. Coe, *A Social Theory of Religious Education*, pp. 92–96; *What is Christian Education?* pp. 122–123, 274. See also Coe, "Bottleneck in Religion," *Religious Education*, Vol. 38 (January-February 1943), p. 10. Coe particularly sets himself against any form of liturgical celebration. "[Again,] when worship has its center in priestly manipulation of supernatural mysteries, it uses suggestion as an instrument for keeping the many obedient to the few, and for repeating the past instead of using the past as material wherewith to build fairer structures of the spirit of brotherhood." *A Social Theory of Religious Education*, p. 96.

24. For an example of this see Lee, *The Content of Religious Instruction*, chapter 2. See also Moran, *Catechesis of Revelation*, pp. 95–102.

25. See Coe, "The Assault Upon Liberalism," p. 88.

26. Coe, *What is Christian Education?* p. 180.

27. Moran, *The Present Revelation*, pp. 267–275. In his earlier writings Moran seems to emphasize a far more traditional position with respect to Christology. See, for example, *Vision and Tactics* (New York: Herder and Herder, 1968), pp. 47–50; see also *Catechesis of Revelation*, pp. 55–65. The picture he presents in *The Present Revelation* is perhaps more in keeping with the irenic and ecumenical intent of the work, and with his plan of reworking Christian doctrine in the light of a new concept of revelation.

28. Lee, *The Shape of Religious Instruction*, pp. 232, 281–283, 24–34; see also *The Content of Religious Instruction*, chapters 3 and 4.

29. Ancient hymn attributed to St. Partick. See Hugh de Blacam, *Saint Patrick* (Milwaukee: Bruce, 1941), p. 60.

30. Fred L. Brownlee, "Social Thought and Action," *Religious Education*, Vol. 47 (March-April 1952), p. 82. Brownlee also quotes Hugh Hartshorne as remarking: "Coe *is* religious education."

31. See George Albert Coe, "The Idea of God." For a discussion of Coe's notion of God, see Major J. Jones, "The Place of God in the Educative Process According to George A. Coe, William C. Bower, and Harrison S. Elliot"; Wayne Rood, *Understanding Christian Education* (Nashville: Abingdon Press, 1970), pp. 200–203; Anne Burgess, "George Albert Coe and Religious Education: An Introduction," *Notre Dame Journal of Education*, Vol. 5 (Winter 1974), pp. 336–340; Fred L. Brownlee, "Social Thought and Action," pp. 80–81.

32. William Clayton Bower, "Contribution to the Psychology of Religion," *Religious Education*, Vol. 47 (March-April 1952), p. 70. See also Jones, "The Place of God in the Educative Process According to George Albert Coe, William C. Bower, and Harrison S. Elliot," p. 184.

33. See Gabriel Moran, "Catechetics, R.I.P.," *Commonweal*, Vol. 93 (December 18, 1970), pp. 299–302. See also *Design for Religion*, p. 9.

34. See, for example, Gabriel Moran, *Design for Religion,* especially pp. 9–48; see also *The Present Revelation,* pp. 18–21.

35. Moran, *The Present Revelation,* pp. 36–38; *Theology of Revelation* (New York: Herder and Herder, 1966), pp. 165–169; *Religious Body: Design for a New Reformation,* pp. 69–106.

36. Moran perhaps best states his position in *Religious Body: Design for a New Reformation,* pp. 158–171.

37. Refer to chapter 1, note 10.

38. Lee had previously given evidence of the direction in which his thought was moving in several of his earlier writings but particularly in three articles entitled "The Third Strategy: A Behavioral Approach to Religious Education," *Today's Catholic Teacher* (September, October, November, 1969).

39. See, for example, Michael Warren, C.F.X., "All Contributions Cheerfully Accepted," *The Living Light,* Vol. 7 (Winter 1970), pp. 20–33; see also James Michael Lee's reply, "Toward a Dialogue in Religious Instruction," *The Living Light,* Vol. 8 (Spring 1971), pp. 109–121. See also Padraic O'Hare, "The Image of Theology in the Educational Theory of James Michael Lee," *The Living Light,* Vol. 11 (Fall 1974), pp. 452–458.

40. Lee, *The Content of Religious Instruction,* chapter 2.

41. Lee, "Prediction in Religious Instruction," *The Living Light,* Vol. 9, (Summer 1972), p. 43.

42. Lee, *The Shape of Religious Instruction,* pp. 265, 272.

43. Lee, *The Flow of Religious Instruction,* p. 293.

44. Ibid. This statement seems to be an "opinion" on Lee's part because it contains his own theological preference and at the same time seems to be in contradiction to his statement that *the* social science approach is of its very nature value free. See, for example, *The Shape of Religious Instruction,* pp. 207–208.

45. Coe, *A Social Theory of Religious Education,* p. 18.

46. Ibid.

47. Ibid., p. 58.

48. Ibid., p. 6.

49. Moran, *Design for Religion,* pp. 49–71, 97, 111; *Vision and Tactics,* pp. 52–54; *Religious Body: Design for a New Reformation,* p. 166.

50. Moran, *Design for Religion,* p. 119.

51. Lee, *The Shape of Religious Instruction,* p. 24.

52. Ibid., p. 26.

53. Contemporary specialists in the teaching-learning process view learning as a construct which may be inferred from observed change in behavior. See, for example, Lee, *The Flow of Religious Instruction,* pp. 45, 59.

54. Coe, *A Social Theory of Religious Education,* p. 55; see also pp. 15–16. Coe, *What is Christian Education?* p. 281. See also George Coe in Edwin E. Aubrey, "A Theology Relevant to Religious Education," pp. 197–198.

55. Moran, *Design for Religion,* p. 64ff.

56. Moran, *Religious Body: Design for a New Reformation,* p. 169.

57. Moran, *Catechesis of Revelation,* pp. 35–36; *Design for Religion,* p. 118. What Moran means by "religious" in this context is an "uncritical attachment to the tradition they [men] were brought up in." *(Design for Religion,* p. 118). In the broader context of Moran's writing, "religious" refers to a person's established relationships to the whole of experience as revelational. As he points out "The religious question emerges as one penetrates all the depths of experience and discovers what is there. If one begins with experience, one is never faced with making a jump from 'man' to God." *(Religious Body: Design for a New Reformation,* p. 89.)

58. Lee, *The Shape of Religious Instruction,* p. 56.

59. Lee, *The Flow of Religious Instruction,* p. 293.

60. For an example of one theorist who holds this, see Lee, *The Content of Religious Instruction.*

61. For example, Gabriel Moran, *Design for Religion,* p. 148. "The assumption," Moran states, "that there is a collection of truths revealed by God that are dispensed by the Church is slowly disappearing."

62. Coe, *What is Christian Education?* pp. 46–59; see also "The Assault Upon Liberalism," p. 88.

63. Moran, *Vision and Tactics,* p. 21. See also, *Design for Religion,* p. 21. See also, Lee, *The Shape of Religious Instruction,* pp. 218, 312–313; *The Flow of Religious Instruction,* pp. 18–19.

64. Coe, *A Social Theory of Religious Education,* pp. 67–68, 102–108.

65. Ibid., p. 74ff.

66. Lee, *The Shape of Religious Instruction,* pp. 72–73.

67. Lee, *The Content of Religious Instruction,* chapter 1.

68. Ibid.

69. The expression "more than human" is Moran's. He uses it to distinguish the divine aspect or divine pole in all of experience. See Moran, *The Present Revelation,* p. 150ff.

70. Moran, *Design for Religion,* pp. 72–95. See also Moran, "Questions for Religious Educators," *Professional Approaches for Religious Educators,* Vol. 4, Trends-Perspectives-A (Winona, Minnesota: St. Mary's College Press).

71. Moran, *Vision and Tactics,* p. 75.

72. Coe, *A Social Theory of Religious Education,* pp. 14–15; Moran, *Religious Body: Design for a New Reformation,* pp. 150–162.

73. The entire volume of Lee's *The Flow of Religious Instruction* is devoted to the structural or teaching aspect of religious instruction. See especially chapter 4, "Toward a Taxonomy of the Teaching Act," in which Lee develops clearly defined meanings for such terms as a teaching "approach" and teaching "strategy." See also chapter 8, "The Nature of Teaching." Lee's theory of religious education has been mildly criticized for being too inherently teacher-centered. See review of *The Flow of Religious Instruction* by C. Ellis Nelson in *The Living Light,* Vol. 11 (Spring 1974), pp. 146–148.

74. Because he claims that the social science approach to religious instruction is value free (that is, appropriate for any religious denomination), Lee offers no concrete statement on what precisely religious behavior is. Presumably, each religious body will determine what for them constitutes religious behavior. Nevertheless, Lee suggests that the behavior to be facilitated by the teaching of religion should be agreed upon jointly by parents, students, and persons representing the church and society in general. Thus, what is "religious" behavior should not be determined by the teacher alone, or by any single authority. On this matter see Lee, *The Flow of Religious Instruction,* p. 354, footnote 2.

75. Lee, *The Flow of Religious Instruction,* p. 293.

76. Lee, *The Shape of Religious Instruction,* p. 281.

77. Lee, *The Flow of Religious Instruction,* p. 226.

78. Coe, *A Social Theory of Religious Education,* pp. 64–108.

79. Coe, *What is Christian Education?* pp. 23–34; *A Social Theory of Religious Education,* pp. 74–85.

80. Moran, *Religious Body: Design for a New Reformation,* p. 164. Moran indicates that his use of the word "language" is not restricted to oral or written words but also includes bodily expression. It should perhaps be noted that Moran claims that the process of language honing belongs to "the highest levels of the educative process." It may therefore be unsuitable for the "lower" or beginning levels of religious education. However, as he points out, a modification of the process can be used successfully with children and with illiterates and therefore can succeed in putting people of all stages of development in touch with the more than human dimension of experience.

81. Ibid. See also *Catechesis of Revelation,* pp. 100–102; *Vision and Tactics,* p. 118; *Design for Religion,* p. 147.

82. Moran, *Design for Religion,* p. 148.

83. James Michael Lee prefers to speak of the "learner" rather than the "student" since he views religious education as centered in the teaching-learning act. The term "student" tends to refer to the learner in formal instructional settings. The term "learner" indicates that people are always learning and that teaching and learning go on in both formal and informal settings.

84. Coe, *A Social Theory of Religious Education,* pp. 6, 35, 168–171.

85. Lee, *The Flow of Religious Instruction,* pp. 135–136.

86. James Michael Lee admits the possibility of infused knowledge which is given directly by the Holy Spirit. Just the same, he claims, the probability of infused knowledge being given is closely linked to and enhanced by the depth of a person's religious lifestyle. It is just such a lifestyle which is the proper aim of religious education. See Lee, *The Content of Religious Instruction.*

87. Moran, *Catechesis of Revelation,* p. 68. Moran appears to take a somewhat different stand on the role of the Holy Spirit later in this same volume. See, for example, pages 116–117.

88. Lee, "Prediction in Religious Instruction," p. 43. Theorists tend to differ on what precisely makes an experience significant and meaningful. Some tend to hold that meaningfulness depends on how closely the experience is related to the here-and-now existential condition of the learner. Others tend to emphasize the critical and intellectual evaluation of experience which will bring about an awareness of the revelatory dimension of experience. Both these approaches (which may be due to differing epistemological stances) correlate with the immanentist theological viewpoint, that is, that God is at the heart of all experience and that all experience is potentially revelatory.

89. Coe, *What is Christian Education?* p. 110ff. See also *A Social Theory of Religious Education*, pp. 335–336.

90. Moran, *Design for Religion*, pp. 29–48, 72–95; see also *Religious Body: Design for a New Reformation*, pp. 158–186.

91. Lee, "Toward a Dialogue in Religious Instruction," pp. 117–118. For a critique of Lee's position see Warren, "All Contributions Cheerfully Accepted," pp. 28–30; see also O'Hare, "The Image of Theology in the Educational Theory of James Michael Lee," p. 454.

92. Coe, *A Social Theory of Religious Education*, p. 13ff., pp. 210–225.

93. Moran, *Religious Body: Design for a New Reformation*, pp. 150, 154–162. See also *Design for Religion*, pp. 151–157. Moran's distinction between teaching and education is to be found on pp. 158–162 of *Religious Body: Design for a New Reformation*.

94. Lee, *The Shape of Religious Instruction*, pp. 74–84.

95. Ibid., p. 17; see also pp. 260–262.

96. Ibid., pp. 81–88.

97. Of the representative immanentist religious educationists whose theories are analyzed in this book, Gabriel Moran has very little in his writings on the place of evaluation procedures in religious education. This may indicate that evaluation is not an integral part of his religious education theory. He tends to limit evaluation to assessment of teacher performance. In this regard he insists that religion teachers should be subject to the same competence evaluative and accountability procedures as teachers in any other area. See Moran, *Design for Religion*, pp. 147–148.

98. Coe, *What is Christian Education?* pp. 142–151, 178; see also *A Social Theory of Religious Education*, pp. 56, 76–80, 238–240.

99. Lee, *The Flow of Religious Instruction*, p. 232ff.

100. Ibid., pp. 274–277.

CHAPTER VI

The Supernatural and the Natural in Equilibrium?

Lest the title of this chapter create some shudders of horror among both theologians and physicists, an explanation of its intent is in order. As was mentioned in chapter 3, not all religious educationists appear to be comfortable with either a fully transcendist or a fully immanentist metaperspective. Some theorists give indication in their writings that they are endeavoring (whether consciously or unconsciously) to hold simultaneously to the diverse emphases of transcendence and immanence and keep them in dynamic equilibrium. Such a position tries, in the words of Marcel van Caster (speaking of Christ's integration of the human and the divine), to "acknowledge[s] both distinction in unity and unity in distinction."[1] Such a position acknowledges the validity and the necessity of the diverse emphases, acknowledges them as distinct, but also wishes to stress that to insist too strongly on one at the expense of the other is to distort the unity and the simplicity of the God/man relationship. It is not enough to accept theoretically that God is both transcendent and immanent vis-à-vis his creation, both aspects must be equally asserted and emphasized in the context of religious education. As was indicated in chapter 3, such a metaperspective might be called *integrationist*.

There is virtually no escaping the tension that is inherent in the dilemma of the Christian God-consciousness. Everyone (and religious educationists are no exception) to a greater or lesser degree experiences the "tearing apart," the malaise, and perhaps the uncertainty and insecurity, which accompany the belief and acceptance that God is simultaneously transcendent and immanent. Some assuage this tension by strongly asserting transcendence and, as it were, looking at the world through transcendist spectacles. Others are happier with the immanentist viewpoint, whether because of intellectual conviction or simply because it makes for a more comfortable personal adjustment to the demands of the Christian life. There are perhaps others (who may be called integrationists) who prefer the more precarious position of striking a balance between the two emphases. The analogy that comes to mind is that of the child's seesaw. The transcendists sit at one end of the plank and are more comfortable when their weight causes their end to overpower the other. Similarly for the immanentists on their side. The integrationists, by contrast, straddle the fulcrum and by a combination of dexterity in balancing and the judicious application of pressure attempt to keep the plank horizontal and in dynamic equilibrium. The question that must be asked is: Is this balance possible? Does it not perhaps represent an alternate dipping back and forth between a transcendist emphasis and an immanentist emphasis? If this is indeed the case, then the possibility exists that there is no real integrationist metaperspective, the position is not distinctive. To use another analogy, the integrationists may well be attempting the precarious walk along the top of a picket fence. Not only are they in danger of falling off into either the transcendist or the immanentist camp, but they must be careful not to be impaled on the fence itself. In any of these eventualities the integrationist metaperspective would have to be considered as nonviable, or at least not sufficiently etched to be called by a separate name.

The present chapter will analyze the theories of three major religious educationists who appear to be attempting some form of integrationism. As will become clear, however, despite what appears to be an integrationist stance, the metaperspective of these three theorists seems to be somewhat closer to the transcendist than to the immanentist position. The basic reason for this may be that the selected theorists give every indication of holding for a clear and sharp distinction between the natural and the supernatural realms, though not necessarily viewed in ontological terms. Given such a clear separation, their major interest is directed toward how these two realms can be integrated in religious education, while at the same time asserting the prior importance of the supernatural. But, is it possible to hold for an integrationist or equilibrist stance while also holding for a sharp distinction between natural and supernatural? Similarly, and by contrast, is it possible to maintain integrationism while adhering to a one-order worldview? Perhaps the questions can better be answered after the evidence has been presented. On one point, however, there should be no misunderstanding, and it is this: throughout this chapter the integrationist metaperspective must be treated as *quite tentative*. The way the evidence is presented in the writing that follows should in no way be taken to mean that integrationism is an established and clearly recognizable position. The intent of this chapter, therefore, is heuristic; it asks questions. It questions whether the selected theorists have successfully achieved a proper balance between the polar emphases of transcendentism and immanentism. It invites all religious educators who may model themselves on the selected theorists to go through the same questioning process. Perhaps the ultimate question this chapter asks is: Can we humans ever achieve an "equilibrium" between the consciousness of our transcendent "other" dimension, orientation, and purpose, and the consciousness of our immanent this-worldliness?

DELINEATION OF THE INTEGRATIONIST METAPERSPECTIVE

1. Revelation

What it is.   Broadly speaking, the selected religious educationists who attempt an integrationist stance see revelation as consisting in God's action in history whereby he communicates personally with man. Revelation, therefore, takes place largely in events in which God's action can be discerned. Revelation is an ongoing phenomenon in human history and experience since God is immanent in all the workings of the universe ("for God is not dead but is the Lord of history"[2]). All this differs little, or not at all, from the typical immanentist outlook. For these theorists, the bible, as a written record of God's dealings with the people of Israel and particularly the culmination of God's self-revelation in Jesus Christ, is "original" or "special" revelation. The bible is *given* to man as God's authentic word. The way to understand how and when God reveals himself in ordinary life situations and events is by reference to God's given word in its biblical, and for Roman Catholics, its traditional forms. The selected theorists appear to be attempting a balanced emphasis on revelation as a continuing immanentist happening whose meaning comes home to one through every human avenue of experience and knowledge, and revelation as a divine once-for-all given which is normative for the interpretation of the meaning of life. "Revelation," one writer states, "is not information about God; it is what happens in the meeting between God who gives himself and man who perceives and responds."[3] The "perceiving" of revelation, the understanding and grasping that God is "speaking" and calling to us to respond in the midst of human life situations, takes place, according to these theorists, principally within the fellowship of the Christian church. Not only does the bible witness to revelation, but so does the church since the church incarnates the person and teaching of Jesus Christ who is God's unique word to man. In sum, the attempted integrationist balance is between revelation as content, and revelation as process. We humans need the content in order to interpret and understand the process. The content is the measuring stick, the criterion by which to make sense out of the process, by which to sort out the jumbled messages of experience. Content and process must be equally emphasized.

Why it is.   In common with the transcendists and the immanentists, the selected theorists who attempt an integrationist stance see the purpose of revelation as being that persons may enter into a personal relationship with the divine. One theorist puts it this way: " . . . When man encounters the Self-revealing God he is confronted . . . by a Person who offers himself to us in love and judgment, and calls upon us to give ourselves a living sacrifice in response. It is a matter of personal communion. If this is the core of revelation so must it be the core of Christian education."[4] Where the immanentists and transcendists differ in their emphasis is not so much on the "why" of revelation but on the "how." But what do the integrationists have to say about this?

How it is. As we have seen, the transcendist-minded theorists emphasize the God-given faith response to an authentic and authoritative divine message of salvation. The immanentists tend more to emphasize the human and humanizing response to the divine revelation in the depths of all experience. In concert with the transcendists, some theorists who attempt integrationism assert that man can only recognize and appreciate the self-revealing God by faith—faith which is itself God's personal gift. The initiative, therefore, is always on God's side. Nevertheless, the integrationists do not appear to envisage this purely as a supernatural impulsion which "seizes" one. Reason does play a part in the appropriation of revelation. There is a "living intercourse" between the mind and historical events. Human reason constantly probes those events to discover their revelatory meaning but, ulitmately, the discovery of that meaning is God's special gift. According to one theorist, God gives us a "natural light" to help us to progressively know the significance of our existence. True revelation, nevertheless, is of a higher quality and enables us to attain to knowledge which transcends our natural capabilities.[5] It appears that the integrationists are attempting to establish a balanced emphasis, that is, an equal emphasis on God's direct role in revelation (its givenness and the grace-induced response to it), and our response and involvement through our own experience and effort. One theorist seems to capture well the striving for balance when he writes:

> Revelation is *not* purely extrinsic to man's life and thought; *but* it is both *intrinsic* to human experience *and transcendental* to this experience. Man's natural experience of his varying cultural expressions are *"mediations"* of divine revelation. God who reveals himself does not speak "outside" of man who thinks, but man's thought receives a *"super-value"* which is truly a special gift of God.[6]

This special gift of God is the gift of faith which is totally beyond all human capacity. But, does not such emphasis on the *givenness* of faith (i.e., faith comes, as it were, from "outside" us) seem to be a reiteration of the transcendist outlook? Do not those theorists who attempt an integrationist metaperspective appear to be making God's unique act the touchstone of their thinking and the focal point of their emphasis?

Finally, some theorists are insistent on the role of the supernaturally founded church in revelation. Thus, " . . . revelation is normally appropriated through participation in the shared life of the Christian community."[7] The possibility of revelation outside the church is not ipso facto excluded but the theorists indicate that the church is the *normal* (and perhaps the *normative)* locus of revelation. The church is also the main instrument of the revelatory interpretation of the bible and of human experience.

What does all this say for the metaperspective of the selected theorists? Can it truly be called integrationist? Although they strongly insist that revelation is intrinsic to human experience and that it goes on through the events of human history, one cannot escape the impression that many theorists who strive for integrationism put more pressure on the transcendist pole of the balancing seesaw. Their insistence on the primacy of the special gift of faith and the key role of the supernatural and Spirit-imbued church tend to give their position a slightly more transcendist than immanentist flavor.

2. Grace

What it is. As far as grace is concerned there is not a great deal of difference between the transcendists and many theorists who appear to be attempting integrationism. The religious educationists selected for analysis in this chapter would go along almost completely with the emphasis noted in chapter 4. True it is that some of them tend to accentuate the fact that grace is a healer of man's split personality and enables man to become more integral and whole.[8] Thus, they relate grace more directly to what, for them, is one of the main aims of religious education, viz., the blossoming of a mature human personality. Nevertheless, their position differs little from that outlined for the transcendists. Grace is a pure gift which confers "superhuman" capabilities and extricates us from the mire of our earthbound secularism.

How it works. As do the transcendists, the would-be integrationists emphasize that grace has its effect in us through faith, that is, faith understood as meaning "the entire Christian way of thought and life[9]"; it thus includes hope and charity. The effect of this faith is to heal our personality, improve our relationship with God and with other persons, and make us believing Christians. Grace acts by causing a Christian *intentionality.* That is, grace enables us to desire and will to direct all our actions toward fulfilling God's purposes. Only when we so direct our actions are we pursuing a Christian ethic. There is no Christian behavior unless human behavior is intentionally placed in a religious dimension. For example, an ordinary human act such as driving a car becomes "religious" and "Christian" by intentionally referring it to God and by doing it for a religious purpose. Nor can we demand, or "induce" God's free gift; at most we can dispose ourselves and others to receive it. One theorist sees grace as acting both from the interior and from the exterior. From the interior grace acts through our freedom to transform and enrich with *meaning* our human techniques (that is, our ordinary, everyday, mundane acts), our human values (that is, those human things which we esteem as worthwhile and desirable), our ordering of values (that is, our morality), and our direct relationship with God. From the exterior grace acts not by changing the laws of nature or modifying the secular structure of the world, but by giving us special signs of God's presence, such as miracles and sacraments.[10] Thus grace " 'transforms' nature, not in what constitutes its 'technicality,' but in what provides its fully human significance."[11] This idea that grace makes human acts more significantly human seems to be a leaning toward the immanentist emphasis that all truly human and humanizing acts are intrinsically graced and gracious. But, it may be too little and too late to really provide the dynamic balance of emphasis that a true integrationist position would seek to achieve. As far as the selected theorists are concerned, on the question of grace they seem to be sitting well to the transcendist side of the seesaw.

The Holy Spirit.   As for grace, so for the Holy Spirit. Selected religious educationists who appear to be attempting integrationism understand the Holy Spirit as so "seizing" the human person that apparent human acts become quasi-divine. The Spirit takes possession of the human person. He it is who initiates, inspires, strengthens, and gives divine value and significance to what would be merely human and secular activity. Human acts become "Spiritualized." If all of this sounds very much like the transcendist emphasis, there is no mistake, for it is.

In their writing on grace the selected theorists give far too little emphasis to the immanentist perspective to maintain a true dynamic balance with their very noticeable transcendentism. If they are attempting integrationism then the evidence coming out of an analysis of their position on grace seems to indicate that they have not succeeded very well.

3. The Church

What it is.   Theorists who appear to be attempting an integrationist stance are agreed that no clear-cut definition of the church is possible because the church is in essence a mystery. (True immanentists tend to be very wary of "mystery.") In concert with the immanentists, the selected theorists emphasize the community aspect of the church. The church is an experience of fellowship and communion with Jesus Christ and with one's fellow members. To be fully known and understood, such fellowship must be experienced from *within*—within, both in the sense of an inner experience engaging the whole person, and in the sense that the experience can only occur as part of the actual *koinonia* of church fellowship. The redemptive experience of personality healing and enhancement can only take place fully within this community where caring interpersonal relationships are established among the members.[12] The church is the witness to the world that Christ's redemption has been given to the world because this redemption is seen to be effective among church members.

To balance this immanentist perspective, the integrationists also insist on the transcendent aspect of the church, its special "other" dimension. Thus, one theorist asserts, "The Church is always an assembly of individuals, and yet it is always more than its members, because it is infused by the spirit of Christ as Lord."[13] The church, therefore, is far more than an experience of human fellowship, it has a dimension that cannot be captured solely by human action. The church is of the world, but far more than the world. It is supernatural, the special and specialized locus of God's self-giving to man.

Worship. In discussing the church's worship the integrationists differ hardly at all from the position taken by the transcendists and, be it noted, even by most Roman Catholic immanentists. Thus, the church's worship is its principal function, the experience above all experiences in which God encounters his faithful people. In the worship of the church, under the influence of the Holy Spirit, a three-way relationship is established: God with his people, God with each individual, and individuals among themselves. Thus, the integrationists emphasize *both* the "vertical" and the "horizontal" component of relationship with God. Each individual can establish a personal vertical relationship with the divine as distinct from, though aided by, a horizontal relationship with others. Such a relationship is both self-affirming and self-transcending in that personal communion with God in the worship of the church is the source of strength and power for dealing with the concerns of daily life.[14] As was noted earlier on, the selected theorists who attempt integrationism tend to see a clear distinction and separation between the natural and the supernatural realms. For them, worship belongs to the supernatural sphere which is distinct from the natural domain in which man must work out his daily problems. We must turn to this supernatural realm where personal relationship with God is established in worship so that this God-fellowship may be incarnated in our secular activity. The nagging question remains: How different from the true transcendist emphasis is all this? Is it possible to establish a distinct third metaperspective while still holding for a clear and sharp distinction between the natural and the supernatural?

The Church and Revelation. All Christian religious educationists agree that in some fashion the church is the specially favored locus of revelation. Yet, many theorists who attempt integrationism appear to lean more toward the transcendist emphasis of pointing especially to the activity of the Holy Spirit. In and through the church the Spirit conveys a meaning and an interpretation of sacred scripture as well as the revelatory dimension of all experience that we could in no way arrive at by our own unaided efforts. In this way God speaks more effectively to his people through and within the church than anywhere else. Likewise, we respond to his word better as members of the church than those outside the church.

In sum, religious educationists who attempt an integrationist stance attempt to emphasize equally (1) the church as human fellowship and as a mutually caring and sharing community, *and* (2) the church as supernaturally formed by Christ and bound together by his Spirit. They attempt to integrate these two emphases by asserting that the supernatural element must elevate and redimension the natural everyday activity of the Christian. The question is: Is this a distinct and clear-cut metaperspective, or is it not some modified form of the transcendist metaperspective? Have the so-called integrationists achieved a sufficiently stable and dynamic balance and equilibrium between the polar emphases of transcendentism and immanentism?

4. Jesus Christ

Statements made by the selected theorists about Jesus Christ seem to be but echoes of those made by the transcendists. Very little in fact need be added to what has already been noted in chapter 4. Perhaps these theorists tend to speak of Jesus Christ less in terms that refer directly to his godhead than do the transcendists. For them Jesus' godhead and lordship should never even *seem* to be separated from his historical incarnation, though it is his lordship which is in fact the primary expression of the self-revealing God. Perhaps these theorists tend to emphasize the "whole" Christ, God and man, whose divinity can only be appreciated through his human self-expression. It is possible that theorists who attempt integrationism do not emphasize, as much as do the transcendists, what has been called the "adoration mode." They can speak of Christ as God without repeatedly resorting to the use of such divinely-flavored and nuanced language as "adorable majesty," "awe-inspiring greatness," "divine dignity," "eternal Son of the Father." Nevertheless, they do not seem to balance their rather transcendist-tending emphasis with an equal insistence that Christ is incarnated in all of human process and experience. And so, once again, it must be remarked that the selected theorists, though seemingly working out of a more balanced and integrated metaperspective, tend to tip that balance in favor of the transcendist emphasis.

Conclusion

What does the evidence adduced above do for the possible existence of a distinctive third metaperspective? It seems clear that the selected religious educationists are attempting some form of integrationism. In point of fact, however, the position they arrive at favors the transcendist position. It has been said before, but seems well worth repeating, that what we are dealing with here is not so much a question of strict theological concepts as it is a matter of *emphasis or accentuation*. Such emphasis takes a person beyond the realm of the merely intellectual theological approach and engages deep sensibilities and personal affect. It is quite difficult to come up with precise criteria of differentiation for issues that have deep personal reverberations. All the same, even though the integrationist metaperspective does not appear to be as clear-cut or as well etched as the other two this does not mean that it does not exist. It could mean that the representative theorists have not thoroughly thought through their position and are not fully conscious of their own metaperspective. They may not be sufficiently aware of favoring one or other theological emphasis. Perhaps the metaperspective which emerges from the evidence adduced above might be more fittingly labeled "moderate transcendist." If such a metaperspective does indeed exist then, one might surmise, there is a corresponding "moderate immanentist" position. In any case, it has already been stipulated, but perhaps should be said again, that the integrationist metaperspective is here put forward as entirely tentative. Whether it is, or is not, a distinctive metaperspective may very well not be the important issue. The real point is that the reader should examine his or her own position in the light of what has been presented and then reflect on how this position works itself out in down-to-earth religious educational performance. The reader will better be able to make this reflection after examining how some of the major theorists who give evidence of trying to achieve a transcendist/immanentist balance work out their own position in terms of religious education theory.

But first, a word or two on three such religious educationists who seemingly project this more balanced metaperspective.

REPRESENTATIVE RELIGIOUS
EDUCATIONISTS

Possibly the most influential of the Protestant religious educationists whose theological metaperspective has the earmarks of being integrationist is Randolph Crump Miller. An ordained priest of the Protestant Episcopal church Miller has held important teaching posts in the field of Christian education, first at the Church Divinity School of the Pacific, and subsequently at Yale University (Horace Bushnell professor of Christian Nurture). No mere academician, Miller has also been deeply involved in Christian education at the parish level, both in teaching and in teacher training. His influence has been exerted through other avenues beside his teaching. A prolific writer, he has authored several major works on religious education together with innu-

merable articles in various journals. Longtime editor of the Religious Education Association journal *Religious Education*, he has also been an advisor in
the development of the Episcopal Church Sunday School curriculum, known
as the Seabury Series. His views and recommendations have been discussed
and assessed by many writers and this fact alone is perhaps a measure of his
importance.[15]

Miller's stated position is that theology is the "clue" to Christian education.[16] Miller asserts that theology is not so much a speculative discipline as it
is "the-truth-about-God-in-relation-to-man." Theology is concerned with the
God/man relationship both as revealed in the bible and as incarnated in life-
situations. Theology must at all times be *relevant* (a favorite Miller word) to
the human situation so that "we can discover God at work in history and in
our own generation, especially in our daily relationships."[17] Miller appears to
be striving (whether consciously or unconsciously) for some sort of equilibrium between the strong and opposing pulls of transcendentism and immanentism. He searches for a symbiosis between an emphasis on the supernatural
and transcendent God who reveals himself and confronts us personally, and an
emphasis on man who is confronted and called to respond in faith. He seems
wedded to a neoorthodox emphasis on special revelation but at the same time
wishes to give due importance and consideration to the insights of science
(particularly of interpersonal and developmental psychology) and to relate
these to the biblical revelation. Though Miller tends to view the God/man
relationship in a vertical Person-to-person perspective, he also emphasizes
that this relationship only effectively takes place in the horizontal context of
person-to-person relationships. The God-in-relation-to-man theme runs as a
constant refrain through all Miller's writings. The transcendent, "other"-
dimensioned God who graciously reveals himself in his special and mighty
acts in history is also the God who is intimately concerned and involved with
our very personal and human development.

Another important religious educationist whose attempt at integrationism is
not unlike that of Miller is Lewis Joseph Sherrill.[18] A Presbyterian minister,
Sherrill's teaching at major centers of Christian education (first at Louisville
Presbyterian Theological Seminary and then at Union Theological Seminary
in New York) ensured his influence on many future religious educators. By
his own admission, his major work on religious education *The Gift of Power*
(1953) attempts to achieve a balance between an emphasis on the God who
reveals himself and to whom man must look for redemption, and an emphasis
on man who is redeemed.[19] Thus, for Sherrill, the transcendent God who
confronts us as creator, as lord, as judge, as provider, and as the object of our
faith, is also he who reveals himself most intimately within the very process of
human sharing and personal participation. A cursory examination of Sherrill's

writings may leave one with the impression that his emphasis is very much an immanentist one as he is so much concerned with the psychology of human relationships and the integral development of the human self. But, even though the self is only formed in relationship with others, for Sherrill such relationship means personal one-to-one relationship with God *and* proper relationships with other persons in the Christian community. He starts with an experienced human need for wholeness and the healing of one's splitness of personality, and answers this need by the development of a Person-to-person relationship with God. Thus, the relationship is primarily viewed in a vertical perspective, as a one-to-one encounter with and response to the transcendent God. Nevertheless, such a personal relationship can only effectively take place through the experienced "horizontal" relationships within the Spirit-animated Christian community. And God is "within" all such true "two-way" human communication.[20] As a result of his personal relationship with God, man lives a "new life" of "openness to eternity" in the very midst of his earthly preoccupations.[21] According to Sherrill's thinking, it seems that the life of grace and union with God are separable and distinct from ordinary human life, though existing within the latter. The life of grace, it seems, belongs to the supernatural realm which is sharply distinct from the natural realm of human life but specifies and animates the latter. This dichotomy of natural and supernatural spheres is strongly reminiscent of the transcendist metaperspective, but Sherrill does not appear to go all the way with that particular overview.

A third religious educationist who tends to integrationism is the Belgian Jesuit Marcel van Caster. Van Caster's influence, particularly in Roman Catholic religious education circles, has been exerted through his teaching at the International Center for Studies in Religious Education (Lumen Vitae) in Brussels, and through his numerous books and articles. Most of his writings have been translated into English from the original French and have reached a wide English-speaking audience. Also, not a few English-speaking religious educators and educationists have studied under van Caster at Lumen Vitae. In his earlier works, *The Structure of Catechetics* (1965) and *Themes of Catechesis* (1966), van Caster tended to follow the kerygmatic pattern of Roman Catholic religious education with its emphasis on the proclamatory transmission of the unique message of revelation. The theological perspective of this type of religion teaching is focused primarily on the supremely transcendent God speaking his word to man in Jesus his Son, the divine savior.[22] At the same time, in his subsequent writings van Caster appears intent on proposing a type of religious education synthesis. The synthesis he aims at is between a type of religious education which has its theological emphasis (and its starting point) in the spoken revelation of the transcendent God, and a type of religious education which emphasizes (and has its starting point in) human experience.[23] In a series of articles written for *Lumen Vitae* (1968–1974) van Caster is concerned with showing that a dynamic unity exists between an emphasis on union with God and an emphasis on human autonomy; between an emphasis on faith in Christ and an emphasis on commitment to the world; between an emphasis on human values and an emphasis on the content of the gospel. This dynamic unity, van Caster maintains, is brought about by a thesis-anthesis-synthesis type of dialectical process.[24] His own tendency in his proposed synthesis is to lean toward emphasis on a personal "vertical" relationship with God as being the important factor in "supernaturalizing" worldly values. Thus, he holds for a sharply-drawn distinction between the natural and supernatural realms. He calls attention to the supernatural as giving meaning and significance to the natural. On the other hand he also emphasizes God's immanence in natural process, sufficiently so for him to be included in the group of those who do not fully subscribe to the thoroughgoing transcendist metaperspective.

THE AIM

The selected integrationist-leaning religious educationists present a three-pronged treatment of aim. Basically, these theorists accept that there is a sharp distinction between natural and supernatural realms, natural and supernatural spheres of influence, natural and supernatural value systems. In keeping with this view they understand the aim of religious education as having, (1) a supernatural component, (2) a natural component, (3) a component which represents an integration of the first two. The supernatural component of aim pertains directly to God and his grace; the natural component pertains directly to man and is within his capacity to produce. The third component pertains to the existential integration in the life of the learner (student) of human values and divine values. Lewis Sherrill seems to neatly encapsulate this three-pronged consideration of aim when he writes

A statement of *ends sought* in Christian education might contain such elements as these: that persons might be drawn into the kingdom of God; that they might attain to increasing self-understanding and self-knowledge and an increasing realization of their own potentialities; and that they might sustain the relationships and responsibilities of life as children of God.[25]

Sherrill himself sees these aims as "bi-polar," that is, as pertaining both to God and to man, as pertaining, therefore, to separate and separable domains.

The Supernatural Component of Aim

"That persons might be drawn into the kingdom of God."

Here, it seems, one is faced with a purely supernatural and transcendent objective which only God can accomplish. To enter the kingdom of God is the final end of man's earthly existence, but it is God who will bring in his kingdom by his free gift of unmerited grace. Entry into the kingdom is beyond man's purely human efforts (and consequently, it should be noted, beyond the reach of any purely psychological or educational procedure). The best that one can do is to prepare oneself and others to be received into the kingdom of God. Thus, Randolph Crump Miller asserts, "The Church, which is the community of the faithful in quest of God's kingdom, seeks to *bring about those conditions* whereby God will act to bring in his kingdom"; and again, "The kingdom is the goal of all human endeavor and stands in judgment upon all human effort, and only by repentance and faith may man enter God's kingdom by his grace."[26]

Another aspect of this supernatural component of aim is, as some theorists state, that religious education should promote an encounter with the Lord. Encounter means being able to recognize God in everyday life, it means being able to read the signs (biblical, liturgical, and life-context signs) of God's presence and enter into a personal union of commitment with him who is recognized. But, this can only come about because of the direct gift of faith. And so, Marcel van Caster asserts, "The direct aim of catechesis is faith, which is knowledge of God in his signs."[27] The knowledge to which van Caster refers is not mere intellectual cognition but rather a discernment and deep consciousness which is self-involving and promotes commitment. We cannot arrive at such a state by our own unaided efforts, "The inner light cannot be coerced. Ultimately the nurturing process must wait on the Holy Spirit."[28]

Although the selected theorists do not identify the kingdom of God with the church but rather with those who do the will of God, as far as Christians are concerned "being drawn into the kingdom of God" means being drawn into the church. And so, the aim of Christian education is sometimes stated as to educate people to be the church.[29] It is within the Christian *koinonia* which is the church that one best encounters God in Jesus Christ. But the church itself is supernatural; it is the body of Christ, indwelt by the Holy Spirit. Only by the grace of God can one enter the church and make a Christian commitment. "We can lead pupils into the community," observes one writer, "and within the community we can lead them to the edge of the abyss, but only by God's grace do they make the leap of faith."[30] Reading between the lines what this effectively says is that we cannot teach for supernatural aims. All we can do is provide the conditions which *seem* best to prepare the student to receive God's grace. This is perfectly in keeping with a thorough-going transcendist metaperspective. Such a metaperspective focuses on God's grace as being *given*—given suddenly, irruptively, supernaturally, from outside human process. The focus is not on grace as working within and through the very scientific process of teaching and as therefore thoroughly enmeshed in human acts. It is a literalistic application of Paul's statement "I did the planting, Apollos did the watering, but God made things grow" (1 Cor. 3:6).

The Natural Component of Aim

"That they might attain to increasing self-understanding and self-knowledge and an increasing realization of their own potentialities."

As a balance to the purely supernatural component of aim, the selected theorists also insist on a purely natural component. The supernatural component corresponds to man's final end and destiny—eternal union with God. The natural component is concerned with man's proximate this-worldly concerns. In order to live a proper human and Christian life one must be mature, self-possessed, and capable of realizing one's full human potential. Growth in maturity can best be achieved through the experience of loving interpersonal relationships within the Christian community. The religion class and the whole church educational pattern must be geared to establishing such healthy and healing relationships. Growth in maturity also requires a basic sense of security. Such security comes within the religious education process from the experience of being accepted, as one is, into a loving community, and being accepted by God.[31] All the above objectives are human enough, "natural" enough, and existential enough to be achieved by human planning and effort.

Another aspect of maturity that some theorists point to is that which has to do with sharpened consciousness and awareness. Sharpening the awareness of one's existential situation (one's basic human experiences) and increasing the depth of this awareness is the basis for recognizing the presence of God in human life and entering into a personal union with him. According to Marcel van Caster, helping the student to increase awareness is a job which the religion teacher can accomplish. The aim is to bring about a change of attitude in the student, a new outlook which is fully appreciative (1) of the presence of God and of supernatural values, (2) of the necessity of promoting human values, and (3) of the necessity of *both* sets of values in a balanced human life. "Nowadays," van Caster notes, "practically all authorities on the subject agree that the purpose of catechesis is not only to increase knowledge but also to bring about a change in the whole person.... Yet... catechesis should give priority to the matter of a change in mental attitude and outlook."[32] Such maturity, change of attitude and outlook, and heightened awareness can be *directly* accomplished by teaching.

The natural component of aim as presented by the selected theorists fits very well into what has been called the "educational" purpose of religious education. If education is understood as a process which is particularly directed toward the total development of the human personality, then to this process religious education must make a specific and signal contribution. If it does not do this, religious education has no place in a balanced school curriculum. Religion is a crucially important factor in the full and mature development of human personality because it provides a system of meaning. It enables the students to answer the ultimate questions which arise in the course of experience, questions about life and death, about suffering, life after death, and about the experience of the power of the divine. Religion enables the students to develop a purpose in life and provides them with symbols which make sense of their experience, particularly in terms of the ultimacy dimension of that experience. Through their experience of community with other church members students are provided with a sense of security and belongingness which pointedly contribute to the development of a balanced and integrated personality. In this view, therefore, the aim of religious education is primarily educational.[33] So stated, it is an aim with which most hard-core immanentists would be quite happy for it highlights their particular emphasis. For them, all that is thoroughly human is also thoroughly divine.

The Integration of the Natural and Supernatural Components of Aim

"To live as a child of God."

In keeping with their striving to achieve a balanced emphasis on both the transcendent and immanent aspects of religious education, the selected theorists point to the need to bring together and to integrate the supernatural and the natural components of aim. To live as a child of God means to live in the world but yet not be of the world. It means that worldly values and ideals have to be respected and promoted but at the same time these values and ideals must be sublimated to nonworldly ones. Supernatural values must take priority. All that is good, all that is human, must be affirmed and acted upon, but Christians must "spiritualize" and "supernaturalize" the human and the natural. This in fact is what living as a child of God means. The ordinary mundane things of everyday life are sublimated to the eschatological purpose of human life. The process is one of intentionalizing. As van Caster puts it, "The spiritual intention behind such acts [acts pertaining to a merely human value] is a transformation of the human intention, because, by working along with the Holy Spirit, we seek temporal values for the sake of their Christian significance."[34] Particularly is this spiritualizing process important when it is applied to the human value of love. It is this supernaturally dimensioned love that members of the Christian church should have for one another and by which they live as children of God.

One of the best means of accomplishing this integrated and balanced emphasis on both supernatural and natural aims for religious education is by membership in the church. Theorists offer three reasons for this. First, it is in the church that we are most readily confronted with the self-revealing God and are drawn to commit ourselves to him in faith. Second, God enters into a personal relationship with each one, but in and through the general church fellowship. As Randolph Miller (quoting Herbert H. Farmer) indicates, "God's purpose is such, and He so made humanity in accordance with that purpose, that He never enters into a *personal* relationship with man apart from other human persons."[35] Third, the sustaining relationships of true Christian *koinonia* within the church enable us to express our faith relationship with God in our very relationships with others.

To what extent the thoroughly integrated aim of religious education can be achieved by any particular educational process or technique is not really made clear by the theorists who appear to be searching for some form of integrationism. Since integrated aims contain a supernatural element which is strictly beyond the reach of mere human striving, theorists are hard pressed to give any clear indication of how such integrated aims can be taught. What it seems to boil down to is "preparing the ground" for the action of the Spirit and the gift of faith. All of which is a harking back to transcendentism.

In fact, the question that has to be asked is: Does what has been described above in connection with the aim of religious education give evidence of a radically distinct metaperspective? *All* religious educationists would probably agree that, in the long run, the principal objective of religious education is to enable the student to "live as a child of God." Granted this general objective, the immanentists would emphasize that living as a child of God means living a fully human life, not only individualistically, but also that such a life must radiate to others' values which make for man's betterment of man. The immanentists would see the action of the Spirit as intimately bound up with and not distinct from such a life. The transcendists, on the other hand, would emphasize a personal vertical union with God and the direct action of the Spirit as necessary for Christianizing and spiritualizing purely human values. Is it clear that the theorists who strive for integration and dynamic balance of transcendentism and immanentism with regard to the aim of religious education succeed in keeping such a balance? Is each pole of the emphasis equally insisted on, or does it not seem that, in final analysis, the integrationists lean towards transcendentism? The selected theorists seem to visualize that love of

God and the promotion of divine values can exist in some sort of separate domain from love of neighbor and the promotion of human values. For them, it is love of God which is the main aim of religious education.

A final word. The aims of religious education which emerge from an analysis of the writings of the three selected theorists lack specificity and clarity. First, supernatural aims cannot be specified in human terms and achieved by specific human endeavor. The Holy Spirit blows where he wills and cannot be manipulated by any human teachnique. Second, even the "natural" or human aims proposed lack specificity because they have to do with such broad, almost indefinable concepts as "maturity" (who or what is a mature person?), "self-integration" (what tests can one apply to assess whether this has been achieved?), "wholeness" (by what standard is a person "whole"?), "sharpened awareness." Third, according to these theorists, all that religious education can do is to lead the student to make a free choice of living as a child of God. Free choice cannot be predetermined by any educational techniques, though it may be aided or promoted by them.[36]

THE CONTENT

In order to propose a content for religious education one must have a clear-cut objective towards which such content is directed. One must know *why* one must teach in order to make a proper selection of *what* one must teach (product content) and *how* one must teach it (process content). As we saw in the previous section, the selected "integrationist" theorists propose a threefold aim for religious education, or rather, attempt to integrate supernatural aims and natural aims by a balanced emphasis on both. As far as content is concerned, the thinking of these theorists is well expressed by Marcel van Caster. According to him "the integral meaning of life is the content of catechesis . . . ." Therefore, "The prevalent desire is to link up more directly, more radically and more progressively with 'experience.' "[37] (All of which, it might be remarked, would be applauded by the immanentists). And so, experience is the full substance of the content of religious education. Not that experience is what is taught; rather, it is from experience that learning arises. For these theorists, religious learning means a change in the self, a change of outlook and orientation in the person which bespeaks a deeper faith and commitment to God and to the Christian way of life. Religious education becomes largely a matter of creating the conditions out of which the students may come to an experience of God—an experience which gives a full and integrated meaning and purpose to life. Experience, however, does not materialize out of nowhere. There must be a starting point, something out of which and from which the students may be engaged by experience. This "something'' from which experience comes is usually designated ''subject matter'' or ''materials of learning.''[38] As they do for aims, the selected theorists conceive of subject matter as existing, so to speak, in a hierarchy of ascending supernaturality. First, that which is purely secular (for example, the story of a nonreligious hero, or the beauties of art and nature); second, that which is influenced by the supernatural (for example, material which arises from biblical or church-oriented sources—the lives of saints, church history, bible stories); third, that which is directly supernatural (for example, Christian church worship and prayer).

Natural life-experiences

The experience of the beauties of the world, or the horrors of the world such as human suffering and man's injustice to man, all can be subject matter for religious education. All can lead to a faith-relationship with God. By far the most powerful of human experiences, however, is the experience of loving, caring interpersonal relationships within the *koinonia* of the church. No experience is more effective in the healing of personal anxiety and in leading to a personal faith-commitment. For, as Lewis Joseph Sherrill puts it, ''God is participant in the community; . . . the processes of interaction are capable of carrying corrective, redemptive, and re-creative power which comes from beyond purely natural processes, not violating these processes, nor setting them aside, but able to transform them.''[39] (Note, again, the peculiar concern these theorists have for the ''supernaturalizing'' of purely ''natural'' processes. Natural processes are good, but they must be ''re-created'' and ''transformed'' by reference to God). If one were to ask: ''How does ordinary human experience become religious experience?'' those who attempt an integrationist stance would probably reply that religious experience grows out of ordinary experience when this latter can be consciously related to God, or to Jesus, his life and his message.

Quasi-Supernatural experiences

Instead of starting with natural life-experiences, the teacher may start with some experience which is recorded in scripture or in some other emphatically church-oriented or God-directed source such as the bible. The theorists, it seems, visualize such material as being in closer touch with the divine than other types of subject matter. The aim is not that the students should merely ''know'' the bible. Rather, the aim is to enable the students to really experience the bible stories and situations as applying to their own lives. Thus, for example, they should really experience Christ healing their own blindness just as he healed the blind beggar and any who came to him believing (Jn. 9:1–38). The students should experience in their own lives the same compassion that Christ showed to all repentant sinners (Lk. 7:36–50, Jn. 8:3–11). Thus, God's workings with his people in biblical times are relevant to present-day life experiences. Similarly, if the lives of holy Christians give evidence of God's presence in the world then the students should be able to experience that same divine intervention in their own lives. Theorists differ slightly on the exact direction this "experience" of biblical material should take. Some, like van Caster, tend to stress the importance of awareness and understanding which are the fruit of careful reflection. "Meaning" will emerge from a meditative consideration of the subject matter. Caught up in the compelling dynamic of the biblical story, the students will be led to a desire to fashion their lives according to the principles which guided the life of Christ.[40] Other theorists, such as Miller and Sherrill, tend to emphasize more the importance of actually putting into practice the type of interpersonal relationships which stand out in the bible or in other Christian sources. The experience of lived relationships with persons leads to the experience of a lived relationship with God. Nevertheless (and this is extremely important), these theorists seem to indicate (in fact, van Caster states it explicitly) that love of God for his own sake is something which is distinct and separable from love for other persons. What this means is that while we cannot love God without loving our neighbor, it is possible to love our neighbor without loving God. Such a love would be mere philanthropy, or humanism, but not specifically Christian.[41]

Once again, it is not difficult to see the leitmotif of these theorists' concern—secular, worldly (that is, natural) values must be Christianized, that is, supernaturalized or spiritualized. It is a concern which flows from a basic assumption that the natural and the supernatural can be viewed as separate spheres of influence—an assumption which would make no sense to a thoroughgoing immanentist.

Special God-Experiences

The selected theorists point to some experiences as more fully communicating the divine presence than others, experiences which "contain" God in a very special and intimate way. High on the list is the special experience of prayer and the worship of the Christian community. The selected theorists contend that the liturgy is an occasion for God's "unusual action," an occasion where revelation is at its highest and most compelling.[42] Church worship "is the experience-centered method [of Christian education] *par excellence*" because here God is more deeply in contact with the learner than elsewhere; worship is the "primary way of establishing a relationship with God."[43] Also, in worship, each one contributes psychologically to the God-experience by turning away from self and affirming God. Thus, worship is also a process of self-transcendence in the midst of which the divine dimension is experienced.[44] With his typically Roman Catholic outlook, Marcel van Caster sees the active presence of God in the liturgy as guaranteed by the fact that the liturgy is of divine institution. God's presence is symbolically visible in the signs and symbols which are used in the liturgy. These signs are, in fact, a prolongation of Christ's work so that we might participate in this work. By participating in the liturgy we actually "put on Christ." The existential act of the liturgy is "the act of the living Christ."[45]

Briefly, therefore, the selected theorists are agreed that all of experience is in fact the content of religious education—a position which would make any thoroughgoing immanentist happy. Like the immanentists also, these religious educationists who give indications of having some type of integrationist metaperspective accept the fact that all experiences are potentially religious experiences and therefore basically useful for religious education. At this point, however, the integrationists shift their emphasis to a more transcendist outlook. They understand experience as becoming religious only when intentionally referred to, or having some intrinsic connection with, the divine. In other words, experiences can be either thoroughly secular, or they can be intentionally "transformed," or "supernaturalized." The integrationists seem to be striving to balance their immanentist emphasis by applying some pressure on the transcendist side. Their position arises from the acceptance of a basic transcendist principle, viz., the sharp and clear distinction between natural and supernatural, between things human and things divine. Does the evidence indicate that the selected theorists have succeeded in achieving a balanced metaperspective?

THE TEACHER

The selected theorists who appear to be tending toward integrationism envisage that religious education simultaneously lives in two worlds and is concerned with two spheres of influence and activity, the natural and the supernatural. These theorists' concern is to give due weight and importance to both worlds, to achieve a balanced emphasis on both spheres of activity. Thus, for them, Christian education engages the natural human capacities of both teacher and student. At the same time, there is also a supernatural and transcendent component to Christian teaching which surpasses the purely natural capacities and resources of the teacher. This component, too, must be given its rightful place in the whole process.

The Teacher and the Natural Component of Religion
Teaching

In keeping with their desire to give due weight and importance to revelation as a continuing existential phenomenon (immanentist emphasis), the selected theorists stress that the main work of the teacher is that of preparing the students to recognize and respond to this revelation. The important word here is *preparing* because these theorists understand that the recognition of God's call and the personal response to that call are due to God's gift of grace. Thus one of the teacher's main tasks is to stir up conscious awareness of the reality of God in the students' daily life. This is something that can be achieved by human techniques and procedures. In this process of stirring up a conscious awareness of the divine, no one method of teaching is so sacrosanct that it should preclude all others. In fact, the theorists recommend that methods of teaching should be as varied as the circumstances demand. The guiding principle is that the teacher should work for the development in the students of those human dispositions and attitudes which aid in the acceptance of divine revelation. Marcel van Caster tells us what these dispositions are. First, a sense of spiritual reality, that is, a sense of the transcendent, the sacred, the "beyond" in human reality. Second, a sense of personal values, such as the value of freedom. Third, a sense of mystery and awe and wonder at the inexplicable marvels that experience reveals. Fourth, a sense of the need for salvation, a sense of the need of help to make up for our deficiencies.[46]

Whatever the method chosen, the theorists insist that the teacher must aim for full student involvement and participation. They are insistent, therefore, that teaching does not merely consist in the transmissive handing on of a divine message (as a thoroughgoing transcendist might hold) for in such a process student participation is reduced to a minimum. Teaching must be a two-way communication, a real process of interaction between teacher and students, not a one-sided imparting of knowledge. Students and teacher must enter into an intimate person-to-person loving and caring relationship. During the religion lesson a spirit of true dialogue must be developed. Some of the selected theorists typically point to the teacher as a true "minister of reconciliation" who mediates for the students God's own loving solicitude.[47] In the teacher the students must be able to see and appreciate the divine intervention in their lives, they must see and appreciate the self-revealing God.

In the context of caring relationships which give the students the experience of acceptance and reconciliation, the role of the Christian community is vitally important. The teacher must make every effort to form each class into a *group,* that is, a real community of those who exhibit caring behaviors for each other. Randolph Crump Miller expresses it this way: " . . . Only the group can achieve the kind of community in which the Christian faith may be assimilated. The Body of Christ is a fellowship *(koinonia)* of believers and not a gathering of like-minded individuals. . . . Group processes, therefore, are essential to Christian education."[48] The teacher is a group leader. In this role of leadership the teacher must exhibit the qualities of a true pedagogue in the original Greek meaning of that word, that is, someone who "leads as head, escorts as supporter, or accompanies as friend."[49]

If group leadership demands certain personal qualities in the teacher this must not be taken to mean that skill and competency in the actual technique of teaching may be relegated to the realm of the unimportant. "Nice" people, caring and dedicated people, do not necessarily make good teachers. There is no substitute for real teaching ability backed by effective training. These theorists insist that the teacher must be resourceful enough to use every human means possible to prepare the students to respond to the God who reveals himself. Such an emphasis gives evidence of the great sensitivity of the selected religious educationists to the natural, or human element in religion teaching. Even though they may view the ultimate aim of religion teaching as supernatural, they see that every human resource must be exploited to the full in order to facilitate it achievement.

The Teacher and the Supernatural Component of Religion Teaching

As we might expect, the selected theorists balance their insistence on the human qualities and technical competence of the teacher by also calling attention to the supernatural component in teaching. They have no doubt that the real Christian teacher is the Holy Spirit acting in and through the Christian church. The actual human person who fills the teacher's role is simply an agent of the church and in fact plays second fiddle to the Holy Spirit. Some theorists see that while the teacher should eschew the exclusive use of transmissive techniques in teaching, nevertheless the role of transmitter and proclaimer of God's message is a very real one. In this sense the teacher is a direct channel of the Holy Spirit to the student. Perhaps even more important is that the teacher's entire lifestyle should be a vibrant witness to the presence of the Holy Spirit. The students must have clear evidence of the teacher's commitment. They must see in the teacher the person of Jesus Christ. "All the expert techniques in the world," notes Miller, "do not channel the Christian faith unless there is faith in the teacher or leader to be channeled. Unless there is a contagious enthusiasm for Christian living, it will not be attractive to the learners."[50] Religion teaching, for those who hold to this position, is not "complete" unless it includes "the testimony of the catechist himself, a testimony which is based on his 'Christian reading' of the historical life of

Jesus Christ, and of the present-day world."[51] What these theorists appear to be saying is that, as the old adage has it, religion is not taught it is caught. (It is an adage which some immanentists view with profound suspicion and others openly scoff at.) In some mysterious way the Holy Spirit, working in and through the faith-commitment behaviors of the teacher, reaches out and touches the students. Such faith-commitment behaviors are, for example, the manifest enthusiasm of the teacher, dedication, reverence for God and evident Christian lifestyle. It is God who acts "from without" in a thoroughly supernatural fashion. In fine, the selected theorists see the teacher merely as God's instrument. God uses the teacher to work his mighty purposes. The teacher is but a catalyst to the work of the Holy Spirit and must never attempt to usurp the functions of the latter.

No matter how much these selected theorists insist on the human qualities and competencies of the teacher, their basic tenet seems to be that, in the long run, Christian teaching is exclusively the work of the Holy Spirit. All that the teacher puts into a religion lesson is but a preparation (albeit a very necessary one) for the personal free gift of the Spirit. Furthermore, they seem to understand this gift of the Spirit not as intrinsic to and thoroughly enmeshed within the very process of teaching (as would the immanentists) but as an "external" given, coming in from outside the process. The Spirit "descends," and Christian teaching is accomplished. Again, what this all looks like is some form of moderate transcendentism, rather than a thoroughly balanced integrationist metaperspective. The theorists appear to have allowed their transcendist emphasis to tip the scales and to overpower their immanentist emphasis.

THE STUDENT

Lewis Joseph Sherrill's view of man in relation to Christian education has been called "theo-anthropocentric."[52] What this means is that Sherrill understands the human person as being a mysterious blend of sharply distinct God-like elements on the one hand and purely human elements on the other. Both these aspects or components of the human person must be given due attention and emphasis in religious education. Nevertheless, the merely natural or human elements must be sublimated to the supernatural elements from which man derives his final destiny and purpose. This view of the makeup of the human person determines much of what Sherrill has to say about the student in religious education. It is a view which also seems characteristic of the other religious educationists whose theories are examined in this chapter. These theorists attempt to temper a fully transcendist approach (which would strongly emphasize and give prominence to the supernatural element) with an insistence on the importance of the merely human (through and in which the immanentists would see the divine as working). May such a metaperspective be labeled integrationist? Does these theorists' position give equal prominence to the transcendist and to the immanentist approach? These questions are more easily answered after taking a look at what these theorists have to say about the student.

The Student and Learning

As one might expect, and in keeping with their by now familiar stance, the selected religious educationists view learning, and particularly religious learning, as both a natural and a supernatural phenomenon. They focus a great deal of attention on the fact that the human person is created in the image of God and therefore bears the supernatural imprint of the creator. But there is no escaping the reality of sin, the disruptive effects of which are all too obvious in the bitter experience of self-alienation and the difficulty of relating to others. It is these theorists' thinking that religious education should be targeted, as far as possible, toward healing the human and personal effects of sin (the natural component of learning) so that the students will be able to freely accept and respond to the grace of redemption (the supernatural component of learning).

The natural component of learning is concerned mainly with two areas. First, mental enlightenment and the development of greater powers of awareness and discernment, and second, personality development and the improvement of interpersonal relationships. No emphasis on this natural component however, can gainsay the fact that the theorists see it as always subordinate to and but a preparation for the supernatural component of learning, namely, the gift of faith. This again points to a basic principle which the theorists adopt, namely, that the final end of religious education is supernatural even though the proximate and immediate aim may be natural and humanly achievable. These two aims are intimately related and integrated in the God/man relationship which Christian education seeks to establish.[53]

And so, ideally, notes Randolph Crump Miller, one of the principal outcomes of religious education is that the student should learn to see the hand of God in the ordinary events of life.[54] To be able to "see" God within the personal fabric of life will push the learner toward making a commitment to the Christian way of life. The capacity to "see," to discern, to read the signs of God's presence is something which can be taught. The student can be brought to ponder and to think deeply, so that new meaning breaks through, by any number of teaching methods. But, when all is said and done, it is the direct action of the Holy Spirit which finally causes "the scales to fall from the eyes," which causes "the penny to drop," which causes true spiritual discernment to take place. Marcel van Caster likewise emphasizes this natural component of learning with which is associated more acute consciousness and heightened awareness. His position is that human activity (which he designates as "technique") always is and remains just that, merely human. Consequently, he argues, there is no such thing as "Christian" cooking, or "Christian" football playing, or "Christian" skiing, and presumably, no such thing as "Christian" learning. No act, according to van Caster, is *merely* technical, it always has a human significance because it is done for some human motive and to uphold some human value. It is this human value which can be spiritualized and Christianized and supernaturalized by the graced acts of the person under the influence of the Holy Spirit.[55] Thus, just as God spiritualizes and supernaturalizes mere human activity when it is performed with a spiritual intention (that is, intentionally referring the act to God) under the influence of grace, so also God can transform the merely human technique of learning into a capacity for perceiving and experiencing the divine. This is religious learning. The thrust of such a position is clear, it is God's direct action, sharply distinct from mere human action and coming in "from outside," which is the determinative factor in "religious" or "Christian" learning.

The pattern presented by these selected theorists is quite consistent and keeps insinuating itself with the clamorous persistence of a hypnotic drum beat. It is this: Emphasize the importance of the natural, the human, the scientific aspects and components in religious education, but always subordinate these to the supernatural and transcendent aspects. Natural and supernatural realms are sharply distinct; the former but leads to and is a preparation for the latter. This pattern is repeated in the theorists' consideration of learning as personality development and psychological maturity. The personal healing of the students' sin-shattered integrity is a learning process with both a natural and a supernatural dimension. Lewis Joseph Sherrill, for example, notes that "changes" in the body can be a religious concern and he cites the frequency with which Jesus associates bodily cures with the faith of the sick person. At the same time, human personality transcends mere bodily functions. Consequently, we are in a realm where scientific learning theory (e.g., trial-and-error learning, token reinforcement learning) can be of little help.[56] The healing which comes to the student comes as a result of the loving interpersonal relationships within the *koinonia* of the church. The student grows and matures as an integral and loving person through the experience of the caring, sharing relationship of the Christian community within which religious education takes place. Ultimately, it is God's healing grace which functions in the community. As Miller puts it, ". . . The presence of Christ affects the group interaction. Things happen which normally would not have happened, because God in Christ moves in a mysterious way to heal the wounds, to break down the barriers of separation, and to give sustaining power for the maintaining of fellowship no matter what strains are present.''[57]

Miller's statement may well be the final word on learning for these selected religious educationists—learning is essentially a mysterious process. Religious learning may perhaps in large part be explained and understood by reference to purely scientific and human processes. Such processes must therefore be emphasized and given their rightful place in religious education. At bottom, however, religious learning is divine, it is the direct work of the Holy Spirit. God's gift of the Spirit produces a "sudden" and mysterious effect which could not have come from mere human striving and sweating. Through the activity of the Spirit in the course of God's self-revelation, the student acquires knowledge[58] which could not have been acquired by human processes alone.

To what extent all the above represents a clear-cut integrationist metaperspective is not easy to say. The immanentists would strongly emphasize that the divine works intrinsically within the very scientific conditions of learning which can be discovered by human research. Scientific learning theory is therefore in no sense *merely* human. God's action cannot be discerned as being sharply distinct from the discoverable scientific process of learning. Learning, therefore, is not "mysterious." The transcendists, on the other hand, strongly emphasize precisely this mysterious element which they attribute to the direct action of the Holy Spirit and which is beyond the reach of scientific procedures. Is it clear that the selected theorists have given equal emphasis to both the transcendist and the immanentist point of view? Or does their position not represent, no matter how much they emphasize the scientific processes of learning, a stronger leaning toward the transcendist insistence on the direct and mysterious action of the Holy Spirit?

Student Freedom

These same questions may be asked about these theorists' treatment of student freedom. For them, freedom, too, has its natural and its supernatural components. The natural must be emphasized and given its due importance, but it must always be subordinated to the demands of the supernatural. Thus, the students' freedom to choose between similar human values (for example, whether to play football or to concentrate on track athletics) may be said to be purely within the ambit of the natural. However, the students' freedom of conscience, the freedom to decide whether to accept or reject God's revelation, touches the sphere of the supernatural. Since freedom is of the very essence of the human person as created by God, and since God will not violate this freedom, then no one should attempt to do so, least of all the teacher whose job it is to promote growth in personality. Consequently, no teaching procedure should be employed which may violate the core freedom of the student to accept and respond to the divine call. The selected theorists have a horror of teaching techniques which are too mechanical, or which are strongly directive and which smack of indoctrination.[59] Employment of such techniques would be regarded by them as trying to upstage the Holy Spirit. Teaching practices, therefore, always should be open to dialogue, discussion, and group processes. Van Caster suggests that one way to maintain and enhance student freedom is to teach the students to interiorize their values by greater reflection. The aim is to come to a proper hierarchical arrangement of personal values. The students should be able to recognize and accept which are the more important and which are the less important values. This in turn contributes to the formation of a balanced and self-integrated personality by minimizing the tension that often results from opposing value claims. The interiorization process is brought to full fruition in the realization that personal relationship with Jesus is the supreme value which gives meaning to all the others. The final choice to commit oneself to the supreme value, and the constant renewal of this choice throughout life, is a choice made in faith; it is a special grace. Such commitment can be prepared for, but never coerced.[60]

THE ENVIRONMENT

By now it should occasion no surprise to discover that the selected religious educationists are inclined to look upon the environment of religious education as having its natural and its supernatural aspects. Man, as Randolph Crump Miller asserts, is in organic relationship with his total environment, but his relationship with God provides an added dimension to man's integral situation.[61] For these theorists it is the added God-dimension of the environment which is the most important and determinative factor as far as religious education is concerned. This is the dimension which deserves most emphasis. But, since this God-dimension is precisely that, viz., a redimensioning of the natural environment through which and in which the divine works, then the purely natural and secular aspects of the environment also are important.

The theorists point to the importance of the general environment, such as good home influence, the physical and cultural environment of the school, neighborhood, and church. For example, good church architecture, proper and tasteful decorations, are mentioned as important for producing the proper atmosphere for worship (one of the foremost of all opportunities for religious education). Likewise, they insist on the importance of the immediate instructional environment. Such things as proper classroom setting and classroom equipment must not be overlooked.[62] For all that, the theorists have a rather broad and ill-defined concept of the environment of religious education and do not advocate using the environment as a crucial factor (variable) in the whole

process. This reluctance to deal more purposively with environmental structuring seems to correlate well with their insistence on a sharp distinction
between natural and supernatural. Too assiduous an effort to create "atmosphere" may be an effort to control the workings of the Spirit.

Thus, while recognizing and accepting the influence of the physical, cultural, and social environment as mediating and preparing the ground for the
entry of God's grace and the commitment of faith, the selected theorists insist
that the major environmental factor in religious education is the Holy Spirit.
The environment in which the Holy Spirit flourishes is the proper environment
for religious education. Particularly important is the good Christian home,
especially in its early influence on the child. Still more important is church
fellowship which is Spirit-filled; God is always a participant in this redemptive fellowship whether in its worshiping capacity or in its ordinary community function.[63] In fact, the whole of the church's life is the word of God, is
God communicating himself, and the religion lesson partakes very specially
of this life. The church's life not only concerns the well-knit *koinonia* of the
small church community, but itself is blended into the wider concerns of the
whole of humanity where God speaks in the signs of the times: *vox temporum
vox Dei.*[64]

In their consideration (or lack of consideration) of the environment as a
crucial variable in religious education, the position of these selected theorists
differs little from the transcendist emphasis. Their attempt to give due importance to what they would consider the natural or secular aspects of the environment cannot balance their strong emphasis on the supernatural or otherworldly aspects which to them seem vital.

EVALUATION

The reluctance of the selected theorists to state aims for religious education
which are specific and behaviorally oriented seems to ensure that they will
find little place for objective evaluative procedures in their overall religious
education theory. For the selected theorists, when all is said and done, the
final aim and purpose of religious education is supernatural and therefore
beyond human assessment. Even though these theorists posit some aims
which are human and "natural" (the achievement of which, presumably, can
be evaluated) they tend very definitely to lean toward the transcendist position
on evaluation. Lewis Sherrill, for example, insists that what we are teaching
for is "faith in faith" and not "faith in works." We aim at inculcating an
attitude of faith, we do not aim at teaching the students how to perform
specific "works." "To fasten attention to the specifics of conduct," Sherrill
affirms, "and to measure success in teaching by the extent to which these

specific outcomes have been achieved... is a relapse towards behavior-ism... [which] means basically that the educator is leading people into moralism."[65] Randolph Crump Miller, for his part, admits that there are certain outcomes of the religious education process which can be measured. He therefore sees a place for such measuring instruments as tests, reports, and profile sheets. Nevertheless, like the transcendists, he proposes that the main criteria for evaluation should be theological. Miller is rather vague precisely on how theological principles can be used to evaluate religious education, but this vagueness seems to be in keeping which his conviction that the major outcome of religious education, namely faith, is unmeasurable. Faith belongs to the realm of an "inner" attitude and is beyond the reach of humanly devised evaluative instruments.[66]

The attitude of the selected theorists toward evaluation in religious educa-tion differs little, if at all, from that of the transcendists. Some aspects of religious education can be evaluated, for example, the acquisition of cognitive content, but the final and substantive aim of the process, which is faith, cannot be evaluated.

CONCLUSION

Does the evidence presented in this chapter indicate the existence of a clear and distinct integrationist metaperspective? Can it be said that the selected theorists give equal emphasis to the transcendist and to the immanentist perspectives and hold them in dynamic equilibrium? The answer appears to be: sometimes they do and sometimes they don't. Where there is an evident lack of balance (as there is, for example, in their consideration of evaluation) the theorists favor the transcendist emphasis. This tendency to lean toward transcendentism possibly derives from the sharp and clear distinction between the natural and the supernatural that these selected theorists tend to draw. They appear to understand God as entering human process "from outside;" they understand grace and the Holy Spirit as working irruptively, as a special embellishment, and not (as the immanentists would hold) as the very natural and human perfection of human process. It is entirely possible that there are other theorists not considered in this chapter who, while attempting some form of integrationist balance, would sometimes tend to favor the immanentist stance. It is possible, therefore, that a pure integrationist metaperspective does not exist, and indeed, given our human propensity for inconsistency and imperfect perception, cannot exist. It may well be better to speak of strict and moderate transcendentism, strict and moderate immanentism. In point of fact, proving or disproving the existence of a clear-cut third or integrationist metaperspective is not really the object of the exercise. The analysis undertaken in the above chapter aims at helping the reader to clarify his or her own metaperspective in the light of what some major religious educationists have to say. Whether one is thoroughly integrationist, or whether one favors moderate transcendentism or moderate immanentism is perhaps not the point. The point is to know where one is. The point is to be aware of the outlook that one brings to religion teaching so as to have a sound theoretical base for what one does. Such a sound theoretical base will not only engender a sense of security, and enhance one's meaning and purpose, but will also provide the jumping off point for the broadening of one's own outlook by the critical examination of metaperspectives different from one's own.

NOTES

1. Marcel van Caster, "Our Faith in Jesus Christ," *Lumen Vitae,* Vol. 25 (June 1970), p. 270.
2. Randolph Crump Miller, *Education for Christian Living,* 2nd edition (Englewood Cliffs, New Jersey: Prentice-Hall, 1963), p. 9.
3. Lewis Joseph Sherrill, *The Gift of Power* (New York: Macmillan, 1955), p. 92.
4. Ibid., pp. 83–84.
5. Marcel van Caster, "Human Experience and Divine Revelation," *Lumen Vitae,* Vol. 22 (December 1967), p. 665.
6. Ibid., p. 666. (Emphasis in text). The word "mediate" is frequently used by van Caster to indicate that all natural (i.e., human and observable) things, events, values, and experiences, are "imperfect embodiments of a more perfect reality." Thus, all experiences can mediate the supernatural provided they are viewed in the light of faith and with reference to God. For a fuller treatment of this aspect of van Caster's synthesis see Jean Le Du and Marcel van Caster, *Experiential Catechetics* (Paramus, New Jersey: Newman Press, 1969), pp. 156–191. See also, Marcel van Caster, *Values Catechetics* (Paramus, New Jersey: Newman Press, 1970), pp. 208–211.
7. Miller, *Education for Christian Living,* p. 96.
8. Sherrill, *The Gift of Power,* p. 192. See also Randolph Crump Miller, *The Clue to Christian Education* (New York: Scribners, 1950), p. 110.
9. Marcel van Caster, *Themes of Catechesis* (New York: Herder and Herder, 1966), p. 121.
10. Marcel van Caster, *The Structure of Catechetics* (New York: Herder and Herder, 1965), pp. 136–137. See also, van Caster, "The Meaning of Life," *Lumen Vitae,* Vol. 24 (June 1969), pp. 292–293.
11. Marcel van Caster, "On Loving God by Loving Men," *Lumen Vitae,* Vol. 28 (December 1973), p. 642. (Emphasis in text).
12. For example, see Sherrill, *The Gift of Power,* p. 12.
13. Randolph Crump Miller, *Christian Nurture and the Church* (New York: Scribners, 1961), p. 12.

14. Sherrill, *The Gift of Power*, pp. 51–55; Le Du and van Caster, *Experiential Catechetics*, pp. 188–191; Miller, *Christian Nurture and the Church*, pp. 104–105.

15. For example, Miller's views are discussed in Kendig Brubaker Cully, *The Search for A Christian Education–Since 1940* (Philadelphia: Westminster Press, 1965); J. Gordon Chamberlain, *Freedom and Faith* (Philadelphia: Westminster Press, 1965); Sara Little, *The Role of The Bible in Contemporary Christian Education* (Richmond, Virginia: John Knox Press, 1961); William Bedford Williamson, *Language and Concepts in Christian Education* (Philadelphia: Westminster Press, 1970); to name but a few.

16. See chapter 1, note 7.

17. Randolph Crump Miller, *Biblical Theology and Christian Education* (New York: Scribners, 1956), p. 5.

18. Similarities between the religious education theories of Miller and Sherrill have been noted by several writers. See, for example, Little, *The Role of the Bible in Contemporary Christian Education;* Chamberlain, *Freedom and Faith;* George M. Schreyer, *Christian Education in Theological Focus* (Philadelphia: The Christian Education Press, 1962); Samuel E. Lo, *Tillichian Theology and Educational Philosophy* (New York: Philosophical Library, 1970); Harold W. Burgess, *An Invitation to Religious Education* (Notre Dame, Indiana: Religious Education Press, 1975).

19. Sherrill's statement in "Bulletin of the Pastoral Psychology Book Club," cited by Roy W. Fairchild, "The Contribution of Lewis J. Sherrill to Christian Education," *Religious Education*, Vol. 53 (September-October 1958), p. 404.

20. Sherrill, *The Gift of Power*, p. 122.

21. Lewis Joseph Sherrill, *The Struggle of the Soul* (New York: Macmillan, 1963), pp. 19–20.

22. While the kerygmatic approach to religion teaching is deeply Christocentric, of itself it need not lead to any particular theological emphasis within the natural/supernatural relationship. It need not lead to and does not demand a specific emphasis on the transcendence of God, rather than on his immanence, or to an emphasis on the divinity of Christ rather than on his humanity. Nonetheless, from its beginnings in Roman Catholic circles as a result of the writings of Josef Jungmann in the 1930s, the kerygmatic movement in religious education became associated with a rather conservative and traditional brand of Catholic theology which Jungmann espoused.

23. See, for example, Le Du and van Caster, *Experiential Catechetics*, pp. 198–225.

24. See, van Caster, "Our Faith in Jesus Christ," pp. 265–278; "On Loving God by Loving Men," pp. 639–648; "A Catechesis for Liberation," *Lumen Vitae*, Vol. 27 (June 1972), pp. 281–303. See also, Le Du and van Caster, *Experiential Catechetics*, pp. 114–118, 156–197.

25. Sherrill, *The Gift of Power*, p. 83. Emphasis in text.

26. Miller, *The Clue to Christian Education*, pp. 164–165. Emphasis added.

27. Van Caster, *Values Catechetics*, p. 215.

28. Miller, *Education for Christian Living*, p. 69.

29. For example, Miller, *Christian Nurture and the Church*, p. 188.

30. Ibid., p. 193.

31. Miller, *Education for Christian Living*, p. 55.

32. Le Du and van Caster, *Experiential Catechetics*, p. 222. See also van Caster, "A Catechesis for Liberation," pp. 282–285; van Caster, *Values Catechetics*, pp. 47–71, 208–215.

33. For a treatment of the educational aim of religious education see, for example, *Religion in Today's School* (Québec, Canada: Service général des communications du ministère de l'Éducation, Gouvernment de Québec, 1974), pp. 30–34.

34. Le Du and van Caster, *Experiential Catechetics*, p. 184. See pp. 177–191 generally. Van Caster proposes that "worldly" values and "religious" values really exist in a dynamic unity. This unity, he states, arises out of the "consciousness" of a faith union with God whereby earthly values are invested with a religious meaning by an intentional act. Thus, for example, love of God for God's own sake is a religious value; love of man is a natural value. Loving another human person for God's sake transforms the worldly value of human love into the religious value of love of God. The purely human act of love is transcended and "supernaturalized" into love of God. Further elaboration of this point may be found in Le Du and van Caster, *Experiential Catechetics*, pp. 130–133, 151–153; and in van Caster, "The Meaning of Life," *Lumen Vitae*, Vol. 24 (June 1969), p. 290.

35. Herbert H. Farmer, *The Servant of the Word* (New York: Scribners, 1942), p. 37, cited by Miller, *Education for Christian Living*, p. 71.

36. See, for example, Sherrill, *The Gift of Power*, p. 83; van Caster, *Values Catechetics*, pp. 133–135.

37. Van Caster, "The Meaning of Life," pp. 277, 278.

38. See, for example, Miller, *Education for Christian Living*, pp. 168, 173; Sherrill, *The Gift of Power*, pp. 174–175.

39. Sherrill, *The Gift of Power*, pp. 80–81.

40. Le Du and van Caster, *Experiential Catechetics*, pp. 206–207; van Caster, "Our Faith in Jesus Christ," pp. 275–276.

41. Sherrill, *The Gift of Power*, p. 182; Miller, *The Clue to Christian Education*, p. 142; van Caster, *Values Catechetics*, pp. 211–214.

42. Miller, *Education for Christian Living*, p. 64.

43. Miller, *The Clue to Christian Education*, p. 4; *Education for Christian Living*, pp. 110, 150.

44. Sherrill, *The Gift of Power*, pp. 51, 58.

45. Van Caster, *Values Catechetics*, pp. 206, 207.

46. Van Caster, *The Structure of Catechetics*, pp. 182–183. It is interesting to compare this position with that of the immanentists who would hold that this very disposing and preparing of the student is itself revelation.

47. Miller, *Education for Christian Living*, p. 356.

48. Ibid., 258. See also Miller, *Christian Nurture and the Church,* pp. 44, 76–80; Sherrill, *The Struggle of the Soul,* p. 94.

49. Van Caster, *The Structure of Catechetics,* p. 205. See also Sherrill, *The Gift of Power,* p. 85.

50. Miller, *Education for Christian Living,* p. 369. See also Le Du and van Caster, *Experiential Catechetics,* p. 155.

51. Van Caster, "Human Experience and Divine Revelation," p. 678.

52. The term "theo-anthropocentric" is used by Charles Kao in his "The View of Man and the Philosophy of Christian Education in the Thought of Harrison Sacket Elliott and of Lewis Joseph Sherrill," unpublished doctoral dissertation, Boston University Graduate School (1969), p. 140.

53. For example, see Miller, *The Clue to Christian Education,* p. 5.

54. Miller, *Christian Nurture and the Church,* p. 62. See also Lewis Joseph Sherrill, *The Rise of Christian Education* (New York: Macmillan, 1944), p. 98.

55. Le Du and van Caster, *Experiential Catechetics,* p. 184.

56. Sherrill, *The Gift of Power,* pp. 147, 151–152. Sherrill's thoroughly "integrated" person is one "who can act as a whole, consistently and over long periods of time, with reference to self-chosen ends. He has integrity in the sense that there is consistency between what he secretely is and what he openly is" (p. 22).

57. Miller, *Christian Nurture and the Church,* p. 79.

58. Knowledge is used here in as broad a sense as possible and not merely as referring to cognitive product content.

59. The question of indoctrination is a sensitive issue in religious educa-tion. The debate goes on as to what extent some indoctrination is necessary to preserve one's own particular religious traditions and to ensure socialization into a particular church fellowship. The word "indoctrination" has odious overtones; for some it is a "dirty" word. What is needed is a clear definition of what precisely one means by "indoctrination." In this regard Barry Cha-zan's " 'Indoctrination' and Religious Education," *Religious Education,* Vol. 67 (July-August 1972), pp. 242–253, is extremely helpful. The article also provides good references for further reading on the topic.

60. Van Caster, *Values Catechetics,* pp. 124–135.

61. Miller, *The Clue to Christian Education,* p. 9.

62. Miller, *Education for Christian Living,* pp. 228, 315.

63. Sherrill, *The Gift of Power,* pp. 82–83. See also Miller, *Education for Christian Living,* pp. 102–103, 396.

64. Van Caster, *The Structure of Catechetics,* pp. 82–85.

65. Sherrill, *The Gift of Power,* p. 182.

66. Miller, *Education for Christian Living,* pp. 388–394.

CHAPTER VII

Conclusions
and Reflections

This book began with a commitment to the importance and indeed the indispensability of theory. One can but view with a certain sadness the inability or the unwillingness of many religion teachers to take time to seriously formulate a personal theoretical position and to examine critically the theoretical underpinnings of the religion texts and practices they use in their teaching. As Peter Enright remarks, "Where teacher, administrator, or legislator is not prepared to advance reasons for his choice we would infer that it reduced the possibility of his work becoming meaningful either to himself or to his clients. Were he *unable* to offer reasons we would consider that, at least, we were confronted with a display of the deficiencies of the trained mind vis-à-vis the educated mind."[1] As with other fields of study, one's personal theory, the development of a personal rationale for action and the establishing of criteria by which to make decisions are more often than not influenced by the major theorists who have done creative and systematic thinking. It is also these major thinkers whose theories influence the development of curricula, and the texts and the methodologies which religion teachers are called upon to use. In the preceding chapters the theories of some major religious educationists were analyzed in order to provide a background and a framework for a personal self-examination by every religious educator.

An important aspect of the thesis of this book is that theorizing about religious education is done within the general pattern of a theological metaperspective on the natural/supernatural relationship, that is, on how God relates to his creation. Not only does one's theological overview have a certain influence on the perception of the relevant laws and facts and presuppositions from which theory is built, but it also affects the way these theories are expressed and the practices one derives from them. The major question that was addressed, therefore, was whether there exists any noticeable congruence or affinity between a particular theological metaperspective and the theoretical position one may adopt with respect to religious education. *The evidence uncovered seems clearly to indicate that when applied to six areas crucial to religious education, namely, aim, content, teacher, student, environment, and evaluation, there is indeed a strong affinity between a religious educationist's religious education theory and the theological metaperspective out of which the particular theorist works.* Which, let it be immediately noted, is not to say that the theological theme of the natural/supernatural relationship is the *sole* determinative factor in religious education theory. There are undoubtedly factors at work other than theological ones such, for example, as the epistemological stance adopted by the particular theorist. Good evidence that other factors also play an important part in the development of religious education theory can be drawn from the consideration of the selected immanentist theorists. While coming out of virtually the same immanentist theological position they propose apparently quite different approaches to many of the six areas noted above. In other words, the *same* theological overview may correlate with *different* theoretical approaches to religious education. Therefore, as was noted in chapter 1, instead of saying that a theological metaperspective is totally or partially *determinative* of religious education theory, it would be better to understand such a theological overview as providing the general horizon against which theory is developed, as providing theory with a recognizable setting. Or again, theological metaperspective may be compared to the light filtering through tinted glass and suffusing the whole with its particular glow and color. Whatever the image one prefers to use, the conclusion remains that a particular theological outlook and perspective does enter as an important theoretical element in religious education theory.

If religion teachers have been brought to a better understanding of their own particular view of how God relates to his creation and are better able to plug their teaching practice into the theoretical position out of which they work, then a major purpose of this book will have been achieved. An added bonus would be if all religious education thinkers have benefited from this analysis in their work of clarifying concepts and categories and in understanding the foundations of a theory of religious education which may serve as a basis for more useful practice. Since these two "ifs" substantially represent the point at which this book began they might well serve as its point of conclusion. Nevertheless, perhaps a final "brooding over the waters," some reflections and concluding remarks, may further help to clarify the issues at stake.

FURTHER REFLECTIONS

On Transcendentism and Immanentism

In the course of analyzing the transcendist and immanentist approaches to religious education, no judgment was made as to the relative merits or demerits of any particular metaperspective. Perhaps the time of reflection is the time to see whether such a judgment can be made. On the other hand, if both transcendentism and immanentism are valid emphases which capture a particular aspect, or nuance, or portion of the profound reality which is the God/man relationship, is there some way in which these two can be reconciled? Before attempting some answer to these questions it may be well to summarize the high points of the difference between the transcendist and the immanentist approaches to religious education.

Like the noisy persistence of hecklers who continually jump to their feet and demand a hearing, two basic issues keep thrusting themselves into any consideration of the selected religious educationists. The first is that of the natural and the supernatural order. The second is really an aspect of the first and a specific focal point within it, namely, faith.

1) The Natural and the Supernatural Order. As has already often been noted, transcendist-minded theorists tend to make a sharp, clear, well-etched distinction between the natural order and the supernatural order, the realm of nature and the realm of grace, natural values and supernatural values, the this-worldly and the other-worldly, the secular and the sacred, the world and the spirit, this life and the life to come. For the immanentists, the distinction between these "dualities" is weak, blurred, or nonexistent. Having radically separated the natural and the supernatural orders, the problem the transcendists have to face is how to bring them together and satisfactorily explain how our natural human life can be "supernaturalized" and become of value for the supernatural existence of the life to come. Human life is good but it is not an end in itself, it only points toward a new, different, and better existence: we have not here a lasting city but seek one that is to come. In other words, how can human life accomplish its eschatological purpose of life with God when this life of eschatological consummation is viewed not merely as different in quality and intensity from earthly life but as belonging to a radically different order? For the transcendists, this bringing together of the natural and supernatural realms is, in its broadest terms, accomplished by "union with God" in this life. In its essence, active union with God consists in a process of intentionalizing and purposing. Grace, which is God present in and sharing himself with us, acts in us through that which most distinguishes us as human, namely, the rational faculty. Thus, life's normal activities are "supernaturalized" by performing them "for the sake of the kingdom," that is, for a supernatural purpose, out of a faith perspective. Human goals and values are good but can never be considered as ends in themselves. Human values are ends *and* means, that is, they are sought for their own sake but also as a means to a higher end. Furthermore, however good human values may be, authentic human life for the sake of the kingdom is always marked by an air of detachment from the purely this-worldly for our true life is otherworldly. Put in another way, we must work, but more importantly we must pray. Prayer develops the individual, personal, spiritual, loving, and transcendent union with God. Prayer develops the interior life which enables us, by intentionalizing and purposing, to add a spiritual dimension to our work for the promotion of proper human values.

What does this particular emphasis say for religious education? Much as the transcendists would insist that their approach aims at the full religious development of the whole person, the accent they favor tends to give priority to the rational and the intellectual as against the emotional or affective aspects of the person. A sharp body/soul distinction goes hand in hand with the clearly etched polarities of this position.[2] If intelligence is the basis of the human self-transcendence by which a mature personality develops, so also is it the avenue through which religious faith acts to bring about a "divine" transcendence in human life which rises above the mere mundane materiality of earthly pursuits and makes life "meaningful" for eternity. The teaching of religion, then, focuses principally on transmission of the specially revealed divine message. Presented with the beauty and moving power of the divine word, the student reaches a state of conviction which translates itself into a life "spiritualized" by the desire and intention of living for the sake of the kingdom. In a transmissionist mode of teaching the emphasis is on deep immersion in biblical texts and lore, on the passing on of the authentic teaching (doctrinal and ecclesiastical) of the church, and on church history. It is a process which tends to minimize student involvement and self-teaching in favor of authoritative pronouncements—the teacher is the authoritative minister of the divine word. It is a process which aims to promote reverence, and respect, and humility before the supremely transcendent God and his word to us.

The immanentists, on the other hand, do not have the problem of bringing the natural and the supernatural orders together because, for them, the orders are never separated. There is only one world order, not two. We are supernaturalized, that is, intrinsically related to God, graced, by the very fact of our creation. All of creation, every human experience, has a depth dimension of ultimacy which points beyond the merely human. In this depth God is revealed. Such experience belongs to the whole person and not merely to one aspect of the person such as the intellectualizing power or affective capability. For the immanentists human life is an end in itself. Human goals are sought for their own sake, for the betterment of life and the promotion of true human values are seen as contributing to the final emergence of God in the eschatological moment. To seek humanity is to seek God. Thus, a truly human purpose, an intention to live authentically and honestly and to contribute to the betterment of the world is in fact a spiritual and supernatural purpose. What is needed is not detachment from the world but involvement with it. Prayer is not so much a personal devotion to the divine transcendent being which develops the inner spiritual life as it is an intensification of purpose to act humanly. The meeting with God takes place not in an inner sanctum withdrawn from the world but actively within the very fabric of everyone's existential situation.

Expressed in terms of the immanentist emphasis at its idealistic best, religious education centers on conscious participation in human experience as pertaining to the whole person in order to plumb the depths of experience's ultimacy. Religion teaching is centered on creating the conditions whereby students come to a personal discovery and appreciation of the divine word, the divine message, spoken through human experience, and whereby they respond to this word in freedom. The teacher is not an authority figure, a mere transmitter of the message, but a companion, a guide, a facilitator, a fellow searcher in this discovery and appreciation of God at the heart of the existential situation. The roles of teacher and student tend to merge in this search for and response to God who is so closely identified with human life and purpose that he calls less for reverent worship than he does for social involvement. All of which points to the most fundamental problem the immanentist has to face, namely, how does one avoid identifying God with his own creation in such a way as to destroy the essential differences between them and thereby destroy the relationship between them?

2) Faith. The second issue about which there is a basic difference of outlook between the transcendists and the immanentists is faith. When the verbiage has been sifted, what the religious educationists are saying (possibly to no one's amazement) is that the purpose of religious education is (to paraphrase the gospel slightly): that the students may have faith and have it more abundantly. This is true whether faith is viewed primarily as an assent to divinely revealed truth, or as a trusting commitment to the person of Christ, or as an attitude which specifies a whole lifestyle, or as all these things. The transcendist-minded religious educationists think in terms of religious education first being directed to the preambles and predispositions to faith. Thus, one can be disposed to faith, one can be prepared for it, but ultimately it is God who comes in and gives the gift. One can be brought to see the beauty of faith by teaching, one can be helped to reason to its necessity, but only God himself by a direct and special act from outside human process can give religious faith. Faith is an *additum ab extra,* an inflow of believing (this includes commitment and action) power from outside the normal process of coming to faith. Thus faith is beyond and infinitely surpasses normal and natural human faculty and capacity. It is thoroughly *super*natural. The transcendists treat grace in exactly the same way since faith is grace-induced and is pure gift. The Spirit "seizes" one and empowers beyond human capability. As for revelation, what the transcendists emphasize is *content.* The message, because it contains and expresses God, belongs to the object of faith. The deposit of faith contained in scripture and expressed in the living, teaching church is the *given* and special revelation of God. The important thing in religious education is to hand on this message and perpetuate the church community. Teaching the message in all its purity, with consciousness of the inner dynamic of the word itself, will enlighten, dispose, lead to faith, and further nourish a faith already given. But always, it is *God who acts;* of ourselves we are incapable of faith.

The immanentist-minded religious educationists emphasize the historico-experiential aspect of revelation. Their emphasis is on the *process* (contrast content above) of continuing revelation. God is revealed as the depth dimension of all experience. Recognizing the presence of God in life and responding to this recognition is largely a matter of recognizing the humanizing factors in life and promoting these. Faith, in this setting, is not a special divine intervention but is the perfection of the human and humanizing process of normal belief. Faith is the deepest dimension of the human quest for meaning in this world as this quest meets with and responds to the "beyondness" dimension of ordinary experience. What religion teachers have to do is to sharpen the awareness of this dimension of ultimacy as, for example, through a consideration of the great questions of human existence—death, life, pain, joy, evil, tragedy, love. Teachers must immerse students in experiential situations which create the consciousness and appreciation of the more than human in all of experience. To be in touch with this dimension is to be in touch with the sacred, with God. God is thoroughly at work within the human dynamic, his special divine intervention is continually being given at the very heart of all human process. Students are "faithed" by an essentially human teaching process; no special divine intervention is necessary. Grace, of course, works in exactly the same way. We are graced by the very fact of our creation. The effect of grace is the natural, human, scientific perfectioning of things human. There is no *distinctive* divine action, except in so far as the very perfection of human process makes it distinctive. Grace acts *ab intra,* from within.

What do these high points of the difference between transcendentism and immanentism tell us? *What they clearly indicate is that rather than being contradictory the emphases are complementary.* Each presupposes the other. Taken to its logical conclusion each points to and leads to the other. They are intimately and inextricably related and both are necessary for a full appreciation of the God/man relationship and for the treatment of this relationship in religious education.

Thus, if the reality of God is to be understood as fundamentally and essentially different from the reality of his creation there is room for understanding that there are fundamentally distinct realms or orders, the natural and the supernatural. This is pretty much how the transcendists view things. Not that these orders or realms should be invested with the strict ontological qualities that some theological systems give them (see chapter 2 above). Rather, that we experience God as different, as other, as superior to ourselves and in that sense as belonging to a distinct and superior order. Nevertheless, these orders cannot be so separate as to be mutually exclusive. Such a separation would put God outside of human experience, which perhaps he is in himself but as such is not in any way beneficial to present human existence. It is the God of human experience that the immanentists prefer to emphasize. They too hit on a valid aspect of the God/man relationship, an aspect which represents the other face of the coin and is complementary to the transcendist outlook.

The relationship and interdependability of transcendentism and immanentism can perhaps be further explicitated by looking at some analogous relationships.

First, transcendentism and immanentism are related in a manner analogous to the way in which ontology and epistemology are related. The former prefers to describe *the way things are* with God, with the world and with people, whereas the latter would rather discover *how we can know* how it is with God, with the world, and with people. The transcendist prefers to start with God, the omnipotent, the transcendent one, the totally other who exists apart from his creation, who reveals himself and tells us about himself by speaking his word. Religious education consists in a telling about this God and what we know about him, as he told it to us. However, in telling us that we know God and what we know about him the transcendist cannot avoid telling us something about how we know him (God). If God is totally other there is no way that we can contact him unless he in some way becomes part of and integrated with our experience. God's word must be fully human if it is to be understood. It must be a word which speaks "in the categories which men had already hewn out of their own direct experience of the reality that is immediately open to their gaze."[3] The immanentist, on the other hand, prefers to address the question: how can we know that it is as the religious person says it is with God? The starting point is experience for this is all we can really be certain of. Thus, religious education starts with experience and one of the principal tasks of the teacher is to put the students in touch with experience. We then embark on a process of discovery. Questing through life's major concerns and plumbing the depths of experience we discover there a depth of ultimacy, a glow of the more than human that is not ever fully captured by experience. Furthermore, this mysterious depth of experience has the qualities which Rudolf Otto ascribes to the holy, the numinous—it is the *mysterium tremendum et fascinans*. It is an experience of the "wholly other" before the power and awfulness *(tremendum)* of which we stand in reverential awe. At the same time this "wholly other" exerts a strange and extreme fascination and attraction *(fascinans)* which draws us on.[4] Thus, out of immanence we reach transcendence and the supremely transcendent one. Similarly, out of transcendence we must come to immanence.

Secondly, transcendentism and immanentism are related in a manner analogous to the way in which faith and reason are related. As was noted above, the transcendist tends to think of reason as supplying solid grounds for faith but that faith and reason belong to different orders and that faith is only possible because of a special act of God. Thus, for the transcendist, faith totally transcends human experience and human believing. Faith is an acceptance of and a response to God's revelation of himself. But the question that the transcendist must answer is: How does one know that this alleged revelation of God (the scriptures, for example) is in fact a revelation of God? The answer that is usually given is: by reason. That is, one judges it reasonable to accept the believing experiences of the Hebrew and early Christian peoples because this experience makes sense for and adds meaning to one's life. Reason, therefore, is not opposed to faith. Rather, faith is an integral part of the reasoning process, is continuous with it and represents its highest peak and its greatest depth—which is a harkening back to immanentism. The immanentist prefers to view faith as arising in the normal course of human belief which is a response to one's experience in life. The immanentist sees God as intimately present within and sustaining the very act of human believing. Thus, human believing always has a religious dimension but specifically becomes religious faith when it comes in contact with the "beyondness," the numinous aspect of human experience. Faith is an ordinary human activity but becomes religious faith when its object is religious. The question the immanentist has to answer is: What is it that assures us that the numinous depth of human experience is in fact God and not some self-delusory subjective state? The problem is well put by Perter A. Bertocci: "Is religious experience a unique and irreducible dimension of human experience? . . . Or . . . is religious experience called 'religious' because the experient already believes on other grounds in a certain kind of God?"[5] Does religious faith, when it achieves its true object, not seem to demand some direct and specific divine intervention from outside the normal process of believing? If one starts with reason and the experience of life (immanentist emphasis), one seems ultimately to reach the point of faith as a special divine intervention (transcendist emphasis). If one starts with faith as God's special gift of believing power in his revelation (transcendist emphasis), one has ultimately to see this faith as having its root in human experience and reason (immanentist emphasis).

What we have here is a dialectical phenomenon. Each pole of the dialectic considered in and of itself appears as the contradictory opposite of the other pole. Nevertheless, if we are to avoid meaninglessness we cannot affirm one pole without implicitly affirming the other. A God who is totally transcendent and beyond human reach must be such if he is to be God. On the other hand, if this God is not thoroughly involved in and present to human life and perceivable in human experience he is of no consequence to the human condition. Each pole of the dialectic must inform, broaden, and enrich the other. What is required, it seems, is an intensive and comprehensive integration of the transcendist and immanentist emphases. Furthermore, integration cannot mean a weakening and watering down of one of the poles of the dialectic at the expense of the other. Nor can it mean a strong affirmation of one pole with a mere "negative" acknowledgement of the other such that its implications do not enter fully into our thinking. Proper integration can only come from a full and total assertion of both transcendentism and immanentism.

Thus God *both* (a) is present to, within, and thoroughly involved with the single order of creation (immanentist emphasis), *and* (b) belongs to and exists in a "supernatural" order or realm which is infinitely beyond and superior to the "natural" human order (transcendist emphasis). Faith is *both* (a) the deepest point of human questing for meaning in life and belief and commitment to that meaning as belief and commitment to God (immanentist emphasis), *and* (b) the inner divine inspiration and motion which transcends human capability and, coming in from outside human process causes belief and commitment (transcendist emphasis). Grace is *both* (a) our gracious acting in a human manner, acts by which we "faith" and "justice" and "compassion" and love (immanentist emphasis), *and* (b) the God-presence without which we could not "faith" and "justice" and "compassion" and love (transcendist emphasis). Revelation is *both* (a) the depth dimension of the personal and community humanizing experience when it comes in touch with the more than human in human experience, that is, a depth which provides new meaning (the immanentist emphasis), *and* (b) the direct action of God through his given word brought about by an inspiration and inner movement which man could not achieve by his own powers, given, therefore, from outside human process (transcendist emphasis).

Is it possible to fully integrate these polar emphases, to reconcile the seeming irreconcilables? Put another way, is it possible to live with the tension which comes from a *full* assertion of transcendence and immanence? Probably not. Which is why we tend to favor one or the other as our personal metaperspective, or perhaps why we waver between them as the needs of the existential moment seem to dictate, that is, as we try to meet the demands of personality equilibrium and well-being. Perhaps one way of assuaging the tension while not relinquishing any of the demands of either the transcendist or the immanentist emphasis is that suggested by F. J. Sheed. In treating of mystery in religion Sheed suggests that we

> accept both elements [of the mystery], and accept them both at white heat without bothering too much about whether one can see a reconciliation. The mind loses no integrity by this, since it is already certain . . . of the truth of each element separately. . . . And the result justifies the method. For al-

though we cannot see the reconciliation, yet some mysterious reconciliation is in fact effected within us. We begin, as I have said, with a steady concentration upon each of the two elements, and a moment comes when we realize that we are living mentally in the presence of not two truths but of one. We still could not say how both can be true at once, yet we truly experience them so.[6]

Even though transcendentism and immanentism are not two truths but rather two aspects of the one truth, Sheed's suggestion can be very helpful for our personal interior balance. Furthermore, the experience of a reconciliation of the transcendist and immanentist emphases is but one of many such experiences which characterize life. Ordinary living is a continuous coping with a tension of opposites, it is a continuous coping with an inbuilt duality which seems to encompass all the important experiences of life. Life leads to death, but out of death comes new life; we can only cope with life if we learn to cope with death. Joy is born of the personal pain of giving; we can only learn the meaning of joy if we learn the meaning of suffering. Losing oneself in the gift of love, one finds self. We can only grasp the meaning of the transcendent God if we live fully in his immanence, and vice versa.

On Religious Education and Religion Teachers

What does all this say for religious education? What it appears to say is that the theories and practices which have affinity with and correlate best with both transcendist and immanentist metaperspectives have equal validity and should be thoroughly integrated if religious education is to be maximally fruitful. Such an assertion may well go counter to much of the current theological thinking and current religious education theory and practice which for the most part favor the immanentist emphasis. In keeping with the modern focus on revelation as principally and proximately sited in ongoing experience, religion programs tend to rely heavily on what is often called (not without ambiguity) the experiential approach. Such an approach, it is claimed, is more suited to an age in which radical questioning and doubt about religious values are rampant, an age which will not easily accept authoritative pronouncements whether about God or the eternal verities, an age which is losing or has lost its sense of the sacred because the religious symbols of a former time have lost their evocative and compelling power. The experiential approach, it is also claimed, is more truly educational. Education must aim at equipping persons to meet the challenges of life creatively and successfully. Consequently, education must aim principally at the development of a mature and balanced personality, persons who know and are in full touch with themselves. Religious education is an integral part of this process for it provides a system of meaning and purpose which sustains personal security and self-integration.

Faith development means the development of a religious attitude and meaning system which will enable persons to reinterpret the world and its experiences in terms of religious reality which is primarily experiential. Good education should rely minimally on authoritative teacher pronouncements, on the supplying of ready-made answers and on the transmission of information. Rather, it should stimulate inquiry, encourage the formation of a personal value system and develop a solid basis for decision making. Religious education, because it is education, should do no less.

Those who favor and promote the immanentist and experiential approach are often critical of the transcendist outlook and the approach to religious education that correlates with it, that is, with the emphasis on transmission of a divine message authoritatively interpreted and handed on by the church. The critics point out that such an approach is basically antieducational in that it tends to stifle personal growth and maturity by authoritatively providing answers instead of opening the students to the freedom to make their own decisions. It is also claimed that the transcendist approach does not easily succeed in putting students in touch with themselves, their experiences and their values, rather it tends to impose a value system. Critics further point out that the approach tends to view religious education as an objective study of religious facts and formulas rather than as a process for promoting and clarifying a meaning system. The approach proposes too mechanical and entitative a view of faith. Faith is understood as something one "has" or "is given" instead of as a "faithing person" who "believes in" rather than "believes that." Many critics sum up much of the above in one pithy statement: the transcendist approach tends to indoctrination. And that, even allowing for polemic exaggeration, is regarded as the final indignity.

The arguments cited in the two previous paragraph are so well known as to probably have made boring reading. It is not proposed to enter here into the controversy of the "new" versus the "old" approach in religious education.[7] There is, nevertheless, a tendency to too easily reject the "old" without sufficient reflection on its values and so throw the baby out with the bath water. The immanentist-experiential approach to religious education is "new" in the sense that it is more in keeping with thinking on education and human development which is currently in vogue. Not everyone would be prepared to uncritically baptize this thinking, and certainly everyone should be open to the possibility that future generations may look upon it as a mistake. The theologians who gathered at Hartford did us a service when they reminded us that we should constantly beware of making the assumption that "Modern thought is superior to all past forms of understanding reality, and is therefore normative for Christian faith and life."[8] New theories develop as new data and new thought patterns and categories become available in keeping with the scientific, cultural, and religious development of people. Nevertheless, the history of human thought and behavior is replete with examples of the swinging pendulum, or of the wheel coming full circle and setting off on another revolution. The human propensity for vacillating between extremes and polar opposites is a fact of personal experience. The real point at issue is that the present concern with immanentist theological thinking and the religious education theories that seem best to correlate with such thinking should not blind us to the real values of the transcendist approach. Transcendentism and immanentism are not logical contradictions but rather imperfect human views of an essentially simple and integral reality that surpasses the human ability to encompass and explain that reality.

And finally, a word for religion teachers. As teachers we must be encouraged to carefully reflect upon, see, understand, and in the end rely on our own particular perspective. Never should we forget, however, that our viewpoint is partial. We almost certainly do not get the whole picture. The reality is bigger than we are. We promote and feel comfortable with certain theories and practices because they probably blend better with our own particular temperament. And this is not inconsequential. A firm basis of personal inner security is very necessary if we are to function successfully as teachers. We do not use this firm basis, however, either as a security blanket which we never let go of, or as the justification for a polemic against those who hold other views. Openness to change is in fact a capital asset of the truly secure person. All good religion teachers must be good empiricists in the sense that they are open to being convinced by the evidence. The problem frequently is that the results of religion programs and the application of certain religious education theories in terms of promoting true and lasting religious commitment are not immediately or even proximately evident. Sometimes they only become evident from one generation to the next. Not infrequently, new theories are hatched and new practices embarked upon before all the evidence is in. It may be entirely possible that religious education theorists are doomed to work in such a milieu, that is, never having fully adequate evidence derived from testing and evaluation of former theories. It has often been said that in formulating clear and precise doctrine the church is playing a ''catch up'' game behind popular evolution of belief and Christian practice. Perhaps something similar is true of religious educationists who have to work out new theories based on evidence supplied by a previous generation. On the other hand, to attribute the cause of the ''faith-full-ness'' or ''faith-less-ness'' of one generation to the religion programs of the previous generation would be naive in the extreme. The point surely is that whatever the possible deficiencies of theory we should be committed to change only when it is based on informed theory which we are able to identify and personally espouse.

As teachers, therefore, we should be committed to our own viewpoint, provided we know and understand what it is. At the same time we realize that this viewpoint almost certainly does not provide a complete picture of the reality before us. In the classroom, or in any educational setting, whatever our personal preference our best efforts to put forward either the transcendist or the immanentist viewpoint should always be conditioned by the honest statement that the polar opposite viewpoint is equally valid. "God is Totally Other; God has entered this world, suffers, and manifests himself in it. *Both* these statements are central to Christian faith; a one-sided emphasis on *either* is distortive."[9] Wholeness is to be found in the teeth of the tension. And what we finally come to in the teeth of the tension is silence—silence before mystery present, the silence of contemplation. If as teachers we can bring our students to an appreciation of and the need for contemplation (in the midst of a full life) before this *mystery* which is *present* we will have gone a long way to fulfilling our role of true religious educators.

NOTES

1. Peter Enright, "Christian Philosophy of Education," *Catholic Education Today,* Vol. 9 (July-August 1975), p. 4. Emphasis in text.

2. Whether one can, or should, dichotomize intellect and affect, thinking and feeling, is a matter of some debate. One merely notes that the transcendist theorists do tend to make this sharp distinction because of their tendency to emphasize a body/soul duality. For an argument against the dichotomizing of reason and feeling see Gabriel Moran, *Religious Body: Design for a New Reformation* (New York: Seabury Press, 1974), pp. 166–171.

3. James P. Mackey, *The Problems of Religious Faith* (Dublin: Helicon, 1972), p. 29.

4. Rudolf Otto, *The Idea of the Holy* (New York: Oxford University Press, 1970).

5. Peter A. Bertocci, "Psychological Interpretations of Religious Experience," in Merton P. Strommen, editor, *Research on Religious Development* (New York: Hawthorn, 1971), p. 6.

6. F. J. Sheed, *Theology and Sanity* (London: Sheed and Ward, 1953), p. 17.

7. The question of the "old" vs the "new" approach to religious education may be more a Catholic problem than a Protestant one. As C. Ellis Nelson remarks, in discussing the Catholic General Catechetical Directory of 1972, "Perhaps the long history of the [Catholic] church existing under all forms of secular government and living through many radical sociocultural changes in the past has made for a built-in sense of the need to change, whereas many Protestants believe they restored the true church in the sixteenth century and now have to defend it. (C. Ellis Nelson, "A Protestant Response," *The Living Light,* Vol. 9 [Fall 1972], p. 88). Furthermore, much of what is "new" in current Catholic approaches to religion teaching bears

marked similarity to some of the liberal Protestant religion teaching of the pre-World War II era. It seems ironic that while many Protestant groups, under the influence of ''neoorthodox'' theology, abandoned the liberal stance in religious education, the Catholics are going in the opposite direction. The phenomenon points to the influence that theology has on religious education and also that often the lessons of history are not attentively read. See Charles Melchert, ''What Catholics Can Learn From Protestants In Religious Education,'' *The Living Light,* Vol. 11 (Spring 1974), pp. 87–96.

8. ''An Appeal for Theological Affirmation,'' *Worldview,* Vol. 18 (April 1975), p. 39.

9. Peter L. Berger, ''Barth and Debunking,'' *Worldview,* Vol. 18 (June 1975), p. 41. Emphasis in text.

Index